HILLSBOROUGH
UNTOLD

HILLSBOROUGH
UNTOLD

AFTERMATH OF A DISASTER

NORMAN BETTISON

Biteback Publishing

First published in Great Britain in 2016 by
Biteback Publishing Ltd
Westminster Tower
3 Albert Embankment
London SE1 7SP
Copyright © Norman Bettison 2016

ISBN 978-1-78590-089-1

10 9 8 7 6 5 4 3 2 1

A CIP catalogue record for this book is available from the British Library.

Set in Sabon and Bell Gothic

Printed and bound in Great Britain by
CPI Group (UK) Ltd, Croydon CR0 4YY

MIX
Paper from
responsible sources
FSC® C020471

CONTENTS

For Olivia and Freya

PREFACE

T his account is offered in the spirit of openness and transparency. Nothing should remain concealed about Hillsborough, for the bereaved families and all of those whose lives were changed by the disaster deserve nothing less than the whole truth. That is so even if any disclosure sits uncomfortably with the popular narratives that currently surround that fateful day and its aftermath.

Nothing here is intended to disturb or challenge the findings of the judicial processes that have examined the facts about Hillsborough. The inquiry by Lord Justice Taylor, which reported within sixteen weeks of the disaster, and the most recent Coroner's Inquest, which took evidence for more than two years, reached the same conclusion. Whilst there were other contributory factors, the disaster was primarily caused by a failure of police control on the day. Since hearing the evidence unfold at the Taylor Inquiry, twenty-seven years ago, I have always agreed with that judgment.

Whilst this account, in places, describes the personal impact of being the subject of an inaccurate and unfair narrative, it does not invite or bear comparison with the experience of the bereaved and others who have struggled against a particular Hillsborough narrative for a quarter of a century.

There are no competing tragedies here. Ninety-six people lost their lives at a football match. Others were permanently disabled by the same events. Thousands were traumatised by what they saw that day. Too many have been obliged to carry the burden of bereavement or bear the responsibility of caring for those who were injured. What happened at Hillsborough on 15 April 1989 affected the lives of countless people. My account is intended to amplify that tragedy rather than detract from it.

CHAPTER 1

ONE DAY
IN APRIL...

1.45 p.m., 15 April – 4 a.m., 16 April 1989

I thought the man was dead by the time I reached him. I had seen death many times during my police career. I also thought that the ten or twelve bodies that had been laid, unceremoniously, alongside a fence, were dead too, although I had fewer close-quarter observations on which to support that presumption.

I have always hoped to talk about this encounter as it

might add to the knowledge, and provide peace of mind, for a next of kin somewhere. Curiously, no one has seemed interested in my direct connection with the Hillsborough disaster.

I was pleased, therefore, twenty-six years later, in the packed aircraft hangar of a courtroom at Warrington, when Jonathan Hough QC, Counsel to the Inquest, seemed as though he might be about to open that door for the first time.

Since being called to the Bar, Mr Hough has acted as Counsel in the Diana, Princess of Wales, inquest; the Charles de Menezes shooting inquiry; Potters Bar and Grayrigg rail disasters; and the inquiry into the explosion and resulting deaths on the nuclear submarine HMS *Tireless*. Then, most recently, Lord Justice Goldring had invited him to assist in his renewed inquest into the causes of the deaths of ninety-six people who had lost their lives so tragically at Hillsborough Football Stadium on 15 April 1989.

My own written testimony was furnished within days of the disaster. It constitutes only a very small piece of the overall jigsaw. Nevertheless, it is difficult to understand why no one has ever enquired about the attention I paid to those who perished.

I was never asked by the West Midlands Police, who carried out an initial investigation into the Hillsborough disaster, nor by the original Coroner's Inquest that sat and reached verdicts in 1991, and which is today regarded as having been an unsatisfactory procedure. Nor was I asked by the campaigning journalists or anyone on behalf of the Hillsborough Family Support Group, who have represented the interests of the bereaved over the years. The question wasn't raised in an interview I gave to Professor Phil Scraton, who wrote the 1999 book *Hillsborough: The Truth* and who went on to become the principal author of the report of the Hillsborough Panel, set up by the government in 2009 to review everything that was known and written about Hillsborough. Nor was it ever brought up by the Independent Police Complaints Commission (IPCC), who have taken a keen interest in me and my Hillsborough past. And finally, my role on the day of the disaster has never been questioned by anyone from Operation Resolve, the massive investigation team set up, at considerable public expense, to reinvestigate precisely how ninety-six people had met their deaths a quarter of a century previously.

Now, though, Counsel to the Inquest, in the most appropriate forum, was on the threshold of asking me about the man on the stretcher to whom I attended whilst waiting for one of the first ambulances to appear.

> WITNESS: '... When I turned around there was a metal stretcher and on that stretcher was a man, twenty-eight to thirty years old, six feet tall...'
>
> JONATHAN HOUGH QC: 'Did you intend to render assistance to him?'

WITNESS: 'Yes, together with a policewoman and a St John's
   Ambulance man...'
CORONER: 'Is it necessary to go into great detail of this Mr
   Hough?'
JONATHAN HOUGH QC: 'I'm just...'
CORONER: 'I don't think it is.'

The enquiry into my personal experience of one of the
greatest postwar tragedies, a story I had been waiting
twenty-six years to tell, was to be closed down before it
had really begun. Mr Hough looked bemused but moved
on following a clear direction from the judge. This vignette
confirmed my suspicion that I had been invited to give evidence at Warrington not as a witness to events that may
be of assistance to the jury, and to a bereaved family somewhere, but as a pseudo defendant at the only forum that
might, figuratively speaking, put me in 'the dock'.

I had been shown the legal arguments that preceded
my calling. Jonathan Hough QC made it quite clear that
I was unlikely to be of significant assistance to the jury
and that I should not be called simply on account of my
more recent notoriety. Others, including those barristers
representing the bereaved families, objected and seemed
determined to bring me to public scrutiny at the Coroner's
Inquest. The judge, I believe somewhat equivocally from
my reading of his decision, agreed to do so. In all of these

considerations, no one made any reference to my experiences on the day of the disaster. They instead argued, for example, that I should be held to account for the manner in which I had applied for the job of Chief Constable of Merseyside, almost a decade after the tragedy, and other esoteric issues. Quite how such issues might assist the jury in determining the causes of deaths of the ninety-six deceased was not clear.

———————

Those ninety-six people attended a football match that day, as did I. An enthralling contest was anticipated. Liverpool FC and Nottingham Forest, arguably the two best teams of the day, were to compete on neutral ground at Hillsborough, Sheffield for a place in the 1989 FA Cup Final. The winning team in this semi would be the favourite to lift the cup. The stage was set.

It was a warm and sunny spring day on 15 April 1989. I have remembered the day, and the ninety-six, on its anniversary each year since and the sun has often shone. I certainly didn't need my heavy wax jacket, but had made a hasty decision to take it when I left the house. I parked near to Hillsborough stadium on the north side of Sheffield at 1.45 p.m. and had reached my seat by 1.54 p.m. I can be precise because I was sitting below the famous old clock set into the canopy of Hillsborough's South Stand, and I also had the electronic scoreboard with its bright-red pixilated numbers shining over my left shoulder.

The short walk from my car took me along Leppings Lane, adjacent to the stadium. The only thing that I noticed that was out of the ordinary was the number of people asking for 'spares' or 'swaps'. I was a seasoned football fan but had been to less than a dozen all-ticket games. The home-and-away, core Liverpool fans, though, had been raised in a culture where the demand for match tickets often exceeded supply. Liverpool FC were at the height of their powers and had dominated English and European football since the early '70s. There was, in short, a more mature secondary market for tickets amongst Liverpool fans than anywhere else in the country. I would enjoy, much later in life, the opportunity of regular visits to Anfield, and European forays supporting the Reds, and so I became used to running the gauntlet of buyers and sellers of hard-to-come-by tickets. It was novel to me, however, in 1989.

I had bought, and read, a programme whilst awaiting the 3 p.m. kick-off. I was sitting in seat NN28 in the South Stand, immediately adjacent to the Leppings Lane end, just twenty-eight seats away from where the tragedy unfolded. I noticed, and said so in my contemporaneous witness statement, that the enclosures behind the goal at the Leppings Lane end of the ground were much fuller than the enclosures to either side. I had been to other games at Hillsborough and this didn't strike me as unusual. Ardent fans always want to be as close as they can to goalmouth action.

As kick-off approached, the centre pens became full. I noticed that a giant inflatable beach ball was being patted around in Pen No. 3, which is where a safety barrier was to collapse in the minutes that followed and where the overwhelming majority of deaths occurred.

There seemed nothing unusual, let alone critical, happening on those terraces in the moments before disaster struck. There were a few individuals climbing up from the central pens to the seated area above but, at that time, I thought the reason was opportunism rather than escape. I was sitting about fifty metres away with an unobstructed view. A public safety professional with a fair experience of football from both a police officer's and a supporter's perspective and I could sense no danger. Of course, I knew nothing of the decision that was being made, at that precise moment, to open a concertina exit gate and allow 2,000 more people to stream in, unmanaged and undirected, to join the throng on the terraces behind the goal.

The ultimate question as to culpability for the deaths in the spring sunshine at Hillsborough is right here. No one has ever advanced the view that it was the wrong decision to open the gate. On most accounts, there were likely to be casualties, and probably fatalities, in the vice-like crush outside the turnstiles. Police officers on duty there had already asked three times for permission to open the stadium gates to effect this emergency relief. The key question is about the extent to which a public safety professional, with an experience similar to or greater than mine, enjoying a similar view to that which I had over the terrace, could or should have foreseen that the decision to open the exit gate, allowing unsupervised entry into the ground of 2,000 more fans, was likely to create a potentially fatal situation.

My honest answer to that most crucial question is that, whilst it was foreseeable, I just cannot know whether it was foreseen – Chief Superintendent David Duckenfield, the police match commander that day, must account to the law and to his own conscience in that regard. What is obvious is that, in hindsight, David Duckenfield, and others around him, should have made that link and acted swiftly. They had adequate time, more than five minutes from the first request to open the gates, in which to contemplate all the issues. Gate C was then in an open position for a further five minutes. Count to 300 in your head and consider how many thoughts flash through your mind during that time.

Whether they did make the connection and ignored the risk, or should have made the connection and froze, or whether it was reasonable for them, in all the circumstances, not to have made the connection, is a matter for judicial determination. It is a question that has been put to such determination once already. The jury in a criminal trial of David Duckenfield failed, in 2000, after five days' deliberation, to reach a verdict on a charge of manslaughter. Superintendent Bernard Murray, who was Mr Duckenfield's very experienced deputy, and who stood alongside Mr Duckenfield throughout those agonising minutes of mutual indecision, was found not guilty of a similar offence. It remains to be seen whether judicial determination ends there or whether the question of Mr Duckenfield's actions and, just as importantly, his thoughts on that spring afternoon in 1989, are to be brought once more to account.

There were, as there always are in the lead-up to any disaster, attendant factors that together created a perfect storm. There is more to the story of the *Titanic* sinking, coincidently on 15 April, than Captain Edward Smith and an iceberg. At Hillsborough, the stadium furniture severely hindered the escape of those who were crushed on the terrace. What on earth were we all thinking in the 1980s when we created impenetrable, unscalable and unyielding steel fences to effectively cage football supporters for the duration of the game?

It wasn't only Hillsborough that had perimeter fences to prevent anyone from invading the sanctity of the playing area. They were common throughout the higher leagues of Europe. Though some continental countries chose netting or moats rather than steel for the job of containing the worst excesses of football hooliganism, which sometimes resulted in rival fans fighting each other on the pitch or attacking the players of the opposing team.

The English first division clubs favoured steel mesh. These fences appeared at most but not all grounds. They were encouraged by the football authorities and by the government, which was dismayed by the constant embarrassment of instances of what the world's press had labelled 'The British Disease'. In the 1980s, hooliganism at football matches was frequent; it was ugly, and it was dangerous. Thirty-nine Juventus fans had been killed at the Heysel stadium in Belgium just four years before the Hillsborough disaster. It provoked sanctions against English football, with all of their teams banished from European competition for the remainder of the decade.

It was Heysel, and other similar incidents, that caused the government to be actively proposing a draconian Football Supporters Bill, designed to curb hooliganism, at the very time that the Hillsborough disaster occurred. There was no hooliganism present at Hillsborough on that fateful day, but the measures put in place to address the threat of hooliganism, and the predisposition of the police and other authorities to anticipate hooliganism, were at least a part of the problem that afternoon. It is a sad indictment that hooliganism, in the minds of the majority, occupied a higher priority than safety.

The steel fences were the ill-considered response of an industry that was trying to limit the potential for trouble by the most economical means possible. 'Take their money at the gate, segregate them, then cage 'em in. That should do the trick.'

The lateral fences in place at the Leppings Lane terraces at Hillsborough were not common across all football stadia. These steel-mesh fences, similar in construction to the perimeter fences, ran at ninety degrees from the edge of the playing surface to the brick wall at the rear of the terrace. There were six of these lateral fences, thereby dividing up the Leppings Lane terrace into seven pens. Effectively, these created cages with only a single gate of less than one metre in width on the front and a gate of slightly larger dimensions on each side boundary. There was a single tunnel beneath the seating area to serve the entrance and exit needs of the majority of the 10,000 supporters who were licensed to stand in those cages. The tunnel could be closed off by the police, and often was when two opposing sets of supporters were being directed into separate cages.

I had stood in the cages at Hillsborough and other grounds as a law-abiding football supporter and it always felt wrong. It was a voluntary confinement for two hours each Saturday afternoon.

I had also, in the 1970s, stood in a capacity crowd at Leppings Lane, when Sheffield Wednesday played Manchester City in the last game of a season that saw Wednesday relegated. The home team needed only a point that night to remain in the first division. They lost. The crush on the terrace was unbearable. And this was before the erection of the perimeter and lateral fences, so I can only imagine, from my own earlier painful experience, how terrible those minutes were for those caught up in the 1989 tragedy, who not only endured a crush, but whose means of escape was prevented by unyielding steel mesh.

Could it or should it have reasonably been foreseen by anyone with a responsibility for public safety that these confines were, in effect, death traps? It was foreseeable that fire, a panic, a terrorist incident or, as in this case, unintended overcrowding, would each create the potential for injury or death. Hindsight offers such perfect clarity.

Hillsborough, and the Leppings Lane terraces, had another, unique, engineering flaw. The crush barrier configuration was unsafe and this contributed to the scale of the tragedy.

Crush barriers are placed, strategically, along any terrace to break up the crowd, to disperse pressure and to prevent a crush. In fact, the crowd packing and pressure were so great in Pen 3 at Hillsborough on the fateful day that a crush barrier, number 124A, bent and finally gave way, causing an involuntary cascade of bodies to pile onto the floor and on top of each other. One thing that the jury in the renewed inquest might have put their minds to is whether this crush barrier failure could explain the disproportionate number of fatalities in Pen 3 compared with the handful of deaths in Pen 4. Both pens were similar in style and design and were equally overcrowded when the tragedy occurred. I know that because I would later be tasked to carry out a headcount from the photographs taken of the crowds in both pens.

Higher up the terrace, directly behind the failed barrier No. 124A, there was, originally, an additional barrier, No. 144. This barrier was designed to restrain people emerging from the tunnel. In order to move anywhere else across the terrace, the incoming spectator would need to find his or her way around that barrier and others, in the style of a children's maze. It was an essential safeguard to prevent a crush from occurring further down the terrace, where barrier 124A was placed.

In 1986, the season after the lateral fences had been installed, a police Chief Inspector, who was a regular commander at Hillsborough football matches, asked the club and its consulting engineer to review barrier 144. He had noticed that people entering Pen 3 from the tunnel were reluctant to move from that point of refuge. It gave a good view of the pitch, central behind the goal, and it was closest to the point of exit for refreshments or comfort needs. It was, however, causing what he considered to be a dangerous backing up of the crowd in the tunnel.

One might imagine that the club and its consulting engineers gave their utmost consideration to the concerns expressed and to the consequences of any action, including necessary mitigation. Unfortunately, those considerations are not well recorded and the consulting engineer has since died. The formal record that remains is of a hastily taken decision to simply remove the barrier, leaving no check whatsoever between the tunnel and the fateful barrier No. 124A, which was near the front of the terrace. A thoughtful observer might wonder why so many people who entered the stadium through Exit Gate C immediately before the tragedy ensued were to be found in the list of deceased (almost a quarter of those who died had entered after 2.52 p.m.). Common sense might have suggested a greater risk to those already in place on the terrace when the overcrowding occurred from the rear. The flow of the incoming spectators, unchecked by the absent barrier 144, might offer a possible answer as to why common sense, in this instance, is confounded.

There are a couple of other contextual points that are worth considering in any analysis of the disaster. Firstly, the overall terrace had a safety certificate capacity of 10,100. That is to say that the local authority licensed it as a public entertainment venue with a maximum capacity of 10,100 in that part of the ground. The local authority, however, did not require to be informed as to how the club or the police would ensure that the 10,100 were to be equitably and safely allocated to the seven enclosures. It appears from the records that, whilst that question had been considered by the club and their engineers had drawn up a plan involving separate turnstile entrances, nothing ultimately was done to address that knotty question. Neither by the club nor by the police, nor by any other statutory representative who sat on the safety committee which issued the certificate. The central pens, Nos 3 and 4, were significantly over capacity at the time that the tragedy ensued. There were, however, no more than 10,100 across the terraces as a whole, even when taking into account the numbers who entered, at police invitation, through Exit Gate C.

On the day of the disaster, Sheffield Wednesday Football Club, the owners of the Hillsborough Stadium, had responded to a police request to ensure segregation of rival fans by allocating separate ends and separate turnstile entrances. It was the 1980s and an undue emphasis was put, by all authorities, on segregation and the avoidance of hooligan flash points. Hindsight compels us to concede that too little concern was placed on the safety and comfort of the paying customer, the vast majority of whom had neither a tendency nor sympathy towards hooliganism. Hooliganism dominated the agenda of everyone who had a responsibility for football and that provides an uncomfortable context for the disaster that ensued at Hillsborough.

On 15 April 1989, Nottingham fans were allocated the Spion Kop, a huge standing terrace at the east end of the ground with a capacity of 21,000, and the South Stand, a two-tiered all-seater grandstand with a capacity of 8,800. Liverpool fans were allocated the Leppings Lane terrace, with a capacity for 10,100 standing spectators, the West Stand area above those terraces, providing 4,456 seats, as well as the North Stand, which was the most modern part of the stadium infrastructure and had seats for 9,700. Liverpool, who had the largest following of the two competing teams, were therefore afforded 24,256 tickets, whilst Nottingham Forest had 29,800.

This was a cause of some disquiet in the Liverpool camp. Peter Robinson, the Chief Executive of Liverpool FC, asked the Football Association (FA) and Sheffield Wednesday to swap allocations. On consulting the police, Chief Superintendent Brian Mole, the experienced match commander at Hillsborough in charge of pre-event planning, rejected the proposal. His reasoning was that most of the Liverpool fans would arrive from the west and north of the ground, whilst Forest fans had to come from the south and east. For him it was a simple question of what provided the most effective segregation arrangements. The club and FA accepted the logic. After all, as previously discussed, everyone was in thrall to segregation in order to prevent hooligan confrontation.

What everyone should have been more concerned about was the impact that this allocation and segregation would have on turnstile configuration. Hillsborough had eighty-three turnstiles in 1989. Every single one would be needed for an event with a capacity crowd of over 54,000. But, with a myopic focus on segregation at all costs, the club, in full view of the police, divided the number of turnstiles so that Nottingham Forest fans had sixty (72 per cent of the total means of entry), whilst Liverpool fans had only twenty-three (28 per cent). Even worse, all 24,256 Liverpool ticket-holders were required to enter the ground at Leppings Lane, where the twenty-three turnstiles were then further demarcated for entry to the different stands, resulting in only seven turnstiles being made available that day for the 10,100 supporters in possession of terrace standing tickets.

The official flow rate through stadium turnstiles is 750 per hour. The club will have known that from the *Green Guide*, which represented, in the late '80s, the bible for safety at sports grounds. The guide was issued by the government to all sporting venues and local authority safety committees. Sheffield Wednesday could also have discovered, from their computerised counting mechanism, the typical flow rates through specific turnstiles.

At 750 per hour, then, the simple mathematics would reveal that Liverpool fans with standing tickets would have to arrive steadily and evenly over at least a two-hour period preceding kick-off if they were to be admitted to the ground safely prior to the start of the match. Of course, like most football fans at the majority of games in that era, they did not arrive steadily and evenly over that timeframe – and why would they?

On the back of their ticket, each spectator was advised to be in their place fifteen minutes before kick-off. With the experience of the previous year, when the same teams played in the corresponding fixture at the same Hillsborough venue, and when the vast majority of spectators got into the ground for the three o'clock kick-off, who could blame any individual spectator for following the advice on their ticket? Coupled to that, it was a sunny spring day. Who would want to stand on a shaded terrace with no pre-match entertainment beyond a self-initiated game of patting a beach ball?

Some fans came later than the ticket advised; some fans – a small percentage of the total – had passed the pre-match period in the pub or drinking al fresco in the spring sunshine on the first warm day of the year. That is not a crime, nor even a cause for censure. It happened a lot at football matches and it might well have been anticipated. The over-whelming majority of Liverpool fans were in the immediate vicinity of the stadium well before 3 p.m. The problem was that the turnstiles couldn't cope. If Liverpool had been allocated the number of turnstiles commensurate with their total allocation, then the spectators might have been admitted more steadily and evenly before kick-off. As it was, the crowds outside Leppings Lane turnstiles became a critical heaving mass. It was estimated that there were 5,000 people gathered outside twenty-three turnstiles with less than fifteen minutes to go before the kick-off of the most anticipated and gladiatorial game of football to be played that season. Who wouldn't be anxious to get in to see it?

Should the kick-off have been postponed? The decision was in the hands of the match commander watching the deteriorating scene on the CCTV screens in match control. What would have been the impact on the crowd outside? What about the even bigger crowd inside, some of whom had been there for over an hour with little more than a beach ball for amusement? To any experienced football match commander the answer should have been yes. Delay the kick-off, try to explain the situation to all the anxious football fans outside and explain it over the public address system to those already in their seats and places.

There would of course be brickbats from terrace critics.

Visiting fans used to packed houses every Saturday at Anfield and Nottingham Forest's City Ground would compare Sheffield to Toytown – a Noddy club employing a Mr Plod clearly struggling with their duties. Any delayed kick-off disrupts public transport at the end of the game. Television executives wouldn't be happy either. They have schedules to stick to and advertisers to satisfy. Furthermore, the two club managers would happily lynch any match commander who decides to delay. They would have spent the day psyching their players to a peak of passion and controlled aggression. They would already have given the *Henry V* speech and they would know that adrenalin levels have a limited shelf life. Virtually everyone is against the match commander delaying the spectacle. They would say not, now, post-Hillsborough. Kick-offs were delayed at the drop of a hat in 1990 and 1991. 'We don't ever want another Hillsborough' was a common refrain appreciated and accepted by even the fiercest critic.

But on 15 April 1989 at 2.45 p.m.? What then? Any match commander worth their salt knows that criticisms of any operational policing decision taken on the grounds of safety disappear, like the morning mist, as soon as a ball is kicked. But David Duckenfield was not a match commander worth his salt. That is not a cheap shot from an armchair pundit who has never been faced with this dilemma – I know that it's a lonely place to be. David

Duckenfield was not a match commander worth his salt because *he* now says so himself.

He tried to mask his failings in the aftermath of the disaster. He told an infamous and ignominious lie suggesting that Liverpool fans had forced their way into the ground. It was an instantly doomed attempt to carry off an air of authority. At the public inquiry that quickly followed the disaster, Mr Duckenfield would also try to share blame with junior officers for not recognising or rectifying his mistakes.

However, in a hushed Coroner's Court on 11 March 2015, the room packed (itself an all-ticket affair with priority seating for the families bereaved by events that surrounded Mr Duckenfield's decisions, actions and omissions), he finally admitted that he was not up to the job that fateful afternoon:

DAVID DUCKENFIELD: 'One of the biggest regrets of my life is that I did not foresee where fans would go when they came in through the gates.'

CHRISTINA LAMBERT QC: 'Do you think you should have done?'

DAVID DUCKENFIELD: 'If I'd have been a fully competent, experienced, knowledgeable match commander with the experience, should we say, of Mr Mole, I no doubt would have thought about it. But I wasn't in their position.'

CHRISTINA LAMBERT QC: 'Understanding, as we do, your limited experience, which we discussed yesterday, is it not a basic principle of policing and, indeed, a basic principle in many other walks of life, where you must think about the consequences of a decision that you make?'

DAVID DUCKENFIELD: 'I accept that, ma'am.'

CHRISTINA LAMBERT QC: 'Why do you think you didn't consider the consequences on 15 April?'

DAVID DUCKENFIELD: 'I think it's fair to say that I was overcome by the enormity of the situation and the decision I had to make, and, as a result of that – this is probably very hard to admit – as a result of that, I was so overcome, probably with the emotion of us having got into that situation, that my mind, for a moment, went blank.'

CHRISTINA LAMBERT QC: 'Did you panic?'

DAVID DUCKENFIELD: 'Ma'am, there is every possibility, but I think others should judge me.'

David Duckenfield may, after all, turn out to be a contrite man who repents of his failings and must live, for ever, with the dreadful consequences. As to an assessment of him as a police officer, he might be viewed as an example of a senior commander uncomfortably straddling two eras. The commanders that I had served under in the '70s were often from a military background (though rarely of commissioned rank) and to a man (for all were men) they adopted an authoritarian demeanour. Many were ranters; those who believed respect and control was gained in direct relation to volume and fear. Most were autocrats; 'my way or the highway', 'shape up or ship out' kind of leaders. And, significantly, they liked to create a myth of infallibility. They of the 'not on my watch' kind of pep talks. A Superintendent, early in my service, had a framed poster behind the desk in his office that sent a less than subtle message to every visitor. It read: 'To err is to be human, to err twice is to be history.'

With many, it was a facade. They had probably worked out that this was the way to get on in their career. Commanders in the twilight of their careers would select protégés in their own image. You'd better be tough; you'd better be ruthless; you'd better not screw up was the zeitgeist of the time.

By the time it got to my generation of commanders in the '90s, we were viewed, by comparison, as a group of lily-livered, laissez-faire dilettantes.

David Duckenfield was in an uncomfortable position in 1989, with a foot on each of the shifting plates. He was educated, he had some emotional intelligence. He wasn't a ranter but he may have still hung on, more quietly than some, to the theory of infallibility. Some who worked closely with Mr Duckenfield would say that he was quick to seize on any perceived slight towards his competence or judgement. A trait, perhaps, of an insecure leader. And eventually, under oath in that Warrington Court room, Mr Duckenfield confessed it to himself and the world.

David Duckenfield shouldn't have even been in charge of policing at Hillsborough on that April afternoon. Brian Mole was the vastly more experienced Chief Superintendent at the Hillsborough Division and was expected to command the operation until nineteen days before the match.

Shrewd, clever, quick-witted and charming, Mr Mole had been a Detective for most of his career and in most ranks. In his earlier CID days, he had been given the nickname 'Soames', which is an obscure reference today. Soames Forsyte is the central character in a series of three novels by John Galsworthy, collectively known as *The Forsyte Saga*, about the life and times of an upper-middle-class family. The eponymous TV adaption of the books became a popular series in the '60s and '70s, more popular perhaps than *Downton Abbey* today. Soames, played by Eric Porter, was a dapper, smooth and self-righteous man who could be crafty in manipulating situations to his own advantage.

Whether he was 'Soames' or not, Brian Mole was popular. He had a loyal following amongst his coterie and he courted and rewarded that loyalty. He was a very good Detective; a very good operational commander; and a very good leader to have around at a time of crisis. He had commanded major events and high-risk football matches and he would have been the ideal man to be in charge at

Hillsborough on 15 April 1989. Unfortunately, however, he had been removed from his post the previous month.

There have been a variety of explanations given to the recent inquest about the reasons for his untimely removal. Some have suggested that it was to assist his career development by giving him additional experience away from Sheffield, the city in which he had served throughout his career. I cannot say whether that was the case or not, but it is not an obvious reason. He was on the top of his professional game and had a wide range of experiences and skills. If he couldn't find a way through the final hoop for Chief Officer appointments, which was via the National Extended Interview for Senior Command Training – and he had been to the interview twice – then perhaps he just didn't have the X factor that was sought. Sending him to Barnsley for 'wider experience' was not a magic key that would unlock further advancement. And anyhow, he was not the most favoured son in the eyes of some at Headquarters. He had been a bit too cavalier; too sharp; maybe a little too charismatic for his own good.

So if it wasn't career development, what was it? Some have advanced the proposition, to Lord Justice Goldring and the jury at the Hillsborough Inquest, that Mr Mole's transfer to Barnsley, weeks before a huge operational event on his division, was a simple and direct punishment. There had been an outrage on the Hillsborough Division more than twelve months prior to Mr Mole's transfer. A despicable, and stupid, initiation prank involving a new recruit had gotten terribly out of hand. The recruit was ambushed at imitation gun point and taken to a quiet location, where his uniform was removed and he was handcuffed to a post and left. There naturally followed an investigation, which was finally resolved in early 1989. Perpetrators were sacked and officers of higher rank, who should have known what was going on, were demoted. There was a clearing of the decks at the Hillsborough Division. Then a gap. Then Brian Mole was moved. I don't know whether he had surreptitiously spoken in support of any of the punished and thereby sealed his own fate. (It would have been in his nature, particularly if any were favourite loyal servants.) But a direct punishment move seems unlikely. That would have been done, if it was felt necessary, in conjunction with the other moves and demotions. It would probably have involved a move to a less prestigious post than that of Divisional Commander. This appeared to be a straight transfer to a post of similar status sometime after the brouhaha.

The clear-out at Hillsborough Division might have triggered a thought in the minds of some at Headquarters to take out the head of the stable. But it was the opportunity, a few weeks later, when the Barnsley Divisional Commander's vacancy arose, to seal Mr Mole's fate.

Of course, his posting could have been deferred, he could

and arguably should have been told to continue with operational plans in train and to command the semi-final game as the Barnsley Chief Superintendent. Though that might have appeared indecisive in the context of the 1980s police culture. Furthermore, any delay in his removal may have given Brian Mole, perceived as crafty and clever, an opportunity to change minds at Headquarters about the whole enterprise surrounding his transfer.

Whatever the reason for Mr Mole's departure, however, the die was cast. The match commander on 15 April 1989 was to be David Duckenfield, a man who now claims, probably accurately, that he was neither appropriately experienced nor sufficiently confident to fulfil that role. It was to be David Duckenfield who would be watching, via CCTV cameras, the swelling numbers gathering outside the turnstiles. It was to be he who would have seen that, at 2.45 p.m., the area was now choked to such a degree that it was becoming difficult for anyone to actually get through the turnstiles.

Imagine a small opening in a bag of coffee beans. The hole might be big enough to let one or two beans pass through easily in turn, but when there is the pressure of other beans concentrated on that same opening then none can escape. There were 5,000 people in a frightening press and their narrow routes to a place of refuge had all seized under the pressure. David Duckenfield was watching this but had no experience of what was normal and what was extraordinary in terms of gathering numbers for a semi-final event. The time for making a decision about delaying kick-off was now.

But he let the moment pass. He had previously given a policy decision to his staff that ruled out kick-off delay except where external factors had prevented the timely arrival of fans. Mr Duckenfield reports that by the time he was resolved to consider postponement it was too late. He might have been petrified, quite literally, at the thought of the criticism that would follow from all quarters at this, his first major operation in his brand-new command.

The topography outside those seized turnstiles aggravated the developing crisis. There was a slight downhill gradient from the road into a bowl and then a funnel-shaped area. The front of the crowd, pressed against the turnstile wall, was maybe thirty-five people shoulder to shoulder but, back at the stadium perimeter gates, it was maybe fifty people and, by the time the crowd was back to the roadway, it was 100 or more across the fan-shaped press.

Some eye witnesses claim that there were some individuals who did not help matters either. This has been a sensitive and controversial aspect of any account of the day. Whilst such claims deserve to be set in a proper context and not exaggerated, they cannot be ignored or concealed.

I raise them here in just two paragraphs only to describe a possible source for the perceptions of a South Yorkshire Police 'cover-up', not to unpick the clear and definitive verdict of the recent Coroner's Inquest.

There has been consistent testimony that a small proportion of fans had no ticket for the game, and had been unable to acquire a 'spare' or a 'swap'. On the sworn evidence of some turnstile operators, it is said that odd individuals sought to use the opportunity of the crush to negotiate their way in. Conscientious turnstile operators sent them back out but this interfered with throughput at the too-few turnstiles even before the crowd became jammed. Several in the crowd – not many – are reported to have become impatient to an assertive degree. Some are said to have pushed, although most in the throng had lost physical control and were simply being carried along by the crowd. One or two are reported to have hurled cans and abuse at mounted police who were perceived to be part of the problem in the crush rather than the solution. According to the unsolicited and unvarnished testimony of some police officers and members of the public, there were some individuals who arrived late at the back of the crowd, albeit a tiny minority of the overall throng, who acted unreasonably. These individual transgressors might have stood out to the junior officers trying, in vain, to restore order and safety even after any chance of control had been lost.

The original evidence of the mounted officers who, against all the odds and at the height of the crush, managed to close the perimeter gates to prevent further entry to the funnel and to protect those inside of the gates, is pertinent. From their lofty viewpoint they claimed to have spotted, in the mass of the law-abiding, sober, frightened thousands, the unreasonable behaviour of a number. The perimeter gates were forced open, the temporary relief was lost and the crowds continued pressing. The mounted officers trapped amongst the throng, incidentally, were predominantly Merseyside officers, shipped in that day to assist with the control of a crowd that would have been familiar to them at Anfield. They made their statements to assist the independent West Midlands Police investigation, not to suit a South Yorkshire Police conspiracy.

Any police interventions at this time were too little, too late. There had been no effective policing strategy to prevent a crush from occurring and no contingency plan or coordinated response when it did occur.

Those junior officers closest to the dangerous crush, which was a precursor to the terrible disaster that ensued in the following minutes, were asked for an early account – by supervisors, by journalists, by families and colleagues, and by a public inquiry which sat within four weeks of the tragedy. It may be no surprise that, having experienced the feeling of professional impotence, and tormented by

their own post hoc guilt at having failed to avert the catas-
trophe, some of them should highlight the behaviour of
individuals who they perceived as not helping the situation
in their moment of failure.

Thus was sown the seed of the perceived and lasting hurt,
felt deeply by the families of those bereaved on this dreadful
day, that 'the police have always blamed the Liverpool fans
for the disaster'. It quickly became clear, particularly once
Lord Justice Taylor's inquiry had heard the wider evidence
of what went on that day, that the fans in that terrible crush
were in no way to blame.

Some people have clung to that false narrative for too
long. They are often people who weren't there on the day,
have heard no evidence from those who were, and have never
read any of the published accounts from the various inquiries. For years I have explained to the occasional jaundiced
commentator that there may have been evidence of misbehaviour by a minority in the crowd but they didn't create
the situation which ultimately led to the deaths of ninety-
six people. The police had lost the situation by 2.45 p.m. on
that Saturday, even if that minority had all stayed at home.

From seat NN28, I knew nothing of these events at the
time. Everyone was standing in this seated grandstand,
at 2.55 p.m., to welcome the players into the coliseum.
An added frisson of excitement was to try to catch a glimpse
of the Forest manager, Brian Clough – the 1989 equivalent

of today's 'Special One'. Clough was under a touchline ban for thumping three fans who had, with hundreds of others, invaded the pitch at a League Cup Quarter Final game in February that year. Clough was allowed to manage the team from the stands with messages passed via runners to his bench. He was to be seated in the South Stand on this occasion and all were straining to witness this 'momentous' event – a football manager sitting in a seat like ours. I thought it was silly and sat down to try to encourage the same in others so we could enjoy the game.

People did, eventually, take their seats and, as the wider scene was gradually revealed to me, I saw that twenty-two men had begun to kick a ball about. But I also saw something much more significant. I saw people climbing from the centre pens at the Leppings Lane end. Dozens were clambering over the top of the perimeter fences and scores were being lifted into the seating section above the terrace. People around me were seeing the same sight but not through my eyes. The man next to me shouted: 'Get the dogs into them! Get them back!' But this was no 1980s-style pitch invasion. No one escaping the cages behind the goal was venturing anywhere near the hallowed playing surface. A number were just sitting, some collapsing, on the perimeter track. This was a safety issue. There were too many people in too small a cage. The utter stupidity of human cages was being made manifest here at Hillsborough.

Even then, I never thought for a second that anyone would be seriously hurt. I imagined that, under police direction, a number would be decanted from one pen to another and the sacred game would continue. I couldn't know about the opening of Gate C outside the stadium and the 2,000 additional people joining an already-full terrace. I knew nothing about the removal of crush barrier 144 at that stage. I didn't realise that barrier 124A had by now collapsed in Pen 3. The tragedy had passed unknown and unseen whilst most of us with an individual seat in the relative calm of the South Stand were looking to see if a middle-aged man, wearing a green sweatshirt, had taken his seat in the stand.

I realised, quicker than many around me, that this was serious. Police officers, some senior, were running. (Police officers don't normally run, as it tends to spook the public.) I saw Superintendent Roger Greenwood stop the game and the referee remove the players from the pitch. My emerging fears were confirmed when I saw a police officer that I knew, PC Keith Marsh, carrying a young boy across the playing surface to a quieter, less chaotic area right in front of where I was sitting. He put him down on the ground and began to give him mouth-to-mouth resuscitation, whilst another man was doing chest compressions on the boy. That little boy was in cardiac and/or respiratory arrest. He was in danger of dying before my very eyes or he may, for all I knew, already be dead. I looked around and took in the wider scene. Hundreds by now were on the playing surface and its perimeter. But, apparently, hundreds of police officers were too. Enough, in my immediate professional opinion, to resolve the most extreme operational challenge. But not enough, it transpires, to prevent the tragedy unfolding behind the impenetrable steel-mesh fences.

Someone had joined PC Marsh and the other man attending to the young boy in front of me. This chap looked up to the South Stand, to no one in particular, and offered a joyous thumbs-up signal. He was obviously under the impression that mouth-to-mouth and CPR had saved the young boy's life. Unfortunately, history tells us that this was a premature, and vain, hope on his part. The boy, Lee Nicol, would be one of the youngest victims of the tragedy.

This was a major incident – anyone would describe it as such. But the emergency services use those two words as a shared code to describe an event that requires coordination of all three services in order to protect life, to search or to rescue. There were literally hundreds of uniformed officers at the point of rescue and I thought that the creation of a rendezvous (RV) point for ambulances might be a pressing need with which I could assist. Intuitively, it seemed obvious to me that if there were casualties on the pitch then they could not be taken out through the still-packed Leppings Lane terrace. I knew nothing of any contingency, and had witnessed no immediate spontaneous decision, to use the gymnasium at the north-east corner of the ground as a clearing station. If the ambulances were going to come – and they must come – then they would come, I reasoned, to the rear of the South Stand. My emergency procedures training kicked in.

I found a large tarmac area between the gable ends of the South Stand and the West Stand. Within the curtilage of these two grandstands it was the closest point of access to the playing surface. The police control room was nearby. This would serve as an RV point for ambulances and the fire brigade.

There was a minor obstruction. A police Land Rover. It was the same Land Rover, I learned much later, that had been used outside, at the Leppings Lane crush, as a plat-form stage by Inspector Stephen Ellis. In an attempt to regain some control close to kick-off, he had climbed onto the roof of the Land Rover and stretched the microphone cord that was attached to a public address system fitted to the vehicle through which he appealed to the crowd. From his unusual and elevated standpoint, he could see that unless the crush was relieved from the back there would be fatalities at the front against the turnstile wall.

There was a gaggle of police officers handily near my imagined RV point. Something that is difficult to under-stand today is that no police force in 1989 held sufficient numbers of police radios to enable personal issue. The Home Office owned and operated the radio network and loaned a sufficient number of handsets to each force for normal day-to-day operations. These officers had no radio between them and probably knew less than I did about what was going on. I showed them my warrant card and dispatched an officer to find the keys to the Land Rover and to move it. The others I deployed to keep the area secure for ambulances that would, I told them, undoubtedly come.

It was then that I encountered, directly, a casualty of the Hillsborough disaster. The day of 15 April would be a long one and my perception of the degree of tragedy involved would multiply many times. I had seen PC Marsh giving mouth-to-mouth to one young boy on the pitch, now here was a second, and then quickly a third, casualty in my personal orbit. I turned around from the issuing of instructions about the Land Rover and RV point to find a man laid out on a metal stretcher on the floor. I can't say how he got there, but the idea of a South Stand ambulance station seemed prescient now. There was a policewoman and a St John's Ambulance volunteer with the man. The St John's Ambulance man was raising his head from what I took to be mouth-to-mouth resuscitation. The policewoman was kneeling at the side of the stretcher. Both uniformed personnel looked frightened and exhausted.

I knelt at the other side of the stretcher and held the

man's wrist. I could find no pulse, but that is a fickle signal. I cannot honestly say that there was no pulse, I just couldn't find one in that urgent moment. But my additional observations indicated that the man appeared to have passed away. He was ashen in colour, a kind of blue-grey of Westmorland slate. His eyes were open and vacant. I could not see, hear or feel any breathing.

Fortunately, an ambulance then appeared at precisely what I was calling, unilaterally, an RV point. Two ambulance personnel immediately attended to the man on the stretcher. I could see now that he was around twenty-eight or thirty years old, of heavy build and about six feet tall. He was having his chest thumped by an ambulance man whilst another tried an oxygen mask. After a few moments they seemed to give up and moved towards putting him in their ambulance. There were sufficient police officers around to help lift the stretcher.

Casualty number three, as listed in my mental ready reckoner, was a walking wounded. He, too, had simply appeared whilst my back was turned. He was holding his arm and I would describe him as more in discomfort than out-and-out pain. In other circumstances he might have received more attention and more sympathy. As it was, there seemed greater priorities. He climbed into the ambulance, whether of his own volition or at the invitation of the ambulance crew I know not.

The ambulance, with one occupant apparently dead and another very much alive, was prepared for departure. I said generally to the group of police officers that I wanted someone to accompany the deceased. Continuity of identification in a case of sudden death is a fundamental tenet of our police training. I didn't need to say why I sought an accompanying officer.

Then something happened which has always stuck with me. I have sought to explain it, or at least verify my recollection of it, since that time without success. I remember, and said so in my first written account in the immediate aftermath, that a uniformed officer stepped forward and said: 'I'll go. I know his family.' That sounds incredible, I realise, but that was my contemporaneous recollection. I have scoured the transcript of the recent Coroner's Inquest but have found no testimony to support that recollection. Perhaps if someone with an overview of all the available evidence had spoken with me about my recollection, then my memory and my own self-doubts about this exchange may have been reconciled.

Whilst I understand, from a purely evidential point of view, that my description of a 28- to 30-year-old man who appeared to me to be dead does not take the jury much further in their understanding, there is, somewhere, a mother, or a wife, or a sister, who might take comfort from the knowledge that professional carers – especially St John's and ambulance personnel – did all they could. Their loved one, within a very short time of the tragedy unfolding, appeared to me to be at peace. Of course, the other thought that has occurred to me since is that, miracle of miracles, the man on the metal stretcher may have been resuscitated in the ambulance, or at hospital, and be a survivor with no knowledge of the emergency first aid that was rendered.

The ambulance left. My so-called RV point was secure and sterile. There were no other casualties at that point. I walked up the service road behind the South Stand and past the gable end of the West Stand to check the route for the further ambulances that were sure to come in response to this major incident.

It was at this point that I reached the next rung on the ladder of escalating astonishment. I had already seen a young boy in difficulty on the pitch in front of me; I had happened upon an apparently deceased man and a walking wounded. Now, as I turned the corner of the West Stand, I saw what I then considered to be the full horror of the tragedy. If only it had been so.

There was a plastic-coated mesh perimeter fence on the south side of the stadium service road beside a river. At the foot of that fence were laid ten or twelve bodies. All appeared, from a distance of five metres, lifeless. The facial appearance of these bodies was disparate. Some were heavily cyanosed, with blue veins apparent on their cheeks.

Some were the ashen colour previously described and some appeared normal. Many, I can't say all, were laid in what is called a recovery position, laid on one side – their right side mainly – with the lower arm outstretched beneath the head and the upper leg bent at the knee to prevent their rolling over onto front or back. It is called a recovery position, but these ten or twelve young people looked, from a distance, to be beyond recovery. I found the sight shocking and was struck by a sense of impotence which was only partially due to my being in civilian clothes.

I saw that this was someone else's busier, and more critical, RV point. Mine had been too advanced. This was a point where ambulances first turned off Leppings Lane onto the service road and the casualties had been brought from the rear of the West Stand. There were at least four or five ambulances parked here. Their crews were dispersed amongst those by the fence and also the walking wounded. There were also dozens of police officers. I saw Chief Inspector Roger Purdy as the most senior officer present. He had a radio and was wearing a uniform with a peaked cap. He had a visible authority – he was clearly in charge. Most of his troop of officers, maybe fifty or more, looked to be in a state of shock.

If this was the full extent of the disaster, as I believed that it was at that time, there was nothing useful that I could add to the professional efforts in train. I acknowledged

Mr Purdy but he was busy organising and rallying. My final act at this place of devastation was to instruct some of the statuesque officers at the service road entrance to stop the general public from entering that scene. They were so much in a state of shock and impotence that they would have taken instruction from anyone, even a stranger in a green wax jacket.

I made my way to my car with the intention of driving the mile or so to the Hillsborough Divisional Headquarters at Hammerton Road. I reasoned that if this terrible event had sucked in all the local resources, then I might be of some further use at the police station. I also thought of ringing home to let my family know that I was safe and well against the context of what must have been emerging news reports of mass casualties at Hillsborough. It was at least a decade prior to widespread mobile phone ownership and I found that all the call boxes on my journey were full with long queues outside.

At Hammerton Road Police Station, there began to arrive a steady stream of visitors. People who had been at the nearby stadium and who, in the ensuing chaos, had become separated from friends. No mobile phones meant a great deal of waiting and worrying in the face of increasingly grave news from Hillsborough. I decided, along with Chief Inspector Les Agar, who had also come to Hammerton Road to see if he could help, that we might treat all of these enquirers as if they were reporting people as missing. We had forms for that, we had procedures, and we could explain it simply and easily to junior officers. This was the best means of getting consistent information about those reported as 'missing'. It seemed obvious that at least some of these reports would tie up with people who weren't missing but were at hospital or worse. Those who had become separated from family members and friends waited patiently for their turn to be collected from the front enquiry office and taken to the ground floor CID office by an officer armed with a report form to be completed.

As the death toll increased with every update, the mood became darker amongst those enquiring about loved ones and so, too, with the cops. There was an unusual silence about the place – no station banter and no clatter of kettles, mugs and typewriters which was the ambient noise of every CID office. The missing person reports kept churning out and they would later be compared with lists emerging from hospitals and, ultimately, with those located at their penultimate resting place – the Hillsborough Stadium gymnasium.

The numbers in the small reception area at Hammerton Road police station grew so that people were standing outside. Someone relieved that pressure point by having the Boys' Club hall next door opened up for those who had made their report and who didn't know what they should do next. Social Services staff supported the families and friends who endured this agonising period of apparent inactivity. The Salvation Army and others appeared out of thin air with sandwiches and drinks. It was all pretty ad hoc. Nobody had a detailed plan of what to do in circumstances such as these.

By the early hours of the morning, the numbers coming to Hammerton Road had dwindled and then ceased. Now was the time for checking hospital lists. I discovered that all those pronounced dead at any hospital had been taken back to the Hillsborough gymnasium, which had been designated, by Her Majesty's Coroner, as a temporary mortuary. The total at the mortuary did not reach ninety-six. Some were being cared for, in extremis, by medical staff at hospitals. One of the casualties, Tony Bland, would only be pronounced dead in 1993, when doctors removed all life support. But there were scores of bodies in a North Sheffield gymnasium – more than anyone who I spoke with had ever seen in one place at the same time. I couldn't imagine what it must be like down there, but I was soon to find out.

I spoke on the phone with Brian Mole in those early hours. Mr Mole, as Barnsley District Commander, had been on duty that afternoon at Oakwell Football Stadium. His first visit since taking over at his new division. Barnsley FC were playing Birmingham City in the old Second Division. There were 6,464 spectators at the game. Brian Mole's extensive football command expertise, and his knowledge of safely controlling large crowds, was being tragically wasted. He was informed of the unfolding disaster twelve miles away from Barnsley and immediately got a driver to take him to the scene. He had eventually ended up over-seeing the mortuary arrangements by the time I rang him to see what he wanted me to do with the sheaf of missing person reports. He asked me to take them to the gymna-sium and to pass them to Inspector John Charles, who was involved in administration at the temporary mortuary.

It is too easy, at this kind of distance, to condemn the mortuary procedures that were hastily put in place that awful night. That came to mind when I saw television foot-age at the time of the crushing in Mecca in September 2015, which left over 2,000 Hajj pilgrims dead. I saw distraught family members sitting on the pavement outside a Saudi Arabian mortuary, three days after the event, who were still uncertain as to whether their loved ones were inside. It caused me to think that early identification in 1989, albeit traumatic and done in a sub-optimal fashion, might have been preferable to a delayed arrangement.

An operational police commander setting up procedures such as those at the Hillsborough gymnasium would natu-rally hope and expect that every single officer involved in each and every encounter with a bereaved family member would demonstrate the appropriate level of compassion, empathy and patience. Not just to get the job done effectively, but to meet the particular needs of the bereaved. I heard some positive reports to that effect but have read compelling evidence from many families who felt that 'getting the job done' took precedence in those dark hours of Sunday morning before the dawn. That is lamentable.

On delivering the missing person reports as instructed, I witnessed for myself the awful, awful situation for all concerned. Around 4 a.m., there was still a double-decker bus parked outside the gymnasium – temporary shelter for those who still had to perform the dreaded task of identification, which would be the final trigger for grief. I could see the people on that bus, illuminated starkly against the surrounding blackness, most of whom were staring blankly into distant space.

I found John Charles easily in the cavernous, echoing gymnasium and I completed my assigned task. But not before I had seen the rows upon rows of zipped body bags laid in an orderly fashion on the floor. To the right of each body bag was placed a chair and on each chair sat a police officer, some in uniform, some who I recognised as Detectives. Every one of them had the same drained and gaunt expression. Even professionals can succumb to shock and trauma. Those who had been deputed as body continuity officers had sat for hour upon hour with their charge, surrounded not only by death but also by the pain of the living.

The anguish of the living is what haunts me about that fateful day. I saw the temporary ante room at the gymnasium into which each body bag was wheeled, in turn, aboard a trolley. The body bag was destined to arrive under the gaze of relatives brought to undertake the dreadful duty of identification. It isn't just the sight of the dead that I witnessed that day that moves me, even now, to tears. It is the sounds of the living and the lost. I handed over my unimportant forms to John Charles, but not before I had heard more than one family cry out in grief at the revelation of their loved one. Their tortured cries echoed around that otherwise silent gymnasium as if they would go on for ever.

For me, at least, this longest day was over.

CHAPTER 2

THE FELLA
IN SEAT NN28

3 January 1956 – 15 April 1989

I have already addressed the curious fact that I have
never been asked to recount my testimony about the
day of the disaster as I saw it unfold from seat number
NN28 at the Hillsborough Stadium. There is another fundamental question, though, that no one has asked me over
the last twenty-seven years… What was I doing at Hillsborough, on my day off, having bought an expensive ticket

to go to a football match that was to be televised and that involved two out-of-town teams?

It was because I have followed the fortunes of Liverpool Football Club since 1 May 1965. There was nothing unique about such an affiliation, for Liverpool FC was the most successful British team throughout my formative years and had a reputation for playing in a swashbuckling style. It was the favourite team of most boys of my generation who read football magazines such as *Goal* and *Shoot*, watched *Match of the Day* on television and decorated their bedrooms with football paraphernalia. I wasn't a diehard 'Red' and it was an attachment that I kept to myself whenever I was invited, in later years, as a guest to Goodison Park.

The 84th FA Cup Final, played at Wembley in May 1965, was the first I had ever witnessed. I watched the whole event, with my dad, on our Bush black-and-white television. In those days there was a televisual build-up to the match which included footage of how each team had reached the final; images of the players eating breakfast at their match-day hotels; in-depth analysis of a few of the key players; a roving cameraman following the team coaches along Wembley Way pausing for vox pop interviews with passionate fans of both teams. During the build-up I folded some paper and wrote out a mock match day programme with the names of all the players of each team arranged symmetrically, on either side of the fold, in the two-three-five formation of the era. It was a spectacle being played out in my own front room and I was gripped by it.

In 1965, the final was contested by Liverpool and Leeds United. (For those watching in black and white, Liverpool were wearing dark shirts, shorts and stockings.) I had no particular allegiance going into the game. My uncle had taken me a couple of times to Millmoor to watch our local team, Rotherham United, who played in the Second Division. But this game was different. There were almost 100,000 fans in Wembley Stadium. Some of the gladiators were household names and television elevated their status, and that of the event, even higher. At the age of nine, I was mesmerised.

The game was nil-nil after ninety minutes but Liverpool had been dominant and threatened on every attack. Extra time, the first in an FA Cup Final since 1947, added even more drama. Liverpool scored first, three minutes into extra time, through a Roger Hunt header. Bremner equalised for Leeds before the teams changed ends for the last time. Midway through that final fifteen minutes, Ian St John headed a whipped cross from Ian Callaghan to score the winning goal. There was pandemonium in the sitting room of 35 Mansfield Road, Rotherham, and I have had a soft spot for Liverpool FC since that moment.

I don't want to overstate my attachment. For the most

part, my support was confined to the armchair in front of the TV or wearing my treasured all-red football kit in park knockabouts. It would only be when I later lived in Liverpool that I came to rarely miss a match. But Hillsborough Stadium was only five miles from where I was living in 1989 and so an important match involving 'the Reds' seemed a natural place for me to be. I went to Hillsborough as a football enthusiast and my only prejudices as I took my South Stand seat were the positive ones held by a supporter of any club.

Nine years prior to my epiphany as a Liverpool supporter, I was born in the front bedroom of 24 Temple Street, Templeborough, on the boundary of Rotherham and Sheffield. The house was within sight and sound of Steel, Peech and Tozer's electric arc furnaces. Steel, Peech and Tozer, known locally as Steelos, was a giant in the South Yorkshire steel manufacturing industry, employing thousands of men. My father was a furnaceman, my mother a housewife, and I had an older sister. We lived, happily, in our two-up-two-down Steelos house between Dad's furnaces and the strip mill, which fashioned the steel for use in the factories that were turning out the cars, washing machines and refrigerators that all postwar families aspired to.

My childhood predated Harold Wilson's 'white heat of technology' era. I lived in a steel-making community at the very heart of the fiery yellow heat and red oxide dust fall-out of the industrial age. Dad, who had been a Coldstream Guardsman, and a tank driver in the Second World War, was earning what he referred to as 'good money' as a furnace second-hander (the number two on the shift). We had a factory house; an Austin A30 car, one of only four cars in our street; and a share in a family caravan at Mablethorpe. Life was OK. We would later move to Mansfield Road, when I was six, to another Steelos-owned house, to make way for the demolition of Temple Street and factory expansion. At Mansfield Road, we would enjoy the novelty of an indoor toilet and bathroom.

I went to Alma Road Infants and Junior School, a stone's throw from home. Even closer, just at the top of the street, was South Grove Comprehensive, a 1,000-pupil educational conveyor belt that produced, each year, the next generation of steel men, coal miners, secretaries and factory girls. I was in the top stream at South Grove and I can only recall five or six of my class going on to university. None of them were the sons and daughters of steel workers. Ours wasn't a school, or a town, that produced academics or captains of industry. We were factory fodder, and the schooling reflected that.

On leaving statutory education, my very moderate

examination results were a little below average for the top stream, well above average for the school. I was luckier than most, however, for I had a vocation. All I ever wanted to be, from a very early age, was a policeman. Not a Chief Constable, but a bobby. School, for me, therefore, was a legal requirement to occupy my time until working age. At sixteen, I became a police cadet in the Sheffield and Rotherham Constabulary. A couple of years later, I fulfilled my ambition when I passed out as a Constable. I built a reputation for being good at my job.

My career choice, like anyone else's, must have been a result of many influences. Some I recall, whilst others may be less obvious. I was always the tallest amongst my pals, over six feet at the age of fourteen, and I had often been given positions of authority at school, in sports teams and in the Cubs. These factors created a trend. I remember my paternal grandfather, who also worked at Steelos, telling me from an early age that I was destined to be a bobby on account of my height. After military service, both he and my father had been tempted by another, civilian, uniform role but took the 'better money' on offer in the steel industry. I knew that neither wanted me to follow in their footsteps.

When I was about thirteen, Dad dressed me as a young apprentice furnaceman in one of his wool shirts and sweat caps and took me onto the floor of the melting shop. The heat and the noise were terrifying. It was like one of Dante's circles of hell. Dad told me later that his intention, in taking me to see where he worked, was to put me off the idea of ever gaining employment at Steelos.

The nationalised steel industry was decimated within ten years of my leaving school: it couldn't compete with cheaper imports. Dad and most of his colleagues were made redundant and, in his early fifties, he never found work again. It seems that my father's influence on my career choice was prescient.

I also had two formative, and positive, experiences of meeting police officers that left a lasting impression. Throughout my career in leading fellow officers, I have always exhorted them to strive, in every encounter with the public, to create a similar positive view of the police service. The average law-abiding person comes across a police officer so infrequently that they will recall, for years, the impact of any meeting. It is therefore in the hands of every cop, every day, to create a positive or negative public opinion about the profession.

One Christmas Day, in the mid-'60s, I was wearing my newly unwrapped football kit and playing keepy-uppy in the back yard when I noticed a torrent of water gushing out of an overflow pipe of the Conservative Association office next door. The pipes had frozen, and then burst, in the empty building. In the steel town of Rotherham, the

Conservative Party needed only a token presence, and they achieved it in a converted end-of-terrace house next to ours. The only up-side of this proximity, as far as I could see, was that Captain Basil Rhodes, the local party Chairman, occasionally parked his green Aston Martin DB4 outside our house, and this created quite a stir amongst my school pals. Anyhow, my report of the burst pipe led to a bobby attending. He had a cup of tea in our kitchen whilst he waited for the key-holder to turn out. He was complimentary about my new kit and about my footballing skills. He impressed me. I wouldn't be very much older when it dawned on me that he was actually only being polite.

A few years later, I noticed suspicious activity on a building site across from our house and ran home to phone the police. I gave a running commentary on the phone that enabled the capture of two thieves. I was praised by a uniformed Inspector who was present at the arrest. The Chief Superintendent in the town wrote a letter of thanks to an impressionable fourteen-year-old boy. My mother kept it for a long time with other family papers.

So, because of this constellation of half remembered experiences, and other unconscious pushes and pulls, it was always going to be a policeman's life for me.

I was a successful cadet and excelled in recruit training. I strove to succeed. My vocation gave me what I had lacked in my school years: desire and ambition.

I was a prolific 'thief-taker' as a young bobby and became a Detective in CID with just eighteen months' service. This was unusual. I wasn't a bad Detective either. Though I had much to learn through working alongside more experienced hands, I was a quick learner.

Some colleagues have tended to look for reasons to explain my successful police career. In the early days, a common label applied to me was 'lucky'. There is an old aphorism which describes the happy coincidence that the harder one works the luckier one becomes. In later years, and in the light of a number of promotions, the labels were to become defined by extraneous factors rather than luck. 'It's because he's a graduate' some suggested – I was, indeed, fortunate to have been given a second chance at education – or, 'It's because he's on the square' – even though I have never been a Freemason or a member of any other exclusive society.

Whilst I was learning my craft as a young Detective, someone, it transpires, was watching me closely. Chief Superintendent Alan Robinson, Divisional Commander at Barnsley in the late '70s, called me to his office one day and asked if I had ever heard of the Special Course at Bramshill. I had heard of neither the course nor the venue. It was a national programme in the police service, he told me, to identify and develop exceptional talent. It was a scheme intended, primarily, for graduate entrants to the service, who had demonstrated immediate potential and, more occasionally, for non-graduate, workaday officers like me. He asked me to apply for the course. My first application form was returned by Mr Robinson, who had corrected my grammar and punctuation. He supported me through the force selection process along with two other candidates. I have always been grateful for that support.

There were two further hurdles. A regional interview, which narrowed the field of candidates from northern forces, and, later, a three-day extended process of tests and interviews in competition with the brightest and best from all forces in England, Wales and Northern Ireland. I was successful in clearing both obstacles – without any additional help from Chief Superintendent Robinson! This opened up, at the age of twenty-six, an undreamt-of avenue of career opportunity for a lad from Rotherham.

There was a full-time programme for twelve months at Bramshill Staff College, the police equivalent of Sandhurst for the army. I studied law, jurisprudence, sociology and politics. As well as the academic input, there was vocational training for the leadership roles that beckoned.

Just eight of the cohort of thirty-six students were non-graduates. At the end of the Bramshill programme, and after we had each proved our potential in the field by successfully demonstrating practical ability in the ranks of Sergeant and Inspector, most of the eight were offered a funded university scholarship. I was amazed to be accepted on my first application to the Queen's College, Oxford, as a mature student to read Psychology and Philosophy. I graduated, in 1986, with an understanding, at last, of the real benefits of education. I have been committed to personal development ever since.

Upon my return from Oxford, I was given an operational leadership role as a Shift Inspector at Rotherham Division. Within fifteen months I was promoted to Chief Inspector, the fourth rung on the police rank structure ladder, which has nine steps ascending from Constable to Chief Constable.

By the time of the Hillsborough disaster, I was a Chief Inspector in a non-operational post at force Headquarters. I had been tasked to create processes, within the Personnel Department, that would identify and develop young talent in the force.

I was just thirty-three years old and, whilst I had experienced three promotions in the previous seven years, my own career still had some distance to travel. I would go on, in later years, to scale the highest peaks of the police service. Chief Constable of two of the 'big five' provincial forces; working alongside ministers on national policy and organisational change; overseeing national police training and development; and supporting the national and international counter-terrorism effort. On 15 April 1989, these all remained chapters of a story yet to be written.

I was sitting that fateful day in what, for me, was a relatively expensive seat anticipating an epic football match. I was not looking down on the terraced pens in which the 1980s football industry segregated the classes of spectator as well as the few who might misbehave. I did not hold a prejudice about football fans generally, nor about Liverpool fans in particular. I stood beside them. On other occasions I had shared the experience of the cages and might have done on that tragic day if the source of my ticket had been different.

The authorities that oversaw football in that era seemed blind to the discrimination that existed in the sport prior to the Hillsborough disaster. The cheaper standing tickets that were made available to the majority of supporters came with fewer, and rudimentary, toilets, inferior catering and other facilities, and a mean and brutal experience that was made tolerable only by the community of others in the same situation. I was a part of that community.

On that spring day in 1989, as the tragedy unfolded, I had no predisposition to besmirch Liverpool football fans. And no one ever asked me to do that in the days, weeks, months and decades that followed.

CHAPTER 3

THE IMMEDIATE AFTERMATH

17 April – 12 May 1989

According to the sworn testimony of ex-Superintendent Clive Davis, I returned to duty twenty-eight hours after leaving the mortuary and, without any meaningful conversation about my experiences at Hillsborough, nor exhibiting any visible sign of distress, I told him that there was to be a team pulled together under Chief Superintendent Terry Wain to collect evidence to begin to defend the actions of South Yorkshire Police. I told him, he recalls, that there would be a briefing of CID officers by Mr Wain at 11 a.m. and that he should accompany me to the briefing if he knew what was good for his career.

His testimony is silent about where I had received that information from and fails to clarify how this briefing was to fit with, or be distinguished from, the acknowledged fact that, on Monday 17 April 1989, the residual tasks of gathering evidence by South Yorkshire Police, prior to handing the whole enterprise to West Midlands Police, was in the hands of a different senior officer, Detective Superintendent Graham McKay. Mr McKay had himself called a meeting with Detectives that day to tell them of the transition of the investigation into the ownership of West Midlands Police. That meeting *did* take place at 3.30 p.m. and was fully minuted. The minutes do not mention Mr Wain or any associated briefing.

It might have made Mr Davis's evidence less credible if he had happened to light upon the same time for these two parallel briefings taking place. Their timings are, rather tantalisingly, four hours apart. Mr Davis recalled these matters from April 1989 with great clarity only after the publication of the Hillsborough Panel Report in September 2012. At the time of the publication, and the attendant press reports, he was on holiday in Mallorca, where he claims that he saw me on television 'continuing to blame

Liverpool fans for the disaster' and he felt compelled, on his return to the UK, to contact the Hillsborough Family Support Group in order to unburden himself about this briefing, which, on his own account, he had not discussed with many people over the intervening twenty-three years.

It wasn't much of a briefing by his account – short and perfunctory. Hardly worth bringing the brightest and best Detectives together from around the force area. I was there, he says, and so too was Chief Superintendent Wain, who Mr Davis reckons had called the meeting. We had both been mentioned by name in the Hillsborough Panel Report, which Mr Davis had read, and had been identified, too, in the media frenzy that followed. Standing beside Mr Wain at the briefing was Superintendent Malcolm Seller. Those were the only three names that Mr Davis could recall at this distance. Of the thirty or so Detectives in the room, whom he thought were mainly Detective Sergeants and above, he could not recall the name of one.

Mr Wain, according to Mr Davis, told the assembled number that he intended to put the blame where it belonged, on the drunken Liverpool fans. It transpires that everyone was then permitted to leave the briefing room to go who knows where without a single person being given a recognisable task. That sounds like an unusual briefing. It was not one that I was at or even knew about.

Mr Davis had given this evidence at the Coroner's Court

in March 2015, and it was very widely reported in the press. After all, his account fitted perfectly with the popular narrative at that time. When I gave evidence, a few weeks later, I was asked whether I considered Clive Davis an honest man and I gave an honest response. I worked alongside him in the '90s and knew him reasonably well. In years gone by he had visited my home with his family. I set out an Easter egg hunt for his children on one visit. I never had any reason to doubt his honesty and integrity until this latest revelation. Mr Wain had been asked a similar question under oath a few days earlier and he had been much more blunt and rude about Mr Davis in his response. Mr Seller had replied by witness statement that he was on holiday in a caravan with his family at the time of the disaster. He had rung HQ on that relevant Monday morning to see if there was anything he might do to assist. He was told no and therefore continued with his holiday. He remembers it vividly.

I was asked if I had any explanation as to why Mr Davis, and others who had delivered such devastating testimony about me at Warrington, might tell an untruth. Again I gave an honestly held response. I think that a lot of people, when history is being written, strive to be 'on the side of the angels'. From my recent experience as an 'accused', I have deduced that some try just a little too hard to achieve this celestial status.

There was no briefing or meeting that I attended on Monday 17 April. I had been, as an off-duty spectator, to a football match, which turned into a disaster. I had no ongoing responsibilities or reason to commit anything more than a professional interest to the question of how it had happened. In any case, I attended day release at Sheffield Hallam University on that Monday, leaving the office around lunchtime.

In 1988, whilst I had the professional development bug carried over from my time at Oxford, I had suggested to my managers in the force that I might be permitted some flexibility to attend Sheffield Hallam University from time to time to study for a Master's degree in Business Administration (MBA). I reasoned that managing police organisations of 10,000 personnel, which have budgets of hundreds of millions, would need business acumen and skills in the future. I would pay the course fees myself and do the necessary work in my own time. I would just need to be able to attend a tutorial day on an afternoon and evening during term time for three years. I undertook to make up the time over the working week somewhere. I was permitted to sign up for the programme, which ran between 1988 and 1991.

On Monday 17 April 1989, two days after the disaster, I was due to leave work early for my class. I was then employed as a Chief Inspector, tasked with creating a new department at Headquarters – the Career Development

Department. It was my job to find ways of identifying, nurturing and developing talent within the organisation. New appraisal systems; mentoring schemes; and promotion board arrangements were early fruits of my labours.

I was back at my desk some twenty-eight hours after leaving the gymnasium at Hillsborough. Of course there was office comment about the weekend's events, but not as much as might be supposed. The force, as a whole, was in a state of shock, if it is possible for organisations to exhibit emotional responses.

It is said of the Taj Mahal that it separates the world. There are those who have seen it and those who haven't. The two camps cannot speak about it with any shared comprehension. Well, the same is true of Hillsborough. There are those who were there or who have been directly affected by it and those who weren't, and haven't been, can have no similar understanding. This was true by 8 a.m. on the Monday after the disaster and has, in my long experience, remained true ever since. Those who were there didn't want to talk very much to colleagues around the metaphorical water cooler, and those who hadn't been there allowed their troubled peers the time and space for personal reflection.

By the time I left for the MBA course, I had learned nothing much more than I had read in the papers and heard on the TV and radio news about the tragedy. I had no clue about its causes, or how South Yorkshire Police intended to respond to it.

There was much more talk about Hillsborough amongst fellow students at university than there had been amongst colleagues at Headquarters. Our custom, on the tutorial day, was to adjourn, at the end of our studies around 8.45 p.m., to the local pub, the Fleur de Lys at Totley. There would usually be a dozen of us, sometimes more, chewing over matters of local or current interest. A general observation about human nature is that the volume of any expressed opinion is often in inverse proportion to the amount of personal experience or research. And so it was in the pub that night. People were holding forth about the disaster and its causes in a bar-room style, and by that I mean an uninformed style. I was no better positioned than anyone else, although I had witnessed the tragedy end of the disaster even if I knew little of the causal end at that time. I remember making it clear that David Duckenfield's intimation that fans had broken down the gates was not true. My Chief Constable, Peter Wright, had said that it wasn't true on national television on Saturday evening within a few hours of the misinformation being propagated. I had read of his correction. I also recall that I knew that South Yorkshire Police were in the process of handing over the investigation of the causes to an independent force and I shared this fact with others who were unaware.

I had not read *The Sun*, which I later learned had published an edition on Monday 17th under a headline 'The Gates of Hell'. The article offered, in typical *Sun* style, ten simple 'Deadly Reasons Why it Ended in Bloody Carnage'. Some of this analysis littered early bar-room-style conversations about the Hillsborough disaster. *The Sun* was to completely overreach itself, however, two days later. Publishing under the banner headline 'The Truth', it quoted unnamed police officers involved in the rescue effort, and it cast some hateful aspersions upon the Liverpool fans who were at Hillsborough. Amongst other calumnies, it alleged that Liverpool fans had stolen from, and urinated on, the dead.

When I left the Fleur de Lys on the evening of Monday 17 April, I was no wiser about the events of the weekend. Furthermore, I had not presented myself as having any particular knowledge other than my experiences after the match was stopped and after the disaster had occurred.

I had not, by this time, begun to write my account about my experiences on the day. A general request was made from Police Headquarters, early that week, for any officer who was at Hillsborough, whether on or off duty, to capture their recollections whilst fresh so that they would be available as an aide memoire when the officer was later seen by the West Midlands Police investigation team. The request was made, in the fashion of the 1980s, by telex to all divisions and departments. No one indicated what should or should not be included. There were no additional instructions about contemporaneous pocket notebooks, which, by the time the telex was distributed, would have been overtaken by time and events. No one told me that I should not make a pocketbook entry. I simply assumed that my written recollection, prepared in several sittings over the next seven or eight days, would suffice as a first account.

It was pointed out in cross-examination, when I gave evidence to the recent Coroner's Inquest, that my detailed written statement produced in the days following the disaster contained neither criticism of fans nor any observation of any bad behaviour in the lead-up to the disaster. That is true, for I witnessed none and therefore could produce no evidence of it. This simple fact in itself might give the lie to lingering suspicions, arising from the Hillsborough folklore narrative, that from an early time after the disaster I was involved in concocting black propaganda.

When I left the Fleur de Lys on Monday 17 April, I had said nothing, to any of my fellow students, about joining a team at South Yorkshire Police to gather evidence for my senior officers and for the lawyers representing the force. I couldn't have done, for that call was still two or three days away.

In the middle of the week, most likely Thursday 20 April, I was at my desk on the fourth floor of Police Headquarters. It was open plan and from my location I had a sweeping view of the whole floor. Beyond the double doors in the far left-hand corner lay the command suite. Individual offices were occupied by the Chief Constable and his deputy and assistants. There were smaller offices for a few Chief Superintendents who oversaw Headquarters activity. My boss, in that regard, was Chief Superintendent Arthur Ball, whose office was next door to that of his boss, Stuart Anderson, who was Assistant Chief Constable Staff Services. Two or three doors further on was the fourth-floor conference room where, although I didn't know it at the time, I would spend most of my waking hours over the next four weeks.

Arthur Ball told me that Stuart Anderson wanted to see me. Mr Ball was always discreet so gave nothing away about the reason. It wasn't unusual to be called by Mr Anderson, as he took a personal interest in the processes and people that were being developed in my department. He asked me to close the door and to sit down. He told me that the Chief Constable had asked West Midlands Police to investigate the causes of the Hillsborough disaster, which I knew. He then told me that he and other Chief Officers had been engaged in a meeting with lawyers the previous day, which I didn't. The upshot of that meeting was that, notwithstanding the West Midlands Police inquiries, the Chief and the force's legal team needed to have some idea about what went on, to make sense of the day, he said, so that the lawyers were in a position to represent the force at a forthcoming public inquiry. He had, with no prior consultation, for that's how it worked in those days, volunteered me to join the team that would support the task. It had nothing to do with me being at Hillsborough on the day. It may have had nothing to do with any particular skill set. Every division had simply been asked to provide a pair of hands. I was deputed from Headquarters. My day job was a non-operational role that could be left unattended for some time with no immediate detrimental impact on the operations of the force. I accepted the secondment. You always did in those days.

One of the projects that I had in train at that time was a review of all Headquarters posts to see which might be civilianised. This was a Home Office requirement arising out of the Conservative government's 'Three Es' programme. The big idea, in the '80s, was that public services should mimic private industry by reviewing their input costs (mainly people) against the 'three Es' of economy, effectiveness and efficiency. Working with me on that project was a bright young Inspector from the Research Department in the force, Clive Davis. I told Mr Davis, sometime after my meeting with Mr Anderson, that I would now be tied up for a few weeks on Hillsborough matters. I asked him to get on with the review of all departments apart from the Radio Control Room at Headquarters, where I had some work in place which I would pick up on my return from this new task. That was my first and, as far as I recall, only conversation with Mr Davis about the force response to the disaster. It was not followed up with any wider briefing to which I invited Mr Davis.

The fourth-floor conference room was about fifteen metres by eight. It had narrow windows at one of the short ends with an unprepossessing view of a local brewery. The smell of the hops sometimes permeated the walls. It had a number of interlocking tables that were usually arranged as a four-sided meeting facility with an island of space in the middle in the style of a G20 gathering (without the national flags). When I walked into the room that was to be my hermitage for the next few weeks, I found that the tables had been pushed together to form a solid working surface in the middle of the room, with no island of space at their core. Most of the meeting chairs were arranged against the walls of the room with only a few dotted, randomly, around the tables.

Dominating the working surface was a scroll of paper like a miniature roll of wallpaper. It was rolled out, as if waiting to be pasted, across the work surface. I knew what this was – I had seen them before as an operational

Detective. It was an ANACAPA chart. Today, if an investigator wishes to capture a complex and integrated series of events and facts so that they can be analysed and understood chronologically, then they would turn to computer software. This was 1989. The way we did it then was to draw a timeline on a scroll of paper and write, in long hand, who did what, when, where and with whom, across the scroll. We used the process of ANACAPA, a long-forgotten acronym if ever I knew its meaning at all, to assist in all major inquiries. If someone was killed in the drawing room with a piece of lead piping, then the cop in charge would roll out the ANACAPA chart and start writing about where the lead piping was last seen, who had it and who can give that evidence. The more complex the investigation, the longer the piece of paper needed to be.

Apparently Detective Superintendent Graham McKay, who was the first senior Detective on scene at Hillsborough, and who had harboured the thought for a day or so that he might have to undertake a criminal investigation, had tasked a Detective Sergeant, Peter Carr, with the job of creating an ANACAPA chart. Of course, the responsibility for investigation was subsequently passed to West Midlands and they would probably do one of their own. But, Peter Carr's early work, drawing on the accounts of anyone so far asked to provide one, was the starting point for our newly defined task.

Already present in the fourth-floor conference room, and with a head-start on me, were Brian Mole and a Chief Inspector from the Hillsborough Division, David Beal. We would be joined shortly by other middle-ranking officers from other divisions around the force. We had not yet been joined by Terry Wain, who would complete the team and the coverage of the force. Sharing out, across the force, the burden of any extraordinary task was a common feature of resourcing in those days.

Mr Mole was in charge on my first day in the conference room. He and David Beal were well on with the work of a review of the planning for the event. They were, though, marking their own homework, for the same two officers had been heavily involved in the operational planning of all major events at Hillsborough Division, and had put together and signed off the operational order for the fateful semi-final. It was their operational order that was handed over to Mr Duckenfield, who did not have sufficient time or experience to revise it or to produce one of his own.

I believe that Brian Mole's closeness to the event planning might have been the genesis for inviting Terry Wain to head up the team. No one ever told me that it was the case. Whilst he was the same rank as Brian Mole, and with much less experience of football and Hillsborough in particular, Mr Wain was assigned to oversee the task. I think someone had noticed, wisely, that the account that was to be furnished for our lawyers, if it came directly through Brian Mole, might not be entirely objective. If that is the case, then the choice of overseer was inspired. Terry Wain was the Father of the House, amongst the oldest, if not the longest-serving, of Chief Superintendents. He is a blunt Yorkshireman who had a reputation for not suffering fools gladly. He was a task master. He had been a long-standing Detective in previous ranks but he had not adopted any of the short-cut, slick, sometimes maverick, ways of many 1980s Detectives. He would doggedly stick to any task given to him through to completion – so long as the task was an honest one. The thought that Terry Wain might ever be involved in connivance or conspiracy is risible. He was amongst the straightest, but also most strong-willed and conservative, of senior officers that I encountered in forty years of policing. When Mr Wain took over as head of the post-disaster inquiry, the team was complete.

An early task, prior to a first meeting with lawyers on the forthcoming Wednesday, was to create a document under six headings, which had been provided by Peter Metcalf. Mr Metcalf was a senior partner in the West Yorkshire law firm Hammond Suddards. He and his firm specialised in public inquiry representation and public indemnity litigation. He had some knowledge about how Cleveland Police had responded in an earlier public inquiry about child abuse.

I am sure that Peter Wright, the South Yorkshire Chief Constable, had not picked out Hammond Suddards, or Peter Metcalf, from the *Yellow Pages*. I suspect he had not picked them at all. Any forensic scrutiny of the Hillsborough disaster would have consequences for David Duckenfield, and other individuals who were in command; for the force as a whole; for the South Yorkshire Police Authority, which set and raised a budget locally and held the force to account in spending it; and also for the Police Authority's insurers. At the end of that long line of interested parties, it would be the insurers who would eventually meet any costs arising from litigation. The insurers, therefore, had a significant influence over the choice of lawyers.

In the first few days that followed the terrible disaster, some things that were done in the name of South Yorkshire Police were wrong. Three of them are seared into the memory of anyone who cares about the reputation of the ninety-six innocent victims of the disaster and of Liverpool football fans in general.

The first was David Duckenfield's scandalous lie about the opening of the gate. The second was the eagerness of a couple of police officers to tell salacious and second-hand stories, in a bar on the night of the disaster, which found their way into the press in the immediate aftermath. That was inglorious. The third was the press interviews given by a Constable who was an elected trade union representative.

He hadn't been present at the tragedy but had listened to his junior colleagues who had. His interviews gave what is regarded to be an exaggerated description of the levels of drunkenness amongst the fans.

As soon as the Chief Constable learned of these three indiscretions he immediately and publicly disassociated himself and the force from those comments. He instructed junior officers to desist from making any comment to the press. Unfortunately, Mr Wright's corrections did not receive sufficient amplification to be heard above the noise created by the *Sun* headlines.

There was a fourth mistake which was, by comparison, simply ill thought through or overly pragmatic. There was a decision taken somewhere between the offices of the Chief Constable and the South Yorkshire Police Authority to retain lawyers approved and briefed by the authority's insurers to represent the interests of the force as a whole. This created the potential for defensiveness when lawyers subsequently convinced everyone involved that they could also represent the individual interests of David Duckenfield and others at the epicentre of the disaster. These various parties – the Chief Constable, the at-risk officers and the underwriting insurer – may not always have had the same interests. And so it has proved.

It is these four actions directly and indirectly that serve, even now, to cause the name of South Yorkshire Police to be sullied. But, just as a couple of swallows don't make a summer, these four regrettable actions do not a conspiracy make.

Peter Metcalf would probably not recognise any tension between his servicing of the Municipal Mutual Insurance (MMI) company in tandem with his named client, the Chief Constable of the South Yorkshire Police. He seemed to me a professional and honourable man who would take instructions from his principal client and who would carry out those instructions in a proper manner. He was at the same time, though, having meetings in the margins with a man called Ken Holmes, who would be rightly concerned on behalf of his employer, MMI, about the costs of representation and the potential for multi-million-pound litigation claims.

MMI, which was incorporated in 1903 to provide insurance to local authorities and other public bodies, would become insolvent in 1993, due to suffering substantial losses in the years 1990–92. The reported £19.6 million compensation arising from Hillsborough fell to MMI during that time. The company, therefore, had every reason to be bothered about who was representing their interests in the aftermath of the disaster.

Whilst Peter Metcalf did nothing substantive, in my assessment, to compromise the interests of his named client in favour of the purse holder, and whilst the insurers' written instructions told lawyers to ignore the potential for future claims in representing the force, there was a tone from the first meeting with counsel, on 26 April, right through to the final submission to the Taylor Inquiry on 17 July 1989, that was defensive. David Duckenfield would need to defend his individual position for sure. The insurers, in a proper manner, would need to mitigate their potential losses. But the Chief Constable might have wanted to say something statesmanlike that may not coincide with the interests of others who were now roped together by this decision to employ common representation.

I have to say that I did not have this thought at the time. Furthermore, I did not witness anyone doing anything that was malfeasant in order to protect the interests of any of those fellow travellers. It is only natural to have reflected upon why South Yorkshire Police, as a body, has been so misunderstood by those who are most aggrieved and hurt by the actions of the people who have represented the force. Those are four things, all occurring in the space of a few days following the disaster, that might individually and collectively help to explain the source of the rancour.

The first meeting with the lawyers, to which the Wain team were invited, was to be on Wednesday 26 April. There had been an early and ongoing dialogue between Peter Metcalf and the Deputy Chief Constable ever since Mr Metcalf's engagement in the middle of the previous week. Peter Hayes, the deputy, is a precise and painstaking man. His natural tendency is towards the intellectual rather than to the intuitive. His first degree is in law. Given his background, and his role as Deputy Chief Constable, it was no surprise that he took a lead with lawyers and oversaw the work of the Wain team. Peter Wright had tasked him to do that. The two Peters met on the evening of the disaster and it was agreed that the Chief Constable would deal with all public-facing matters and the politics that would obviously follow. Whilst Peter Hayes would deal, in his cerebral and organised way, with meeting the requirements of the inquiries, inquests and other formal proceedings that might ensue.

Peter Metcalf had sent to Peter Hayes, on 20 April, six headings under which he needed more information in order to prepare an opening submission to the Taylor Inquiry. First, the force, its history and organisation; second, the general responsibilities that fall to the police for policing sporting events; third, the history of the force approach to such operations and any standing instructions; fourth, the specific planning for the 15 April semi-final; fifth, the details of the staffing, deployment and organisation for the event; sixth, the events which occurred, to be drawn from police officer accounts. It was this shopping list from the lawyers that caused the Chief Officers to realise, after standing down Mr McKay's investigation team, that they needed a resource to fulfil this and all future requirements of the lawyers. It precipitated my meeting in Mr Anderson's office, when I was assigned to the task.

It was assumed by Peter Metcalf that the sixth requirement would probably not be available in time for the 26 April meeting, but he hoped the other five could be. In fact, the sixth requirement, albeit a narrow, police-only perspective on the events that occurred on that day, was substantially available through the work that had been done by DS Peter Carr using his ANACAPA chart. The work was well underway on all six areas before Mr Wain took over the leadership of the task. Brian Mole, already au fait with the planning of the event and by now familiar with DS Carr's early work, did most of the work either directly, or indirectly through tasking some research here and there. I was given lots of these mini tasks but was given, in my own right, a quite straightforward job – to draft a piece that met the first of Peter Metcalf's tasks – an account that would explain to the uninitiated the structure and organisation of a police force, and South Yorkshire Police in particular. It took me less than a day. I was carrying out ancillary work and undertaking specific tasks from Mr Mole elsewhere. The working routine quickly settled into a pattern of ten to twelve hours each day, six days per week.

With section one of the report for the lawyers already in the bag, I broached with Mr Wain, on his first Monday in charge, the question of my day release commitment to the Sheffield Hallam University. I had worked for Mr Wain before so I knew there was unlikely to be any misunderstanding on his part about my commitment to the task in hand, but I also knew that it would be untenable, given what faced us, to take every Monday off. I asked if I might be allowed to go that afternoon to explain the situation and absent myself from the programme temporarily. He agreed.

The reason I felt it important to explain in person is that I had been struck by a warning given to all students by the course leader in our first week on the programme back in the autumn of 1988. He told us of a typical 25 per cent attrition rate and urged us to ensure continued support from our employers for day release. He correctly pointed out that we would all consider ourselves to be in critical jobs and informed us that he was unimpressed by any special pleading regarding professional commitments as an excuse for being unable to complete a project or the programme as a whole. If I was to successfully complete this postgraduate course, then it seemed important that I should explain myself, in person, at the campus. 24 April 1989 is the last time that I attended the university until very near the end of the spring/summer term.

I told all and sundry, tutors and fellow students alike, of my recent tasking. Not boasting, as was implied by a witness who was to give evidence about this day, twenty-six years later. I did say that I had been seconded to a team which would pull together evidence for the forthcoming public inquiry, which was due to start in three weeks. I did not say, as it is alleged, that I had been tasked to concoct a story to put the blame for the disaster onto the drunken Liverpool fans.

John Barry was a fellow student, although I could not recall him when he became prominent, after a round of television interviews, in October 2012. He was a civil servant with the Manpower Services Commission, which had a headquarters in Sheffield. I think his department was paying for one or two people to go through the MBA programme at Sheffield Hallam University. I had nothing in common with John Barry except the business course and, it transpires, our attendance at the same football match. Mr Barry had been at the Hillsborough semi-final and, on his own testimony, he was traumatised, and remains traumatised to this day, by what he saw.

He alleges that I spoke to him in the Fleur de Lys pub after a day at university together. Given that he was absent, suffering the effects of shock trauma, on Monday 17 April, and given that I was absent for the remainder, or majority, of the term after 24 April, it could only have been on that day that a conversation, if there was one between us, took place.

He said that I told him, in a boastful way, that I had been selected to join an important team that was looking at the disaster. Without the boast and hyperbole that sounds like one of a number of conversations that I had on that day. Mr Barry goes on to testify that I made an announcement, for there was no two-way interaction, no contextual conversation and no response from him, just, he says, my outburst at the bar of the Fleur de Lys as we collected our drinks at the same time. I volunteered, he says, that my specific task was to concoct a story that all the Liverpool fans were drunk and that we were afraid that they were going to break down the gates so that is the reason we opened them. Leaving aside that there is not one scrap of evidence that I ever did any such thing, and leaving aside my denial that I used such foolish words, Mr Barry is also in some difficulty with his timings.

He says that this pronouncement definitely did not take place on 24 April, which would fit with my recollections of widespread conversations on the theme of my recent tasking. Mr Barry says it happened within a week or two after 8 May. The reason that 8 May is so central to his account is that he was seen by the independent West Midlands Police investigators on that day. They took a statement from him about what he had witnessed in the lead-up to, and the aftermath of, the disaster. Mr Barry had been sitting directly above the site of the crush. Any pro-forma for statement takers has the suggested prompt 'Is there anything else you want to add about this incident?' Unless Mr

Barry had a good reason for withholding his very serious allegation about me from the Detectives who were undertaking the formal investigation, then he is obliged to place the occasion of my alleged disclosure sometime after his interview with West Midlands Police. I was not in a position to have any conversation with Mr Barry after 8 May because I was not attending university. Furthermore, my work with Mr Wain was completed and handed to lawyers by 9 May. For what it is worth, it isn't likely that I would have been speaking in the future tense about a task that had already been completed. Mr Barry is mistaken.

Taking into account the devastating effect that his public denouncement, on national television on 23 October 2012, was to have for me and my family, I am afraid that he is very seriously mistaken.

I can't know of his motivation, although he told the Coroner's Court that he had, in the late '90s, made financial contributions to support the private prosecution of Messrs Duckenfield and Murray. I only know that he is wrong about me. After one drink in the Fleur de Lys on 24 April, I left for home and an early night to prepare for the rigours of the task in hand.

The next twenty-one days were to be frenetic. Lord Justice Taylor would open the inquiry and begin taking oral evidence on 15 May. We had yet to meet the counsel retained by Peter Metcalf but the Deputy Chief Constable had warned us that the demands from lawyers were likely to be onerous.

One of the early tasks that fell to me was to bring together copies of all CCTV material that was available (the original tapes had been taken by the West Midlands Police) and to review it to see if it might assist in making sense of the day. In real time there were dozens of hours of footage, although it was possible to fast forward the less relevant material. I made a 113-page summary of what the CCTV images revealed and submitted it, through Mr Wain, to the lawyers. Again, there is nothing within those 113 pages that hints at bad behaviour on the part of Liverpool fans. There was no such evidence revealed on the video and so I would not have included it in my summary. A further, simple counterpoint to the assertion that I was somehow employed in a 'black ops' squad.

Another task that I undertook during that three-week period has always remained with me because of the poignancy of the process and the significance of the result. The lawyers were keen to know, before the start of the public inquiry, whether the central pens, Nos 3 and 4, were full around the time of the opening of Exit Gate C at 2.52 p.m. With the help of a colleague from the force's Scientific Support Department, I assembled a montage of photographs taken across the two pens at the relevant time. They were put together like a jigsaw puzzle, matching a column or a row of spectators on two adjoining images. Scientific Support rephotographed the montage and blew up the images into two panels, each approximately four feet squared. They delivered the panels to the fourth-floor conference room on a Friday evening. I recall that Chief Superintendent Wain received them and asked me to calculate the headcount by the following Monday morning.

I took Saturday as a rest day but came into Headquarters on the Sunday to complete the task. Armed with a red marker pen, I pinpointed and counted each spectator caught by the camera's lens. I took care to avoid counting anyone twice who might have been found on two abutting images. Sometimes I could only detect a shoulder or a raised arm but I tried to be as accurate as possible. In carrying out this task, which took me most of the day, I was conscious that my red marker pen was occasionally lighting upon the last image that would ever be captured of many young lives. On Monday morning, I was able to report that both pens were equally over capacity around the time that Gate C was opened on police instruction. A fact that was to go to the very heart of the public inquiry.

By far the most pressing task that occupied the Wain team over the next two weeks came as a result of the first meeting with Bill Woodward QC. Mr Woodward was the counsel retained by Peter Metcalf to represent the Chief Constable but his brief also included the at-risk officers such as David Duckenfield and Bernard Murray as well as the Police Authority's insurers, MMI. We met him at Police Headquarters on Wednesday 26 April 1989, eleven days after the disaster. As well as the Deputy Chief Constable, Mr Hayes, and Assistant Chief Constable, Mr Anderson, there were members of the Wain team present; Mr Woodward and his junior Mr Patrick Limb (who has subsequently become a Queen's Counsel); Peter Metcalf and his assistant Belinda Norcliffe. The meeting was chaired, nominally, by the Deputy Chief, but it was dominated by Mr Woodward QC.

Bill Woodward was, like every QC I have met, impressive. Some parade their impressiveness, intellectual sparring being a way of flirting with their client. Some are more impressive by being understated and only reveal, by way of a crucial point made in conversation, submission or witness examination, a mastery of the subtleties of the brief. Bill Woodward was in the latter category. There was no doubt that he would lead for the Chief Constable at the public inquiry. He had lots of experience of them, whilst the police officers in the room had none. Our job would not be to manage him but to feed him. He presented, at this first meeting, as a man with a voracious appetite.

This meeting on 26 April lasted for almost five hours. It is remarkable, particularly for those who know me in recent times, that, whilst I was present throughout,

I made no contribution to the meeting whatsoever. It was the opportunity for Mr Wain and Mr Mole to deliver the six-point report that had been requested by Mr Metcalf a few days previously.

When setting the task, Mr Metcalf had said that, within the week, the lawyers needed a document of sufficient breadth so that they could submit it or draft for themselves a written submission to the public inquiry. So either Mr Mole or Mr Wain had given the document the title: 'For Submission to the Judicial Inquiry'. It was never clear that it was to be submitted as it was drafted and, in the end, Peter Metcalf prepared the submission that was delivered by Bill Woodward QC at the opening of the inquiry.

At this, our first meeting with counsel, Mr Woodward complimented the team on the material provided. In and amongst many other requirements, he asked, however, that we provide him with the fullest picture possible of what evidence the officers who were on duty at Hillsborough might give about the events of the day. He wanted their feelings, fears and opinions as well as facts. He made it clear, and it is a matter of record in Belinda Norcliffe's file note of the meeting, that such information was for him and Patrick Limb only and not for submission to the inquiry. A deadline was set with Mr Wain outside of the meeting. This information was to be made available for lawyers by 9 May, six days before the start of the public inquiry.

Mr Wain opened a Major Incident Room, not because he was leading an investigation but because there are procedures and systems in any Major Incident Room that would complement his task. The HOLMES (Home Office Large Major Enquiry System) was a computerised way of indexing and storing witness accounts to enable an investigator, or someone answering a question of counsel, to drill down or retrieve the requisite information. If, for example, a blue car was to become pertinent to any enquiry, then, providing that the indexers had done their job correctly, HOLMES allowed the retrieval of all statements that mention a blue car. Free text retrieval, whilst commonplace now, was not easily achieved in the 1980s. Peter Sutcliffe, the Yorkshire Ripper, who was caught and convicted in 1981, had been mentioned numerous times in the thirteen parallel inquiries but no connections were made. HOLMES was developed as a direct result of a review of the Ripper case. The letters HO, at the front end of the acronym, signify Home Office ownership and reveal the source of funds to develop the national computerised system, which was beyond the resources of individual forces.

The Deputy Chief Constable, Mr Hayes, had, a couple of days after the disaster, asked all staff involved to record an account, as an aide memoire. These accounts, it will be recalled, were intended to assist officers' recollections when later interviewed by West Midlands Police. Chief

Superintendent Wain saw that copies of these self-prepared accounts would serve his purpose, too, in meeting the requirements of the task set by lawyers. He arranged for them to be recovered in a prioritised fashion: Supervisors; followed by those on duty at the Leppings Lane end of the ground; those who addressed the crush outside; those involved in rescue and so on. He deployed a number of officers to collect copies of these self-written accounts from around the force. The original document would stay with the officer pending West Midlands Police interviews. The couriers did not take statements. It wasn't their job and there wasn't time. Furthermore, there was no process of vetting or emendation at this point. Mr Wain received, and thereafter his team were furnished with, unadulterated accounts prepared by the persons giving them.

Some of these accounts contained expressions of emotion and intemperate language. Not the kind of thing normally seen in professionally taken statements. Mr Woodward QC had expressly invited such content and it had clearly been a cathartic experience, in the days that immediately followed the tragedy, for some officers to vent their feelings when writing their accounts.

All the accounts were first of all indexed and entered onto HOLMES and then passed into the fourth-floor conference room to be read and analysed. The reading was done by various members of the team although the accounts sometimes arrived with highlights and marginal comments from Mr Wain, who spent most of his time in the Major Incident Room.

The accounts were indexed against the key events of the Hillsborough disaster as identified on the ANACAPA chart, first created by DS Carr. For example, if we wished to know who could give evidence about the opening of Gate C at 2.52 p.m., we would have a list of officers and a short summary of their evidence. The team read hundreds of accounts of South Yorkshire Police officers. That is all that we had access to, for it would have been quite wrong to tread on the toes of West Midlands Police by going beyond these in-house accounts.

As the deadline approached for the information to be fed into the lawyers, we stopped reading and began to assess the product. Mr Wain chaired a meeting in the fourth-floor conference room, where, with the contributions of others from his team, he distilled the emerging picture. Mr Wain settled on eighty-one accounts that were considered to have the most objective evidence to capture the essence of what South Yorkshire Police officers could say about the events, as they had unfolded, on that spring day.

On this point I wish to be very clear. The hundreds of accounts that had been provided were available to both West Midlands Police and the counsel to the inquiry at the Taylor Inquiry. They could interview and call anyone that they wished. Mr Wain's list of eighty-one represented what he considered to be the best attempt at giving Bill Woodward QC an illustration of the overall police officer evidence. I was given the task of summarising the eighty-one accounts.

Any file prepared for the Crown Prosecution Service is always accompanied by a summary. Preparing a summary was meat and drink to an experienced Detective. Although this was novel in that it concerned only a limited part of the evidence (the South Yorkshire officers' aspect only) and was for barristers at a public inquiry not Crown Court, we set about producing the summary in a familiar fashion.

I was always aware that what we had in our hands was not an analysis of the causes of the disaster. It wasn't even a comprehensive account, limited as it was to only the self-prepared accounts of police officers. Furthermore, they were officers who, perhaps because of the trauma of the events and their shared sense of impotence and failure, had sometimes been emotional in their testimony, and had often highlighted, disproportionately, the unhelpful behaviour that they claimed to have witnessed.

I wasn't aware of Werner Heisenberg at the time, but was aware, professionally, of the limitations that he spells out so clearly about the nature of evidence. Heisenberg, the father of quantum mechanics, warns that 'we must remember that what we claim to observe is not nature in itself, but only those aspects of nature exposed to our means and method of enquiry'. Lord Justice Taylor was going to be in a much better position, very soon, to subject the Hillsborough disaster to a greater depth and breadth of enquiry. What the Wain team had produced, in contrast, was an internal document on the direction of Bill Woodward QC, so that he could know what evidence officers might give if they were called at the Taylor Inquiry.

This is an important point of emphasis because the Independent Police Complaints Commission (IPCC) appear to have misunderstood the purpose of this internal briefing document.

The Hillsborough Panel had referred to the document, which had been carefully preserved in the South Yorkshire Police archive for their subsequent discovery, as 'The Wain Report'. We never called it that. If we had ever thought of giving it a name we might, more accurately, have referred to it as the Woodward Report, for it was he who commissioned it. The Hillsborough Panel were struck by the one-sided view offered by the report but seemed pretty clear that it was only ever an internal report. It was never submitted to any judicial inquiry or proceedings. From the outset, Mr Woodward QC had deemed that it should not be submitted anywhere.

In spite of these well-documented constraints on its scope and purpose, the Independent Police Complaints Commission (IPCC), when giving their written and televised response to the Hillsborough Panel's report on 12 October 2012, four weeks after its publication, hit out publicly at the so-called 'Wain Report' and my contribution to it. Deborah Glass, the forthright Deputy Chair of the IPCC, declared that she intended to consider whether 'the Wain Report was a biased report which sought to divert criticism from South Yorkshire Police'. That is an entirely appropriate line of enquiry given the Hillsborough Panel's concerns about its one-sided nature. But Ms Glass went on to conclude: 'At its highest this could amount to perverting the course of justice, and at least raises questions of discreditable conduct, and honesty and integrity.' And so, four years ago, before an investigative stone was turned, the narrative of conspiracy and cover-up, insinuated by the Hillsborough Panel and asserted by some campaigners and politicians, was reinforced publicly by an early judgement of the Deputy Chair of the IPCC.

On 9 May 1989, Mr Wain delivered the document that had been commissioned by Mr Woodward QC in two twelve-inch cubed document boxes. The covering document alone was about two inches thick. It was accompanied by the eighty-one statements in full, from which the summary had been drawn, and many other appendices, which, together, filled the boxes. There is ample evidence, in comparing the summary to the eighty-one original statements, that we had not misrepresented the first-hand accounts. Some were left on the cutting room floor because they were considered to be heavy on rhetoric but light on objective facts.

I also offered the following caution to Mr Woodward QC under the heading, 'Behaviour of supporters and actions of ground staff':

> In the preceding paragraphs a number of references have been made to the unruly behaviour of some of the spectators. It is important, however, that a sense of perspective should be maintained as it would appear that this behaviour was limited to a relatively small minority of the total number of spectators in attendance.

Hardly the tone of a 'black propagandist'.

It ought to be acknowledged that on the final draft of the document someone higher up the food chain had appended a set of observations. It is implied in the opening paragraph that they were the observations of the Chief Constable who was not, by raising them, seeking to draw any definitive conclusions as to the cause of the tragedy. These observations have been described at the recent inquest as a less dispassionate analysis than the rest of the report. That is coy. I believe that there are aspects of those observations that go beyond the evidence known and presented to Mr Woodward in describing the behaviour amongst football fans on that fateful afternoon. Certainly, the so-called observations were not fully supported by my summary of the evidence that was to hand at that time.

I don't believe that the Chief Constable wrote those observations. They are written in a curious, self-righteous manner that was not the style of Mr Wright. I do not know who wrote them. Whether they influenced the thinking of Bill Woodward QC I cannot say, but I would doubt it very much. If he attached any credence to the observations then it would have been quickly dispelled by the broader evidence that was presented to Lord Justice Taylor's public inquiry, which opened six days after Mr Woodward received the report.

As far as my own contribution to the post-disaster/pre-inquiry tasks are concerned, I responded professionally, and in good faith, to the requests of lawyers. That is also what I witnessed in those around me. We were, however, working in a bubble. The so-called Wain Report was completed within twelve days. We had no connections to the wider world of evidence and only had, in preparing for the pressing public inquiry, the self-prepared accounts of officers who were closest to the traumatic events, and the contemporaneous photographs and CCTV footage from around the stadium.

Might my contribution have been written differently once I had discovered more about the tragic events? That is a fair question, for I was about to learn a great deal more over the next few weeks… and I would share that more developed analysis with Mr Woodward QC.

CHAPTER 4

HELPING WITH INQUIRIES

15 May – 17 July 1989

I had been a junior member of the Wain team. I was seconded to that role from a Headquarters post where my three-week absence had caused no immediate problem for the operations of the force. I had also demonstrated, during this short secondment, a talent for fulfilling parallel tasks set by multiple masters. These three criteria meant that the gaze fell upon me when the Deputy Chief Constable was looking for someone to be a runner for the legal team that would be representing the force at the Taylor Inquiry.

It was only a few days before the start of the inquiry when I was told by Mr Hayes to clear my diary for its duration. I was to perform two functions. Firstly, the Wain team was to be wound down and I would act as a point of liaison with the legal team in order to furnish their ongoing needs for information or documents from the force. Secondly, I was to follow the proceedings at the inquiry and update the Deputy and Chief about its progress.

I felt, even then, to be in a privileged position to have the opportunity to observe a public inquiry at close quarters and to learn and understand much more about the recent dreadful tragedy. My experiences over the next six weeks would give me insights that would enable me to analyse the Hillsborough disaster in a broader context and to reach deeper conclusions about its causes.

Lord Justice Peter Taylor had been asked to conduct this urgent public inquiry. He was from the north-east, a keen Newcastle United fan. He understood football and knew what it was to be a football supporter in the 1980s. His interests and talents stretched much wider though. I recall a conversation, years later, with Dame Fanny Waterman, a distinguished impresario of piano concerts and competitions. She thought that Peter Taylor was one of the most naturally talented pianists that she had ever taught.

He could have been a concert pianist if he hadn't chosen the law. He went on after the Hillsborough Inquiry to
become Lord Chief Justice, the most senior judge in the
UK. He also, in my experience of the inquiry, understood
the human condition. Most judges demonstrate an understanding of human nature but can't always, within the
straitjacket of legal procedures, respond to basic human
needs. The Taylor Inquiry, whilst a formal judicial tribu-
nal, felt also like a humane response to aid the processes of
grieving and understanding. It might have had something
to do with the immediacy of the inquiry to the tragedy.

By the time of the inquiry, ninety-five people were known
to have been killed at a football match and there were two
pressing needs for some early analysis about causation.
Firstly, the new football season would open in August of
that year and the government wanted to be in a position
to implement any safety recommendations before it began.
Secondly, the government were actively debating a Football
Spectators Bill to curb the real and present threat of football hooliganism. They wished to know whether the public
inquiry could inform that nascent Bill.

For these two reasons, Lord Justice Taylor was asked
to open the inquiry at the earliest possible date and to
deliver a report and recommendations before the beginning of the 1989/90 football season. With the experience
of the Chilcot Inquiry and other recent public scrutinies of

historical events, it is perhaps difficult to imagine the pace with which Taylor assembled and concluded his inquiry. It opened on 15 May 1989, exactly one month after the disaster occurred. Oral evidence was heard from 174 witnesses, and hundreds more statements were referred to by the inquiry. The inquiry stopped taking evidence on 29 June and Lord Justice Taylor delivered his interim report on 4 August 1989. All in all, less than three months from start to finish.

Well, not quite. One concession demanded by Lord Justice Taylor, as he scoped the inquiry, was that he be allowed to deliver an interim report by August and a final report later on. The interim report would deal with the specific causes of the disaster whilst the final report would deal with the wider context in which the disaster had occurred and his recommendations to government.

Some commentators ignore the final report, published in January 1990, because of its sombre chapters dealing with the blight of football hooliganism and how that blight created a context for some of the bad decisions, by various parties, which led to the disaster at Hillsborough. It had a chapter on the problems of ticket touts and recommended legislation to keep them and non-ticket holders away from the curtilage of football stadia. It had a chapter on how football clubs, which make a significant profit from public entertainment, must share the burden of responsibility for crowd safety, and it recommended that this be spelled out in formal written agreements with the police. Indeed, of its seventy-seven recommendations, the overwhelming majority were directed at football authorities and government, not at the police.

The final report from Taylor is damning of the perilous state of football stadia in 1989. It was to lay the foundation for a revolution in the experience of the paying spectator. The removal of dangerous cages; the creation of all-seater stadia; and the provision of facilities to ensure customer comfort as well as safety were all presaged by Taylor's final report.

Taylor's final report analyses, very carefully, the interlocking pieces of a complex jigsaw that create a picture of how a tragedy such as the one at Hillsborough was possible. Furthermore, it lays out a plan as to how, through the thoughtful redesign of those interlocking pieces, disaster might be prevented in the future. It was a tour de force.

In the considerations of Hillsborough over the years, media sub-editors, constrained by copy length, and politicians contributing to time-limited debates, aren't always able to do justice to Taylor's multi-faceted final report. Instead, they find what they are looking for at paragraph 278 of Lord Justice Taylor's interim report, published sixteen weeks after the disaster. One sentence in paragraph 278 seems clear enough: 'Although there were other causes, the main reason for the disaster was the failure of police control.'

A lot of commentators quote only the last twelve words.

Having sat through the oral evidence phase of the inquiry, I too had reached a similar conclusion to Lord Justice Taylor. Before his published report, I was able to brief the Chief Constable and Deputy that this was likely to be the conclusion. I was also able to write a more rounded summary for Mr Woodward QC to the one that is contained in what was to become known as the Wain Report.

The final day of oral evidence at the Taylor Inquiry was Thursday 29 June 1989. The following day, I gave a personal briefing about my analysis of the evidence to Peter Wright, the Chief Constable. On Monday 3 July, I sent a similar written account to Mr Woodward QC, who was preparing his closing submission that was to be provided in writing to Lord Justice Taylor by 7 July.

It was unsolicited. I was a middle-ranking police officer with no experience of public inquiries bar this one. Bill Woodward was an eminent leading counsel with lots of experience of representing clients at public inquiries. He had been called to the Bar in 1964; took silk in the '70s; was head of chambers by 1989; and went on to become a recorder and then deputy judge of the High Court. He knew perfectly well what was needed in any closing submission and hadn't directly invited my analysis. He knew that I intended to brief my Chief Constable at the end of the oral evidence phase and expressed mild interest in what I would say to him. That opened the door for my faxed correspondence to Mr Woodward.

Under the heading, 'A few thoughts about the nature of the police role at Hillsborough and the evidence that has been received at the Inquiry', I set out my analysis of what I had heard and understood from the testimony presented to Taylor. I mentioned, in summary, that there had been evidence about club irresponsibility, local authority ineptitude, engineering flaws, and unreasonable behaviour by many hundreds of fans. But that wasn't where blame was settling. In particular, I set out how, in my view, the evidence had fallen for South Yorkshire Police and for the match commanders. On the third page of that unsolicited analysis I wrote the following:

> I turn now to the aspect of the operation that presents the greatest difficulties for the South Yorkshire Police case – the link between the difficult situation outside (in Leppings Lane) and the disaster that occurred inside.
>
> There are potential criticisms that are difficult to counter:
>
> No contingency plan for dealing with such circumstances as those which arose at Leppings Lane.

Delay in appreciating the likelihood of problems occurring (e.g. 2.17 p.m. road closure requested. 2.40 p.m. reinforcements requested).

Little and poor communication between outside and inside.

Five minutes between request to open gate and the instruction to open them.

During that time no steps were taken to gather additional information; to communicate the intention to other police officers and club officials.

No plan was made for the systematic (controlled) opening of the gates. 'Open the gates' appears to have been a panic reaction.

No check was made after the instruction to see whether the gates had in fact been opened.

And finally and most crucially:

No other attempt was made to monitor the movement of the fans inside the ground.

All of these evidential features of failings in police command that I highlighted in my note of 3 July 1989 can be found in the interim report of Lord Justice Taylor, which he published on 4 August. I had had the opportunity, like Lord Justice Taylor, of hearing the testimony of 174 witnesses over thirty-one days of the inquiry. My perspective was no longer one-dimensional and constrained by a few days spent examining and condensing only police-officer testimony. It was rich and complex and would influence the way that I thought about and talked of the disaster from that time forward.

The evidence of my early enlightenment at the Taylor Inquiry is overlooked by those who are keen to promote a narrative of a force in denial, conspiring to rewrite the Taylor Report and deflect any blame from the match commander and onto the shoulders of the fans.

That is the picture that is consistently created by Maria Eagle MP in her contributions to any parliamentary debate about Hillsborough. The first time that she painted this picture was in 1998, a year after being returned as a Member of Parliament for Garston and Halewood, a Liverpool constituency. Parliament had, in 1997, commissioned Lord Justice Stuart-Smith to review how South Yorkshire Police had gathered and presented evidence about Hillsborough at judicial proceedings, and to also review the conduct of those proceedings. He presented a report to Parliament which broadly provided reassurance about the approach that had been taken by South Yorkshire Police.

From her own reading of the original papers, lodged by Lord Justice Stuart-Smith in the Commons Library, Ms Eagle reached a very different conclusion to the learned judge. Her contribution to the debate about Stuart-Smith's report in 1998, like all parliamentary debates, attracts parliamentary privilege. This is an immunity enshrined in the 1689 Bill of Rights, which defined the role of Parliament after the English Civil War and states that an MP can say whatever they please in Parliament and this may be reported more widely without risk of their being sued, impeached or questioned in any court. That is an awesome privilege which should not be used lightly or wantonly.

On 8 May 1998, Maria Eagle told Parliament that

> South Yorkshire Police behaved abominably leading up to the Taylor Inquiry.
>
> They orchestrated what can only be described as a black propaganda campaign which aimed to deflect blame for what happened onto anyone other than themselves ... That campaign continued after the Taylor Inquiry reported when it should have stopped ... The committee's purpose changed from supplying black propaganda to achieving historical revisionism but its aim has always been the same – to deflect blame. It is time it stopped.

Ms Eagle, in campaigning on behalf of the Hillsborough Family Support Group, has often repeated the invective contained in this speech – but only ever within the protected confines of the House of Commons.

It is difficult to square Ms Eagle's rhetoric with my own

analysis of the policing failures at Hillsborough that was submitted to both my Chief Constable and the QC representing his case. They accurately predicted Lord Justice Taylor's findings.

It needs to be said, however, that none of these aspects of the evidence found their way into Mr Woodward's closing submissions. He had, as might be expected, written his own submission. There was a private meeting between Mr Woodward and Peter Wright, the Chief Constable, after his written submissions had been delivered to the inquiry. Mr Woodward had agreed to meet the Chief Constable to 'take him through' the submissions. Neither man spoke to me about what was discussed. I can have no way of knowing whether the police command failures that I had clearly identified to each of them were considered in their discussion.

Lord Justice Taylor rebuked those representing South Yorkshire Police in his interim report for 'failing in their submissions ... to concede they were in any respect at fault in what occurred ... It would have been more seemly and encouraging for the future if responsibility had been faced.'

I have tested, with lawyer friends, the question of the professional obligation on the part of Bill Woodward QC. They all agree that, whilst respecting the comments of Lord Justice Taylor, the fundamental obligation of representing counsel is to submit the best case on behalf of their client to the best of their ability and not to mislead the court in any way. Mr Woodward QC cannot be said to have fallen below that professional threshold.

I reflected earlier, though, on the wisdom of having a single legal team attempting to represent the interests of parties who may not have had common interests. By default, rather than positive decision, Hammond Suddards, and counsel retained by them, were representing the interests of three distinct parties before the Taylor Inquiry: the Chief Constable of South Yorkshire Police; individuals at risk of personal liability such as David Duckenfield; and the Municipal Mutual Insurance company, which was underwriting the financial consequences of any future litigation. Just whose interests were best served by not conceding any fault before the public inquiry is difficult to determine. Counsel may have thought it was in the best interests of all three. The Chief Constable might have agreed with it, although I was never aware of any declared strategy of the Chief Constable to deny or to shirk from responsibility.

Indeed, on 4 August, after Lord Justice Taylor had published his interim report, Peter Wright publicly acknowledged and accepted the blame apportioned to the South Yorkshire Police and apologised for its significant role in the disaster. He announced that he would be submitting his resignation to the South Yorkshire Police Authority.

I had witnessed in my personal contact with the Chief

Constable, during the time of the inquiry, how the dawning realisation of accountability for the tragedy had weighed increasingly heavy on his shoulders. He was particularly appalled by David Duckenfield's misinformation, which immediately sought to blame the fans for breaking down the gate. Peter Wright attended the inquiry, in person, on just a couple of occasions during the thirty-one days that it sat. I made arrangements for his visit on each occasion. One of those occasions was to witness, first hand, the evidence given by Mr Duckenfield. I left with Mr Wright at the end of the day and travelled back to Headquarters with him in his staff car. He was seething over what he had heard at the inquiry. I worked for Mr Wright for over seven years and this was the only occasion that I heard him swear. In the privacy of the staff car, he vented his feelings: 'Why the fucking lie? That will be all that people remember about South Yorkshire Police whenever they talk of Hillsborough.' It was a rhetorical question that did not invite any response from me. A psychologist might have been able to explain the lie in the context of a spontaneous response to a traumatic situation, but no one could ever justify or excuse it.

There is a disturbing trend in society at the moment to seek to put the dead on trial. It was a serious consideration, even contemplated by a retired Director of Public Prosecutions, in the case of Lord Janner, who was never tried, whilst alive, in relation to accusations of sexual abuse against children. Since the publication of the Hillsborough Panel Report in 2012, a year after Peter Wright's death, there have been some dreadful aspersions cast about his integrity that he is in no position to defend. In the recent Coroner's Inquest, and with heavy references to the popular TV drama *Wolf Hall*, there were knockabout exchanges between counsel and a witness suggesting that Peter Wright played a Henry VIII-esque character: presiding over a corrupt Tudor Court, having his every whim fulfilled on the basis of fear and misplaced loyalty. The witness was never asked to provide a single example from his personal experience that enabled him to draw such a powerful and demeaning simile. The unsubstantiated slur just entered the court transcript and remains there for posterity.

In my own personal experience, I always found Peter Wright to be an honourable man. I can say with certainty that he did not commission or command a black propaganda exercise after Hillsborough. He was as appalled by David Duckenfield's dishonesty as the fiercest critic. He accepted the blame apportioned by Taylor although he was always frustrated that others criticised by Taylor failed to share that burden. I believe that he was sincere in offering his resignation on behalf of the force that was found to have failed so lamentably.

It would have been better if Peter Wright had been

specific about the reasons why he thought he must go. For example, he had agreed to move Brian Mole within nineteen days of the semi-final. He had appointed David Duckenfield without contemplating the consequences for the forthcoming major event. He presided over a force that had failed in their duty of care so tragically at that event. His chosen commander had disgraced himself publicly, and gratuitously, in telling a scurrilous lie. In order to restore confidence in the institution called South Yorkshire Police, it was right that its head should go.

It would have been even better if the Police Authority had accepted his resignation. They should have done so recalling the many good things that Peter Wright's tenure could be remembered for. Resignation represented an honourable act that might have begun to atone for all of the wrongs that were properly laid at the door of South Yorkshire Police.

Unfortunately, that didn't happen. The Police Authority declined to accept the resignation. I know of no evidence, however, to persuade me from the view that the offer of resignation was genuinely made.

———

There has been a great deal of moral outrage generated by the recent disclosure that over 200 police officers' accounts were amended before they were submitted to the Taylor Inquiry. Whilst the outrage is relatively recent, official knowledge of the process has been documented since 1989. It is an issue that should be addressed here for it is one of the issues within the current popular narrative that taints anyone connected with South Yorkshire Police from that era.

I can address this issue confidently. I knew of the process. My own account was amended. I never, at the time, saw anything done as part of this process that caused me any concern.

On the other hand, given that this is one of the key issues that attracted such opprobrium after the publication of the Hillsborough Panel Report, and given that the Independent Police Complaints Commission has been investigating these matters for more than four years and is still to conclude that investigation, I should be circumspect in discussing any particular allegation in detail.

In general terms, the emendation process was initiated by Hammond Suddards lawyers, not by the force. It was in response to an urgent and late request from West Midlands Police to furnish self-prepared factual statements for the Taylor Inquiry. Both the original account and any amended version remained available to West Midlands Police. Lord Justice Taylor, and counsel to the inquiry Andrew Collins QC, now the Hon. Mr Justice Collins, a High Court

Judge, were each aware of the process. The original and amended accounts were preserved and catalogued in the force archives and the practice was reviewed, in 1997, by Lord Justice Stuart-Smith, a High Court Judge.

Those general and uncontroversial facts alone might put a slightly different emphasis on the practice than the one which has been created since the Hillsborough Panel Report. A little more detail that is already in the public domain may explain more.

On the day after the disaster, West Midlands Police were asked to conduct an independent investigation into the causes of the disaster and any criminal offences arising. A day or two later, the Deputy Chief Constable asked that everyone in the force be made aware that West Midlands Police were undertaking the investigation and that anyone who had anything to do with the Hillsborough disaster should prepare an aide memoire on plain paper to support their recollections when later seen by West Midlands Police investigators who would be taking statements.

West Midlands were not quick in getting out to see officers for statements.

On 26 April 1989, Mr Wain and his team, of which I was a member, were tasked by Mr Woodward QC to provide a summary of the available evidence from South Yorkshire police officers only. Mr Wain considered the aide memoires to be the only means by which the task could be fulfilled in the time available. He had copies of them proactively collected and gave additional information to any officer who had not yet produced an account about what was required. This requirement, based entirely on Mr Woodward's proposals, sought the inclusion of any opinions and any fears and concerns felt by any officer. Copies of the aide memoires, or self-prepared accounts, were dutifully collected and used for this limited internal purpose.

Then, on 7 May, only eight days before the start of the public inquiry and *after* the self-prepared accounts had been used by the Wain team to furnish the summary for Mr Woodward, West Midlands Police asked for self-prepared statements from a significant number of South Yorkshire Officers. West Midlands claimed that they had neither the time nor the resources to complete the urgent task themselves.

Peter Metcalf, the senior lawyer from Hammond Suddards, took the view that what was in his possession was not a statement obtained for this new stated purpose. Furthermore, officers had been invited to write all kinds of things not normally associated with a fact-only statement for the purpose of judicial proceedings. He undertook to vet the aide memoires to determine what was needed in order to meet the requirement of the West Midlands Police.

My own account, for example, had referred to my being crushed at Leppings Lane terraces as a spectator in the early '70s. That was a fact and could stay in if I wished it to once I understood the new purpose that was envisaged for my account. The account went on, though, to proffer my unsupported opinion about the inherent danger of the Hillsborough stadium design. That was comment and pure speculation, not fact, and Peter Metcalf suggested that it should be removed from the statement that I provided to the Taylor Inquiry. I agreed the amendment without demur. I understood the reason. I suspect that that is the way that many of the amendments were secured.

This vetting and emendation exercise was intense. It involved lawyers reading scores of accounts each day and handing their advice on each one to a team of officers working under the direction of Chief Superintendent Don Denton at force Headquarters. It mostly took place once the Taylor Inquiry had started and so there was a time pressure on Mr Metcalf and Chief Superintendent Denton to complete each day's tasks for urgent delivery to West Midlands Police and to the counsel to the inquiry, Mr Collins QC, by close of business each day. I was, by this time, working at the public inquiry, at the beck and call of Mr Woodward QC and Mr Limb, the counsel team. I had no involvement with the exercise of transposing aide memoires into statements.

That describes the context of what was going on. I witnessed no clandestine plot involving a conspiracy at South

Yorkshire Police Headquarters to tamper with evidence destined for a public inquiry.

It would have been better if West Midlands Police had taken their own statements. It would have been better if there was more time to complete the exercise. It might have even been better to let the original account go in, complete with comment, hearsay, opinion, emotional content and finger-pointing, to let the inquiry sort out with any particular witnesses what was admissible and what was not. Even then it could have only been done with the permission of each officer, because the original request for an aide memoire did not envisage its use at judicial proceedings.

These alternative ways of responding to the West Midlands Police request were not followed. Mr Metcalf has conceded, to both Lord Justice Stuart-Smith and the recent Coroner's Inquest, that there were a handful of accounts where he suggested that content be removed that in retrospect should have stayed in. There are also a small number of examples where police officers fulfilling Mr Metcalf's recommended changes appear to have gone further than he was suggesting. Those, and maybe other discovered examples, are now, quite properly, subject to forensic investigation by the IPCC.

Lord Justice Taylor makes it clear, though, in his interim report that he can be satisfied, as one of the leading and most experienced judges of his generation, that he had heard sufficient and reliable testimony, in both oral examination and written statements, to draw conclusions about the causes of the disaster.

> To have called more evidence would have prevented me from presenting an interim report in the required time and would not have added significantly to the relevant evidence I have been able to take into account. I should like to thank all those who made it possible for this hearing to take place so soon after the event and for the evidence to be efficiently presented to give a full and fair account of what happened in all its aspects without irrelevancy.

Lord Justice Taylor's sixty-page interim report is a model of analytical report writing. It is clear, well-argued and succinct. It manages to cover the various and complex features of the disaster in a concise fashion.

As mentioned earlier, 'the main reason for the disaster was the failure of police control' is the oft-cited partial sentence from paragraph 278 of Lord Justice Taylor's interim report. I agree with that assessment. However, the words that precede that familiar quote are relevant too: 'Although there were other causes...'

Lord Justice Taylor documents these other causes in his erudite report. It suited the popular narrative then, as well as now, to ignore or pass over them quickly. People are generally more comfortable with binary explanations of things and events than they are with complexity. The media delivers black and white; heroes and villains; saints and sinners. It makes news easier to digest.

The press headlines on 5 August 1989, the day after the interim report was published, were all one-way and pretty one-dimensional:

The *Daily Mail*, on its front page, had 'Damned: Police bear the brunt of the blame'.

The Independent led with 'Police blamed for Hillsborough'. This same newspaper also had a cartoon on the front page, drawn by Colin Wheeler, with three mock police epaulettes arranged as a representation of the rank structure of South Yorkshire Police. On the Constable's epaulette, in place of insignia, was the word 'guilty'. On the Inspector's it said 'more guilty'. And on the Chief Superintendent's it said 'most guilty'. The cartoon might raise a smile, perhaps, with anyone who was not one of the Constables or Inspectors at Hillsborough, who bore a deep and traumatic sense of guilt about their inability to avert the disaster or rescue the victims from the impenetrable cages.

In order to understand the psyche of the South Yorkshire force at that particular time, it is necessary to understand the impact that this media reporting had on the individual, junior, members who had been involved on the fateful day. Forget, for this exercise, the Chief Constable – he had offered his resignation and it was right for him to do so, as the symbolic head of an organisation that had failed in its responsibilities. Forget Chief Superintendent Duckenfield – he was in command at Hillsborough and his actions and omissions had been directly, and properly, criticised by Lord Justice Taylor. Chief Superintendent Duckenfield was suspended from duty on the publication of the Taylor Report pending a criminal and disciplinary inquiry and, by then, he was a professional outcast. Forget people like Superintendent Bernard Murray and Superintendent Roger Marshall, the commander outside in Leppings Lane – they could all take care of themselves and each had direct access to legal advice.

Imagine, just for one moment, how this reporting was received in the family home of the Constable who was the officer on the gate of Pen 3 – the 81-centimetre-wide gate that quickly became clogged with the tangled bodies of the dead and dying. Or the Inspector who was there in charge of a serial of officers behind the Leppings Lane turnstiles, with no view of the terraces, but who could, with the right instruction from match control, have easily and quickly blocked off the tunnel to prevent overcrowding and ninety-six deaths. Imagine how it felt to the 1,100 other men and women who were involved that day, the majority of whom had done their professional best in an appalling situation.

The popular narrative was driven by the media and the media had made two significant errors in their initial reporting of Lord Justice Taylor's judgment, which have persisted to this day in folklore. Firstly, the 'other causes' aspect of Taylor's definitive account was absent, left on the sub-editor's table, or at best indistinct. Secondly, there was a fallacy of definition common in the reporting of policing matters. The failure of individual officers is frequently ascribed to the police as a body.

Lord Justice Taylor had spoken of a failure of commanders to control and respond to the situation when discussing blame. The press reporting, and the popular narrative, transposed this to a simpler message: 'the police were to blame'.

It is not unique in general conversation and media reporting for the specific, e.g. the racist attitude of an individual officer, to be reported as a generic problem, e.g. the racist police. However, when the context of such generalisation is the Hillsborough disaster, from which many officers were personally traumatised, the assertion of generic blame was to have a devastating impact within the force.

Officers, such as the Constable at the gate to Pen 3 and the Inspector behind the terrace, and many others who were directly involved, assumed that this would mean a homicide investigation into their own actions and omissions. West Midlands Police were in charge of the inquiries and so no assurances were available from within the force. Anxiety, self-blame and anger were common and widespread psychological responses amongst the junior ranks of the force.

It was against that context that I was set one of my final tasks arising from the Taylor Inquiry. I was tasked by the Deputy Chief Constable, Mr Hayes, to produce a compilation video to demonstrate all the aspects of the disaster in which the junior ranks had played a part. It was to be shown at a meeting being organised by the South Yorkshire Police Federation.

The Police Federation is the trade union for the ranks of Constable, Sergeant and Inspector, who pay a monthly subscription for membership. The Federation is charged with two statutory functions. The first is to protect the welfare of their members. The second is to work with the force management to ensure its efficiency and effectiveness. The Federation generally has a full-time secretary and Chairman in each force and then elected representatives at each work place and for each of the three ranks, who come together on a regular basis to form what is called a joint branch board.

South Yorkshire Joint Branch Board intended to hold a meeting to address the anxiety created amongst its membership by the popular narrative that was abroad since Lord Justice Taylor's Report. The Chief Constable had agreed to 'address the troops' so to speak, but then delegated the responsibility to the Deputy, Mr Hayes.

Each officer who had been at Hillsborough would be recalling the disaster through the narrow window of his or her personal experience that day. I therefore produced a video, on Mr Hayes's instruction, that would take the audience through the day from build-up at the turnstiles; opening of Gate C; overcrowding in the pens; the rescue effort; and finally to their gruesome duties in the gymnasium. The material was drawn, primarily, from three main sources – the inquiry compilation video produced by West Midlands Police and shown at the Taylor Inquiry, the BBC images, and the CCTV footage recovered from cameras at the stadium, which depicted the crowds at both the 1988 and 1989 semi-finals (many junior officers had been given the same duties at both).

Chief Superintendent Mole introduced me to a training video that he had come across, that had been produced by another force prior to the Hillsborough tragedy, called 'Plan for disaster'. He felt that the front end of that video, which included details of previous football tragedies, would be a useful and contextual addition to the compilation.

I went along to the Federation meeting. I had no knowledge of who would be there. It was their meeting.

I recognised the full-time secretary and Chairman of the Joint Branch Board, Paul Middup and Bob Lax, who were conducting the meeting. Other members of the Joint Branch Board were present. Mr Hayes was there, of course.

Then there were some people I didn't recognise: two lawyers retained by the Federation to represent the interests of the junior ranks; a member of the National Police Federation Executive Board; the editor of a national Police Federation magazine; and a Member of Parliament and his secretary.

Michael Shersby was a Conservative Member of Parliament who was paid a retainer by the National Police Federation to represent the interests of the junior ranks in Parliament. It was typical of similar arrangements of that time adopted by trade unions, which commonly sponsored MPs. The Federation, unlike some trade unions, is non-party political and it changed its retained member whenever the government changed, making sure they always had someone from the party in power who was able to champion their cause.

The Chairman of the South Yorkshire Police Joint Branch Board opened the meeting and, amongst his welcoming remarks, he said that he wanted to give Michael Shersby information that may be helpful to him. He introduced Mr Hayes, who made it clear that the force had accepted, unequivocally, the findings of Lord Justice Taylor.

He said that the Chief Constable had agreed to him speaking on his behalf to do two things. Firstly, to enable everyone to have a better understanding of what happened at Hillsborough, including a video and photographic presentation. Secondly, to spend time listening to junior officers' fears and frustrations.

I played the video, which had no narration from me and showed photographs and diagrams of the engineering features of Hillsborough Stadium that had been scrutinised, and found to be sub-standard, at the Taylor Inquiry.

My overriding impression of the meeting was that it created an opportunity for catharsis. There was some unseemly rhetoric from the floor about the contribution of the fans to the crush at the turnstiles. Individual officers and their federation representatives were very emotional and raw about the emerging popular narrative that implied that it was they, the junior ranks, who had each been complicit in the deaths of ninety-five people. The force Welfare Officer was present so that she could pick up the pieces afterwards with any officer who might, at the meeting, exhibit signs of stress and anxiety. On the evidence of what I saw that day, she would not be short of clients.

After the meeting, Mr Hayes had lunch with the Joint Branch Board and their invited guests, including Mr Shersby. I was not present. Mr Shersby asked Mr Hayes if the same video, photographs and diagrams might be shown to a number of MPs who were then active in the consideration of the Football Spectators Bill. Mr Hayes consulted the Chief Constable, who decided that I should be tasked to do that.

On 8 November 1989, I visited the Houses of Parliament on the instruction of Mr Hayes. At a meeting called and chaired by Mr Shersby, in one of the committee rooms there, I fulfilled my task. There were just twelve Members of Parliament present and two left midway through the presentation. There were few questions and, ultimately, little interest.

———————

My full-time employment on Hillsborough matters had ended before the visit to London. It had come to a natural conclusion after the Taylor Inquiry was over. I returned to my day job in the Career Development Department at Headquarters after what had been an absence of three months. Occasionally I was given additional tasks or responsibilities because of my grasp of the findings of the Taylor Inquiry.

I was the secretary of a task group, for example, which met occasionally under the direction of the Deputy Chief Constable, to implement the recommendations of Taylor. There are five professional football teams, and associated stadia, in South Yorkshire. The senior officers responsible for each stadium were called to a series of meetings at Headquarters to understand, discuss and roll out the recommendations emerging from the Taylor Inquiry. The group ensured that the force was ideally positioned to ensure the safety of spectators at football matches in the future.

The work of the task group reflected the corporate acceptance of Lord Justice Taylor's criticisms and recommendations. I had seen those criticisms crystallise during the time spent observing the public inquiry. From the regular briefings provided to the Chief Constable, he was able to produce a draft press release in advance of the publication of Lord Justice Taylor's interim report. It did not alter significantly in the terms of the statement he issued immediately after the 4 August 1989 publication. In that statement, Mr Wright said that he wished

> to make it clear to all concerned ... that I accept the findings and the conclusions of the public inquiry in so far as they relate to South Yorkshire Police ... I once again extend my heartfelt regret to those who have lost loved ones or suffered injury.
>
> Lord Justice Taylor and all concerned may be assured that the South Yorkshire Police will pursue every action to ensure that such an event could not occur again ...

In my report to the Police Authority in the immediate aftermath of the disaster I accepted full responsibility for police action in connection with this event. In pursuance of this responsibility, and in the light of Lord Justice Taylor's findings, I have written to my Chairman and offered my resignation … My office is now at their disposal.

The popular narrative in the twenty-first century implies that South Yorkshire Police never accepted any responsibility in the aftermath of Hillsborough. Mr Wright's acceptance of responsibility was immediate and clear. It was accompanied by his 'heartfelt regret' offered to the bereaved and the injured. He suspended Chief Superintendent David Duckenfield that same afternoon pending a criminal investigation by an independent police force. Acceptance of responsibility was reinforced later by the settlement of all civil liability claims regardless of whether any of the other parties blamed by Taylor were prepared to step forward to contribute to those claims.

The argument is already advanced that it would have been better if Mr Wright had been allowed to resign. It might have registered, and resonated, as a tangible and appropriate response to Lord Justice Taylor's damning indictment of South Yorkshire Police.

The Taylor Inquiry had influenced my own understanding

and knowledge about the disaster in ways that would forever colour my thoughts and judgements about the event. The various phases of my tasking, from being seconded as a member of the Wain team right through to my last act as secretary of the Taylor Implementation Group, had encompassed only six months. Six intensive months perhaps, but I could now move on from this inquiry and the disaster. Whilst I would be occasionally asked to respond to ad hoc requests for information from lawyers representing the force in subsequent proceedings, my immediate work was done.

The bereaved and the injured had also learned more through the Taylor Inquiry, though it did not for them represent a conclusion. Their toil and struggle was only just beginning. Theirs would be a long and arduous journey lasting twenty-seven more years. Whilst all the other actors on the stage at the Taylor Inquiry would move on and play many different roles in life, the families would be obliged to carry for many years the burden of grief and injustice...

CHAPTER 5

AN ENDURING HURT

15 April 1989 – present day

Hillsborough claimed ninety-six lives, and hundreds were injured. Thousands more were directly or indirectly affected by the tragedy. But tens of thousands share the pain of the victims and their families.

The capacity crowds that have attended the memorial service at Anfield in the middle of April each year are a demonstration of that breadth and depth of unity. There are dedicated journalists and film makers who have kept the memory of the ninety-six alive for a quarter of a century. Some campaigning politicians, traditionally fickle in their allegiance, have remained steadfast to the cause of the bereaved families. The enduring flame motif will be for ever emblazoned on the team shirt worn by every future Liverpool player as a tribute to the terrible loss.

Some recent events emphasise the phenomenon of social bonding that follows in the wake of disaster. The spontaneous 'Nous sommes Charlie' manifesto, for example, that followed the bombing, in January 2015, of the offices at Charlie Hebdo – the French satirical magazine. There was also the global demonstration of fraternity and solidarity that coalesced around Paris in the wake of the simultaneous terrorist outrages in November 2015, which left 130 dead and many hundreds injured. These are more than mawkish sentiments in an instantly connected world of social media. They seem like authentic claims of mutual hurt.

Many of these mass social movements typically demand 'justice'. Though there isn't always clarity or agreement about what 'justice' might look like if it were to be achieved.

There are two broad responses to any claim for justice. First of all, retribution, or punishment of individuals who are found to have done wrong. Secondly, reparation to those who have been wronged or hurt. We sometimes underestimate the power and importance of reparative justice because of a 21st-century obsession with blame.

In the context of Hillsborough, it was undoubtedly just to

respond to twenty years of hurt, as Parliament did in 2009, by setting up a process to review and share everything that could be known about the disaster and its aftermath. It was also just to set aside the verdicts in what had clearly been an inadequate and hurried Coroner's Inquest held in 1990. This was replaced with an altogether different inquisitorial process, which has sat for more than two years and has succeeded in winning and maintaining the trust and confidence of all. The fact that the jury have reached a different majority verdict on the causes of death is a vindication of that decision. These actions have begun to repair a terrible wrong.

Now the claim for 'justice' is once again attached to calls for a retrial of David Duckenfield on a charge of manslaughter. It should be noted that the legal definition of 'unlawful killing', arising as a verdict of a Coroner's Court, does not amount to the requisite legal burden of proof sufficient to convict an individual for homicide. No verdict of the Coroner's Court can be framed in such a way as to appear to determine the question of criminal liability on the part of any named person.

That is, though, to temporarily split hairs of jurisprudence, because it is obvious why, at an emotional level, any call for 'Justice for the 96' might encompass an ambition to see the retrial of an individual whose actions and omissions were so closely connected with the disaster. Widespread anger remains around the fact that no person appears to have been punished for the untimely deaths of ninety-six people.

Retribution, according to the philosopher John Stuart Mill, has three moral justifications: to ensure the deterrence of others; to achieve the rehabilitation and changed behaviour of the offender; and to secure the safety of the majority. These limited moral grounds are the reason why retributive justice must always rest upon sober judicial decisions, based on all the evidence that is currently known, rather than be driven by popular demand or a political imperative.

Whilst the issue of retribution is a live issue, particularly around David Duckenfield, it may be that further reparations remain necessary for justice to finally prevail in respect of Hillsborough.

'Justice for the 96' is a flag that has bound people to a common cause, and the campaign arose because of what happened to ninety-six innocent people who lost their lives at Hillsborough. There may, however, be some issues more directly connected to the bereaved that have sustained the campaign. It might be that what happened to the families and friends of the ninety-six at Sheffield, and in the aftermath of the disaster, is a source of hurt and anger in addition to that arising from the tragic loss of a loved one. As well as failing in the duty of care to ninety-six victims, South Yorkshire Police *and many other* institutions may have also failed in their duty of care to the bereaved.

If that is the case, then the law courts might not be the most appropriate venue at which to seek redress. The redress that is owed to the bereaved, as opposed to the deceased, must begin with an acknowledgement that they were let down by the procedures that followed their loss and by those who devised and managed the procedures. Acknowledgement of injury is the necessary first step on any journey towards reparation and reconciliation.

At a very fundamental level, I think it is significant that Liverpool supporters travelled away from home on 15 April 1989. The procedures that immediately followed the disaster were therefore alien and de-humanising to everyone caught up in them.

I have often wondered why, in the context of the Bradford City fire in 1985, there have been no similar and persistent calls for 'Justice for the 56', the number who perished at the Valley Parade football stadium. There appears, at the very least, to have been negligence and an irresponsible disregard for the risks in relation to the potential for fire in a wooden stand that was known to be packed underneath with combustible litter. There existed a report to the club safety committee which warned that decayed boarding, and the felt which covered the roof of the stand, created an unacceptable fire safety hazard. The report went unheeded.

There were no fire extinguishers in that part of the ground. There should have been but they were removed to prevent hooligans having access to them. The water pressure was reported to be insufficient to deal with the resultant fire because the water board reduced the pressure at weekends.

When the fire took hold there was, apparently, misdirection of some fans who perished beside exit gates that were locked and unmanned. They shouldn't have been. It was reported that there were untrained stewards on duty as young as twelve and as old as seventy-five.

There seems to have been a sub-optimal response from the emergency services, too. There were ad hoc and extraordinary mortuary arrangements which were imperfect.

There was a public inquiry which took evidence for a matter of days. The judge in charge of the inquiry was asked to also make recommendations about dealing with hooliganism at football stadia as well as fire risks. As at Hillsborough, there was no hooliganism on the day of the Bradford disaster. But it was everyone's obsession in the 1980s.

There was an inquest which lasted only a few weeks and returned a verdict recommended by the Coroner. 'Death by misadventure', not 'unlawful killing'.

There was mourning and there are annual memorials held. But there was no outrage and no collective sense of injustice. Although it should be acknowledged that there is a recent campaign launched by Martin Fletcher, who survived the Bradford fire disaster whilst his father, brother, uncle and grandfather all perished. He is now seeking a public inquiry along the lines of that undertaken by the Hillsborough Panel, but his campaign does not appear to be gaining significant traction and support.

At a simplistic and humanistic level, Valley Parade, Bradford was 'home' to the local fans. Fifty-four of the fifty-six people who died that afternoon were regular City fans. Most were sitting in familiar seats in a familiar stand. Whilst they may have been unaware of, or inured to, the risks present in that football stadium, they felt at home in the fabric of Valley Parade.

Bradford folk and Bradford cops were caught up in the conflagration together. Whilst no officer died, several were badly injured that day. The footage of a dazed officer staggering out of the burning stand with the back of his jacket ablaze is just one of the striking television images from that dreadful event.

The injured and dying from Valley Parade were taken to familiar Bradford hospitals. The mortuary was in Bradford. The inquest was held in Bradford under the direction of a Bradford coroner. The police investigation was conducted by Bradford Detectives. In Bradford, the disaster was terrible and shocking but it was a disaster that unfolded and was addressed within the community.

In stark contrast, the Hillsborough disaster in Sheffield created, at almost every turn, a feeling of alienation amongst the bereaved. At least 5,000 Liverpool supporters endured a frightening and shocking crush outside an unfamiliar stadium. That will be, for those thousands, the lens through which the disaster is always seen.

They witnessed unfamiliar police officers failing to sort out the problem as Merseyside cops always seemed to be able to do at Anfield. Cops, too, who had a barely hidden prejudice. Not against Liverpool football fans, as is so often alleged, but against out-of-town football fans in general. Visiting football fans, in the context of 1980s policing, were often associated with trouble. Whilst they were generally happy to take the overtime payment that rewarded football duty, most officers hated close-quarter deployment amongst the fans, particularly at the away end of the ground, where they regularly emerged with spittle-covered coats and worse. I've worked in three different police forces and there was nothing unique or endemically worse in the underlying prejudice felt by South Yorkshire officers towards visiting football fans. But just because an attitude might be widely held, that does not excuse it.

As the disaster unfolded, those present saw police officers standing, helplessly, at the unyielding fence whilst people were suffering and dying a few feet away. They saw the cops form a cordon on the half-way line rather than assisting the rescue effort. They witnessed fans, their neighbours from Merseyside, working tirelessly to ferry the dead and injured on advertising hoardings fashioned as makeshift stretchers. The occasional brave and instinctive response from junior officers was overshadowed by the general impression of impotence.

In the chaos that ensued at Hillsborough immediately following the disaster, Liverpool fans lost their friends. For the lucky ones, it was only a temporary loss. It meant, for each of these thousands of individuals, a frantic search to locate their loved ones. Many of the police officers they met were unhelpful. Not intentionally so. They knew little more than the fans about what had happened to the injured and the dead. Most of the officers had been bussed in from outer divisions to bolster the police numbers at what was expected to be a large public order event. They didn't have radios and didn't have the least clue about what was going on. Many who had seen anything of the tragic consequences of the crush were in a state of shock themselves.

A lot of the bereaved and the separated found their way, perhaps via the local police station, to the Hillsborough Boys' Club. This was little more than a space enclosed from the elements and, whilst there were well-intentioned volunteers on hand, the abandoned were fed a diet of curled-up sandwiches but starved of information. At Hammerton Road Police Station next door, the police on duty were simply filling out forms and they appeared to be treating their loved ones as if they were temporarily lost. Whereas the person making the report knew their loved one wasn't lost. All of the 'missing' had been at Hillsborough Stadium, less than a mile away, as recently as three o'clock that afternoon. All they wanted to know was whether they were OK. It was a reasonable request. We couldn't tell them, so the officers continued filling out their forms.

Not everyone who found their way to unfamiliar hospitals in an unfamiliar town was allowed to see their loved one even if there was reason to believe they were there. Those who arrived at a hospital late in the evening were told that all the deceased had been returned to the Hillsborough gymnasium on the order of the Coroner and that they would need to see the police, now acting on the Coroner's instructions, to confirm whether that number included the one they really cared about. A crazy and inhuman game of pass the parcel.

Only when the Coroner and the police were organised and ready did the music stop. And then what happened? A number of double-decker buses, commandeered from the local bus garage, were loaded up at the Boys' Club and hospitals. The passengers, by now broken and numbed by the isolation, the lack of information and the bureaucracy, were driven silently through strange streets to arrive outside the Sheffield Wednesday gymnasium where they were parked. The people as well as the buses.

One by painstaking one, the bereaved were invited from the bus to be tortured at the Polaroid wall. All the known deceased, photographed in their body bag, were on that wall. Each next of kin was invited to scrutinise more than eighty post-mortem images. It must have seemed, to someone, an efficient way of linking bodies to next of kin, but think about it for more than one second; put yourself in the shoes of these families who may never have seen a single dead person in their entire lives. Now, in a state of traumatic paralysis, they were being asked to look at pictures of scores. They were families who had been waiting hours to perform this dreadful task and families who were praying not to find any hint of recognition amongst this sea of Polaroid images. It is unsurprising that the majority of identifiers had to be encouraged to look again when declaring their dearest to be absent from the board.

Some of the deceased had identifying documents – a bus pass or a working men's club card or a bankcard. How much more humane might it have been to have shown just one photograph in those cases where there was corroborating evidence that pointed towards identity?

Imagine sitting on that bus until nearly dawn hearing the accounts of those who had been to hell and back in the nearby gymnasium. I would have wanted to storm the door and tear open the zip of each body bag until I knew the answer that I most feared to learn. Yet, unfamiliar police officers in this unfamiliar town and in the most horrific of circumstances were inviting families to sit on a bus and wait.

Coronial procedures always have professional and dispassionate requirements which were, in the 1980s, even stricter and less humane than they are today. It is easy to understand how lots of individual decisions were taken to arrive at this detached and alienating process.

Affording the slightest degree of compassion and empathy towards those caught up in these bureaucratic processes, however, one can see that it was so obviously wrong. It magnified their suffering and it created within hours of the disaster a foundation for mistrust and disaffection. Each link may have been forged with good intentions but, in hindsight, the finished whole created an inhuman chain.

I am eternally sorry for those arrangements. I offer this regret and an apology as a middle-ranking South Yorkshire Police officer who was, twenty-seven years ago, ignorant about most of the arrangements put in place in the immediate aftermath of the disaster. Objectively, one might therefore conclude that it is not my place to apologise ... but someone should and I do.

The Liverpool homecoming, by contrast, was warm and familiar. Liverpool has, I recall from a survey in the early twenty-first century, the highest proportion of church-going citizens of any city in England. There are two cathedrals in Liverpool. Firstly, an imposing Anglican Cathedral, the largest Anglican church in Christendom and the kind of church that inspires a sense of awesome wonder, where both visitor and God feel more important and closer to one another. This was to be the place where families were to gather for the publication of the Hillsborough Panel Report in 2012.

Then, within sight of the Anglican Cathedral, there is the Roman Catholic Metropolitan Cathedral of Christ the King. A cathedral of such contemporary circular design that it gives rise to the affectionate Liverpool nicknames of 'Paddy's Wigwam' and 'The Mersey Funnel'. Two cathedrals are joined, as they say in Liverpool, by hope: the two great buildings stand, like bookends, at opposite ends of Hope Street.

Both cathedrals, and most of the local churches on Merseyside, threw open their doors, and the congregations their hearts, to the grieving and the confused. A televised requiem Mass held in Liverpool on the Sunday night, and attended by over 3,000 people, was a moving testament to neighbourliness and humanity.

It should be acknowledged that there were dead and bereaved, and injured and grieving, in towns other than Liverpool. The last day for some had begun in Derbyshire; in London; in Staffordshire; and even in Sheffield. But Liverpool became the spiritual home, and so it remains, for all who were hurt at, and by, Hillsborough.

The City Council made resources available immediately and without question of cost. Social services; emergency financial relief where necessary; and, subsequently, legal support to represent the interests of those hurt by Hillsborough. An aid fund was set up and it grew quickly to a substantial sum.

Anfield and Goodison Park are the third and fourth cathedrals in Liverpool. Saturday Mass and the occasional midweek evensong attract bigger crowds than the two on Hope Street. They too threw open their doors to the lost souls who could make no sense of Saturday's tragic events. It is estimated that over a half a million people visited Anfield in the week that followed seeking solace, love and the companionship of their wider family.

It was fitting that, on Saturday 15 April 1989, Everton had won the 'other' semi-final match against Norwich and, three weeks later, Liverpool FC beat Nottingham Forest in the rearranged tie to set up a Merseyside FA Cup Final – a 'friendly final'. The score didn't matter. It didn't really matter who carried home the cup to Liverpool. What mattered was the provision of a suitable venue for 82,000 neighbours to come together in shared grief and a spirit of renewal.

In the days and weeks after the disaster, Liverpool, both as a city and as a football community, had demonstrated how to look after 'its own'. Whilst many Sheffield residents had responded to the needs of people in the immediate aftermath of Hillsborough, the whole homecoming experience was in stark contrast to the torments the bereaved had suffered in Yorkshire.

If the poor treatment in that first twenty-four hours had been the full extent of the hurt imposed upon the bereaved, then the failings of the police and other institutions in Sheffield might by now have been overwritten. Never forgotten, but diffused in the shade of the love and support demonstrated by the people and the institutions of Merseyside. But it wasn't the end. It was just the beginning of their anguish.

The issuing by anonymous officials, in a foreign town, of ninety-six approvals for burial or cremation was a task that seemed to be once more tied up with bureaucracy. There was to be a public inquiry back in Sheffield, and an investigation by people from the West Midlands. This all seemed to be disconnected from home and familiarity. There would also have to be an inquest at some stage after the public inquiry and that too, it was decided on high, would be in Sheffield, overseen by a Sheffield coroner sitting with a South Yorkshire jury.

Most of these arrangements had been put in place within forty-eight hours of the disaster occurring. The inquest would not begin for more than a year but all the other tasks were begun immediately. They were procedural arrangements that were being done *to* the bereaved families, not *with* them.

Even then, you know, it might have been possible to find a way through these callous processes without lasting injury being caused (leaving aside the verdict of the jury in the first inquest, to which I shall return later). But then, on Wednesday 19 April 1989, *The Sun* went to print with its front-page headline: 'The Truth' – a headline that was created, recklessly, by *The Sun*'s editorial team late on Tuesday evening after the copy had been filed by the journalist Harry Arnold. Arnold had researched and produced a story but had doubts about the veracity of some of the source material. The editor decided to publish and be damned. He was, and he deserved to be. *The Sun* infamously besmirched the whole Liverpool fan base by accusing their number, amongst other despicable acts, of picking the pockets of victims and urinating on the bodies and the 'brave cops'. I have never seen a shred of evidence to support such shameless accusations. The headline of 'The Truth' sat above a great lie. In and amongst this vile account, anonymous South Yorkshire Police officers were quoted as the source for some of the allegations and the secretary of the Police Federation (the Trade Union for junior officers) is quoted as saying: 'I don't doubt these stories are true.'

One long-retired officer has admitted at the recent inquests that on the night of the disaster he gossiped in a bar about mainly second-hand information in a way which got into the hands of a local MP and then a news agency.

He was a Police Inspector speaking on his own account, not an officially sanctioned spokesperson. The gossip had little credibility, it had no place being published without verification, and it created an injury that would never heal.

Those affected most deeply by the disaster and who were isolated from the whirl of post-disaster activity would have every reason to wonder just what was going on in Sheffield. Were those South Yorkshire Police voices, quoted in *The Sun*, speaking on behalf of the force? Was that to be the Sheffield version of events? Those who had been there knew that it wasn't 'The Truth'. It was, in fact, a travesty.

The Taylor Inquiry, even though it was conducted in Sheffield, made it absolutely clear where the blame lay for the ninety-five deaths that were registered at that time and for the hundreds of physical and psychological injuries sustained at Hillsborough. It was just sixteen weeks after the disaster when Lord Justice Taylor, after hearing 174 witnesses give sworn testimony and reading hundreds more written accounts, stated clearly that the cause of the terrible tragedy was mainly due to a failure of police control.

It was a vindication for all who had been out-of-town visitors to Hillsborough on that April afternoon. Most hadn't witnessed any misbehaviour by Liverpool fans, and there was certainly nothing that resembled the hooliganism familiar to all who followed football in the 1980s. The abiding memory for most is of football fans reacting as quick, if not quicker, than the public safety professionals to the unfolding disaster and doing all they could to help. *The Sun* was wrong. Their story wasn't the truth after all. Those gossipers were exposed. The blame for the ninety-five deaths, and the countless injuries, that were known of at that time was 'mainly' due to a 'failure of police control'. Lord Justice Taylor had said so at paragraph 278 and no one needed to read beyond that.

If we could stop the clock on the afternoon of Friday 4 August 1989, the day that Lord Justice Taylor delivered his interim report, then the bereaved families and the wider Hillsborough 'family' might have felt content with the way that the post-disaster wheel was turning. The test cases for civil litigation could now begin.

The fight for justice was never about money, but the judgment of the civil court is one of the ways that the state recognises when, and to what degree, someone has been wronged. The people who had lost a source of income, and the people who had simply lost the most precious person in their lives, would now be able to claim compensation. The people with physical injuries were the next most clear-cut of claimants. Then there would be the psychological trauma cases. Some of these claims would arise from novel and indirect circumstances. For example, the police officers who were traumatised by what they witnessed at the fences, or the people who saw terrible events unfold on television.

Each would stake their claim. Their claims would all be against South Yorkshire Police. For it was they that were held to be 'mainly' to blame by the judicial inquiry.

The test cases progressed, and they generally found in favour of the plaintiffs. One of the anomalies of civil litigation that has always stuck in the craw of some bereaved families is the differential categories of compensation recognised by the law. If someone was a breadwinner and is precluded from earning in the future then they can be awarded much more compensation than the family who have lost a child, even if the first claimant is alive and relatively well.

Some South Yorkshire police officers, against the wishes of the Chief Constable and many colleagues in the force it must be said, made claims for psychological trauma and loss of earnings in being unable to return to frontline work again. There are examples of some who were financially compensated more generously than the legal tariffs would allow for the parents of a deceased dependant. At a human level, that doesn't seem right. The law is sometimes rigid and rule-bound and can often seem to act contrary to common sense.

'The police' caused this disaster and then 'they' get paid out more than a grieving family? What's going on? Rack that injustice up with the expanding list of grievances felt by the bereaved and their supporters.

The South Yorkshire Police Authority insurers, MMI, accepted liability and agreed settlements that were reported to amount to almost £20 million. It was a sum that would contribute towards the demise of the insurance company in 1993. They were looking to recover a part of these costs from others criticised by Lord Justice Taylor: Sheffield Wednesday Football Club; Eastwood and Partners, the stadium engineers; and Sheffield City Council, who issued a defective safety certificate permitting the event to be staged at Hillsborough Stadium without appropriate measures to protect those in attendance. There were no contributions sought from any other parties. The only parties that were enjoined in these proceedings were those institutions that were each roundly criticised in Lord Justice Taylor's interim report. The fact that there were other parties criticised by Taylor as contributing to the causes of the disaster is, even now, not a familiar part of the popular narrative. It confuses the simple, one-dimensional picture of where blame resides.

It is sometimes implied today that South Yorkshire Police were trying to wriggle out of their responsibilities in these contributions proceedings. Such inferences can only be drawn by those who are blind to the careful judgment of Lord Justice Taylor. The police were 'mainly to blame' for the disaster, but so were others, he said. Those others ultimately accepted, in an out-of-court settlement, a part of the liability and made contributions to the costs that were carried, unilaterally, by MMI.

By 1990, two important post-disaster procedures were running in parallel. The results of each are perceived to have denied the Hillsborough families the justice they have sought for a quarter of a century. The West Midlands Police completed their criminal investigation in 1990 and submitted their file to the Crown Prosecution Service (CPS). At the same time, the South Yorkshire Coroner was contemplating how to conduct the necessary inquests into the deaths of the ninety-five (Tony Bland would survive until 1993).

The Coroner, Dr Stefan Popper, had a dilemma. It is a dilemma with many precedents. A key question for all coroners is about when to hold an inquest if there are criminal matters that are being considered in relation to anyone who might be a significant witness at the inquest. The driver of the car that kills a pedestrian, for example. The way that coroners usually deal with this dilemma is by staying the proceedings until the criminal matters have been resolved. The disadvantage is that it delays the process for distressed families but, on the other hand, it generally makes for a more streamlined inquest when it is finally convened.

Lord Justice Goldring had to address the same dilemma at the start of these more recent proceedings. It was submitted that it would be unfair, to David Duckenfield and others, to take evidence, including theirs, in a court whilst the question of criminal proceedings was, once again, under active consideration. The Coroner noted that the deaths occurred twenty-five years ago. The families were not getting any younger and some of them had passed away in that passage of time. He acknowledged the legal difficulties that might ensue but, on balance, he wanted to start the renewed inquests as soon as possible and decided to go ahead.

One of the potential consequences for a Coroner's Court, in deciding to go ahead before CPS have reached a decision, is that any witnesses may assert their lawful right not to incriminate themselves and therefore decline to answer some or all questions. Neither David Duckenfield nor anyone else from South Yorkshire Police raised any objection to giving testimony on oath at Lord Goldring's inquest, despite a criminal investigation being conducted in parallel.

Coroner Stefan Popper was faced with this same procedural dilemma in 1990 and arrived at a novel and controversial solution. Instead of applying the typical caution of coroners and staying the proceedings, or adopting the bold approach of Lord Justice Goldring by starting proceedings in the face of potential difficulties down the line, Dr Popper instead proposed a third way. He would hear the 'who', 'when' and 'where' evidence about the ninety-five deaths at a preliminary stage and then he would adjourn the proceedings until after the CPS decisions in order to hear testimony as to 'how' the deceased had met their deaths.

These two parts of the inquisitorial process became known, respectively, as 'ninety-five mini inquests' and the 'Generic Inquest'. I shan't seek to explain the justification for the Coroner's decision or some of the arbitrary rulings that he gave along the way. For example, his ruling that he would only admit testimony about events up to 3.15 p.m., as he accepted preliminary medical evidence that people were either dead or irreversibly dying by that time. Whilst his procedure, rulings and eventual verdict have been over-turned by the High Court, which ruled in 2012 that there should be new inquests, all but the fiercest critics accept that he was acting in good faith in trying to move on a pro-cess in which delay is so often a source of concern for the families involved.

Indeed, there is evidence that the Coroner's proposals about how he might open the inquisitorial process in this limited way were warmly welcomed by the Hillsborough Steering Committee (HSC), the collective body of law-yers representing the bereaved families and the injured. Dr Popper met with Doug Fraser of the HSC on 26 Feb-ruary 1990 to discuss the way forward. Mr Fraser, on behalf of all those represented, agreed that anything that could be done quickly to 'get information to the families in a non-adversarial way would be warmly welcomed'.

The mini inquests might have been proposed with the best of intentions, but they left the families with a deep sense of dissatisfaction. Their loved one was described at the inquest, in life and in death, by an unfamiliar third party, a West Midlands Police Officer. The family had no part in the proceedings, and questioning of witnesses was limited. All ninety-five mini inquests were concluded in thirteen days, between 18 April and 4 May 1990. The Coroner, armed chiefly with the West Midlands Police summaries, raced through several individual deaths each day. Legal representation was prohibitively expensive for individual families, who were therefore observers of, rather than participants in, the procedures. The bereaved families would feel that these mini inquests had been conducted superficially and with no opportunity for their concerns to be addressed. They received the impression that their loved one was simply a number in a bureaucratic process.

The families were given reason to believe that any inadequacies in the 'mini inquests' could be addressed in the resumed 'generic' inquest stage that would follow the decision on criminal proceedings. The CPS decision was published on 30 August 1990. Their press release read as follows:

> Following a lengthy and detailed investigation by
> the West Midlands Police and close consideration of

Lord Justice Taylor's report, the Director of Public Prosecutions has concluded that there is no evidence upon which a prosecution for manslaughter or other criminal offence may be brought against the South Yorkshire Police, Sheffield Wednesday Football Club, Mssrs Eastwood and Partners [the consulting engineers who designed the Leppings Lane stadium configuration] or Sheffield City Council in connection with the disaster at Hillsborough Football Stadium Sheffield on 15 April 1989.

The Director has also concluded that there is insufficient evidence to justify the institution of proceedings against any officer in the South Yorkshire Police force or any other person for any offence.

The decision enabled Dr Popper to resume his inquest into the deaths of the ninety-five. It is clear that he did call and re-call some witnesses in the resumed inquest with the intention of addressing some points of concern or contention raised by the families. It is also clear, however, that this generic phase of the inquest failed to satisfy everyone.

There were two major constraints imposed by Dr Popper that were each an impediment to meeting the needs of the families. Firstly, the 3.15 p.m. cut-off for all evidence. It meant that families who noted that death was certified at a later time, and who may have noticed conflicting or ambiguous evidence in witness testimony or video footage, could not get to the bottom of their concerns.

Secondly, the determination of Dr Popper to keep the generic part of the inquest relatively short. At one time, prior to the start of the resumed proceedings, he had expressed the hope that it might start in early November 1990 and be finalised by Christmas. In fact, this phase began on 19 November 1990 and concluded on 28 March 1991. Whilst this inquest was, at the time, the longest on record, it had only sat for thirteen days at the 'mini inquests' stage and for fifteen weeks when it resumed. In total, fewer days than the number of deceased.

Furthermore, in subsequent High Court proceedings in 1993, when six of the bereaved families applied for the inquest verdicts to be set aside, it was considered that Dr Popper's conduct of the inquest had been unorthodox and that he had failed to comply strictly with Coroners Rules. Yet the High Court rejected the application to dismiss the proceedings and the verdict.

The question about the adequacy of the process was enquired into yet again in 1997, when Lord Justice Stuart-Smith was asked by the incoming Labour government to undertake a review of the residual contentions of the families and other campaigners. Lord Justice Stuart-Smith agreed with the High Court about the unorthodox nature of the original procedures and he also formed the view that, under Dr Popper's direction, the complexity and enormity of the process had caused the generic hearing to become out of control. Lord Justice Stuart-Smith concluded that, in hindsight, it might have been better for the Coroner to have avoided the need for any generic inquisition into how the ninety-five died by simply adopting the Taylor Inquiry report as his guide. That would have satisfied the bereaved families much more than Dr Popper's fragmentary process.

Some relatives found, after this whirlwind procedure in a strange town, in which they had felt excluded from the proceedings, that they were still no wiser about how their loved one had died. By contrast, the recent inquest conducted by Lord Justice Goldring has sat for almost 300 days and has tried to put the families at the heart of the process.

Those families that did go to hear the proceedings at the resumed, 'generic', inquest back in 1990 also heard a tired and familiar story: that some unruly fans had precipitated the disaster.

'The police', as a body, had been represented at the Taylor Inquiry by a single legal team and barrister. By the time of the inquests, 'the police' were a more disparate group of separate interests. There were five legal teams at the inquest representing the interests of individual police officers who considered themselves to be at risk in the proceedings. Whilst the arguments adopted by individual counsel are independent of each other, it must have felt, to the families, like a concerted and corporate strategy to defend any criticism of 'the police'.

Notwithstanding their disappointment about the way the inquest was conducted, by the Coroner and by 'the police', the families gathered in Sheffield to learn the verdicts as to the cause of the ninety-five deaths. When the jury were sent out by the Coroner in late March 1991, they had available to them optional verdicts. 'Unlawful killing', where death was deemed to have been caused through the gross negligent acts or omissions of persons or organisations, or 'accidental death', where a person has died as a result of actions by others that had unintended consequences. There was nothing in between these two verdicts that was permissible in the coronial proceedings of that time. An 'open verdict' would also be available, where doubt remained in the minds of the jury as to how the deceased came to their death.

The jury took some days to reach their verdicts. By a majority of nine to two, the jury considered that all ninety-five deceased had met their deaths through accidental causes, as a result of actions or omissions of others that had unintended consequences. We are left to assume that the minority supported an alternative verdict of 'unlawful killing' but we can never know what went on behind the jury room door.

The families were outraged. They felt let down by the Coroner, by the jury and by their own collective legal representation, the Hillsborough Steering Committee, which was all that they had been able to afford. How could the newspaper images, which depicted the life ebbing from faces pressed up against the fence in Pen 3 at Hillsborough, be reconciled with a verdict of accidental death? This was another monstrous insult from which the families would never recover.

Reasonably content with Lord Justice Taylor's version of events from two years previously, the families, and their supporters, were now reeling from two reversals in the space of a few months. No proceedings were to be taken against any individual for any act or omission surrounding the deaths. And now they were being asked to live with the notion that somehow their loved one, who had set off to watch a football match, had had an accident and wouldn't be coming home. Furthermore, there was at least an insinuation that they were members of a group that was partly responsible for the 'accident' that occurred.

The fact that the families could not rest with these conclusions is perfectly understandable. People who only know, vaguely, about a tragic loss of life at a stadium a quarter of a century ago may fail to understand why the bereaved haven't moved on. This goes to the heart of my earlier 'Taj Mahal' point. One can only really understand how it feels if one is affected by it. When faced with what the families consider to be an affront of this magnitude it actually makes the notion of 'moving on' even more difficult or impossible.

It was on the steps of the Coroner's Court in Sheffield in 1991 that the families discovered a shared purpose and a campaigning zeal. It is there that they found the fortitude that would sustain them for twenty more years and enable them to enlist the support of others along the way. They had to fight or give in... But for them there was no second option: they would fight.

In 1993, when six of the bereaved families' application for the inquest verdicts to be set aside was rejected by the Divisional Court, this may have added further salt to the wounds.

By 1996, the fight for justice was gathering pace, predominantly in Merseyside. The renowned Liverpool dramatist Jimmy McGovern wrote a TV drama called *Hillsborough*, which was produced by Granada Television and aired on 5 December that year. The film told the story of the disaster through the eyes of three of the bereaved families: the Hicks, the Glovers and the Spearritts. It followed the experiences of the families from the day of the disaster up to the day in 1991 when the inquest verdicts were announced. The McGovern film was a moving account and had a profound effect in raising public consciousness about the families' struggle. It won the BAFTA award for best drama of 1996 and many other industry plaudits. It has been broadcast since on the twentieth anniversary of the disaster, in 2009; on 15 September 2012, three days after the Hillsborough Panel Report was published; and after the recent inquest verdict of 'unlawful killing'.

The public outcry that followed the first screening of this film caused Jack Straw, the incoming Home Secretary in a new Labour government, to order a review of Hillsborough. There were allegations raised in Mr McGovern's screenplay which implied that there was evidence that had been withheld or obstructed in the proceedings before Lord Justice Taylor; in the files submitted to the Director of Public Prosecutions and the Attorney General; and in the testimony that was heard by the jury at the Coroner's Inquest. The Home Secretary appointed Lord Justice Stuart-Smith in June 1997 to enquire into these matters.

Lord Justice Stuart-Smith reported in February 1998 that he had considered all the matters that had been brought to his attention by the families and other parties. He had met or received submissions from thirty-four families. He had also received oral and written submissions from counsel and solicitors representing the families, and from Professor Phil Scraton, who was, at this time, leading the 'Hillsborough Project' at Edge Hill University College.

The Hillsborough Project, part funded by Liverpool City Council, was commissioned in 1990 to conduct research into the causes of the disaster and its aftermath. The research would culminate in 1999 with the publication of the book *Hillsborough: The Truth* written by Professor Scraton. This book, according to the Hillsborough Project website, concluded, a full thirteen years before the publication of the Hillsborough Panel Report, that the Hillsborough disaster represented a serious miscarriage of justice and a cover-up by the police.

The families, and those supporting them, could not comprehend, therefore, why Lord Justice Stuart-Smith had not agreed with this view when he reported to Parliament in 1998.

Lord Justice Stuart-Smith did reach the conclusion that it was not satisfactory for an inquest to inquire into the causes of deaths in relation to a major disaster when an inquiry chaired by a High Court Judge had already covered the same ground. The families might have taken some solace from the fact that Lord Justice Stuart-Smith was reinforcing the primacy of the Taylor Inquiry in apportioning cause and blame. They remained stuck, however, with the formal verdict of 'accidental death', and that sore would fester for a further eighteen years.

After the decision of the Director of Public Prosecution, in 1990, to not institute proceedings against David

Duckenfield or any other person or body in connection with the disaster, the families had been considering their options. In 1998, they began private proceedings against Mr Duckenfield and Bernard Murray, his deputy at Hillsborough on the fateful day. The families were able to contemplate this financially daunting step because of funds raised in support of their cause. A significant source was from the proceeds of the Hillsborough Justice Concert held in 1997 when, once again, Anfield hosted a capacity crowd with all proceeds from the concert going to the Hillsborough Family Support Group. The headline act was the Manic Street Preachers, who later released a recording of their song 'South Yorkshire Mass Murderers'. The question of whether the concert and the recording might influence the jury became a contentious issue in preparing for the subsequent trial of David Duckenfield and Bernard Murray. Mr Justice Hooper, the trial judge, decided that a jury would be capable of discounting the prejudicial effect of such peripheral matters.

Getting the two officers to court was a tortuous process. The case was begun by laying a formal criminal allegation before a Merseyside Magistrate's Court thus triggering a private prosecution. It was, ultimately, and after several legal wrangles, adopted as a public prosecution and the case was heard at Leeds Crown Court in June 2000. It is typical of the determination of the families that they overcame all kinds of legal obstacles that were put in their way.

The two faced charges of manslaughter and misconduct in a public office. In the course of the proceedings the trial judge ordered that the misconduct charges be withdrawn leaving the indictments of manslaughter. Having heard all the evidence, the jury in the case deliberated for five days before returning their verdicts. In relation to Bernard Murray, the jury were unanimous that he was not guilty. In respect of David Duckenfield, the jury failed to agree, in either unanimity or majority, whether he was guilty or not guilty of homicide.

This was yet another setback in the families' long struggle for justice. Furthermore, Mr Duckenfield had retired from the police service in 1990. He had been unable to work due to the effects of stress since the conclusion of the Taylor Inquiry. He retired prematurely, on the grounds of ill health, a year later. He was therefore beyond the reach of any disciplinary proceedings and this gave the families an added grievance. No one has ever lost a day's pay, let alone their liberty, for any acts and omissions at Hillsborough. Given the stinging rebuke, by Lord Justice Taylor, in relation to the police command and control at Hillsborough, it is hard to argue against the families' sense of grievance.

After the double disappointment of the Stuart-Smith

rejection, and the failed prosecution of the main targets, the families might have been forgiven for giving up. It had been eleven long years of struggle in the face of public complacency beyond Liverpool and closed institutional doors. They have always seemed, however, to draw strength from adversity, and succour from the steadfast support that they have received closer to home. A response posted by the Hillsborough Justice Campaign in the aftermath of the failed prosecution speaks volumes: 'The bereaved families of the Hillsborough Justice Campaign will continue to fight … with the aim of having the true facts of Hillsborough officially recorded. We know that this will take a long time. We are used to waiting.'

It would be nine more years before there would be a further glimmer of hope for the families. That would appear, fittingly, at the twentieth anniversary memorial service, held at Anfield on 15 April 2009. A panel would be formed to review the whole history of the disaster and its aftermath. Their report would create a spark to ignite the public consciousness and lead, finally, in 2012, to a quashing of the original inquest verdicts and the reinstatement of a new inquest under the direction of the former Senior Presiding Judge for England and Wales. The running sore might be finally healed because of the determination of the families and through the efforts of the Hillsborough Panel.

There would emerge a consequential glimmer too. In the

shadow of that reinstated Coroner's Court at Warrington, an opportunity for conciliation arose.

After David Duckenfield had completed his evidence on Wednesday 18 March 2015, he was met outside by Barry Devonside. Mr Devonside had been at Hillsborough on the day of the disaster with his son Christopher. He returned home alone. Christopher's was one of the young lives lost on that April day. Mr Devonside has been a constant and articulate driving force for justice for twenty-six years. He had been ever present at the Warrington Inquest and had listened carefully to the testimony given by each of the witnesses, including the evidence over the seven days that David Duckenfield spent in the witness box.

As Mr Duckenfield left the court house after the last day of his evidence, police officers accompanying him readied themselves as Mr Devonside made a beeline for the witness. They were there to give Mr Duckenfield unhindered passage into and out of the court. They had no need to be anxious for his safety, however, for something remarkable occurred.

Barry Devonside had been waiting twenty-six years to hear an expression of contrition delivered by David Duckenfield. It seemed as though he wanted to tell the man, who had owed him a significant debt for a long time, that his evidence at Warrington had been a step in the right direction. It is sad that Anne Williams, Eddie Spearritt and countless other bereaved family members did not live long enough to witness that day for themselves.

CHAPTER 6

IN MY LIVERPOOL HOME

11 October 1998 – November 2004

'W hat's the definition of rock hard?'
    'I don't know. What is the definition of rock hard?'

'It's a copper from South Yorkshire who becomes the Chief of Merseyside, and he's with us in the studio.'

This gentle banter ushered in the happiest and most fulfilling six years of my policing career. The exchange took place between Billy Butler and Wally Scott on a Radio City live broadcast. Radio City FM is the commercial radio station for the Liverpool City region. Alongside its BBC equivalent, Radio Merseyside, City FM is a much-loved source of news and entertainment throughout Liverpool and beyond.

Of all the places where I have lived, including many towns and cities across South and West Yorkshire and also in London and Hampshire, Liverpool is the place where localism and the spirit of community have felt most tangible and real. It might have something to do with the Irish Sea. If anyone goes to Liverpool, then they can't go any further without a swimming costume or a ferry ticket. You have, as the sat nav says, reached your destination. It is a city, the sixth largest in terms of population, but it feels like a village or, to be more precise, a series of villages creating a single homogeneous community.

The *Liverpool Echo*, the local daily newspaper, has always prided itself on having the biggest readership of any local paper outside of London. I remember claims, during my time there, of a daily readership of 250,000-plus, which must have assumed multiple readers of the copies sold. Merseysiders, as a general rule, take a passionate interest in local news and events. The football, local crime, politics and the 'family announcements' section of the paper are all more topical and talked about, in my experience, than elsewhere in the country. The local newspapers are well read and the local radio well listened to.

Because of a furore around my appointment to the post of Chief Constable in Merseyside, in October 1998, I asked the Merseyside Police Press Office to arrange a round of media interviews to coincide with my first days in the job. I gave more than twenty interviews over two days. Inspector Ray Galloway, who was the head of the press office, told me there were three, key, local touchstones. The *Echo* of course; *The Roger Phillips Show* on BBC Radio Merseyside – aka 'The Voice of Merseyside'; and *The Billy and Wally Show* on Radio City. He had lined me up for all three, and many more besides. Billy and Wally were to be first up.

I felt some trepidation as I walked into the Radio City studio. It was my first opportunity to speak directly with the people of Merseyside. This would make a change from having had lots said about me in the local media in the five weeks since the announcement of my appointment.

Billy and Wally were the Ant and Dec of Merseyside entertainment. Physically distinct, but that wasn't obvious on radio. They were inseparable and had spent years sparking off each other on the airwaves and in the local theatres and clubs. Was it Billy who asked Wally for the definition of rock hard or was it the other way around? Whatever the case, it was a good interview: welcoming and positive.

I found myself talking about the future and not just the past, trying to engage in the joshing that was the hallmark of *The Billy and Wally Show*. Although another lesson that I quickly learned as I settled in to Liverpool life is to never try to have the last word with a Scouser. Naturally quick-witted, with acerbic humour and a lyrical grasp of the spoken word, they, as a general rule, will out-josh all comers. Just smile and take it in good part – there is rarely any offence intended.

I had arrived. It seemed like touch and go for a week or two but now, here I was, in the home of the Beatles. A city which boasts the finest architecture outside London and the most extensive range of cultural opportunities. Whilst a resident of the city, I would often go to a gallery opening in the morning, watch premiership football in the afternoon and hear the Royal Liverpool Philharmonic Orchestra in the evening. This was going to be my kind of town.

———

I had visited Liverpool only twice in my life before 1998. Once to a game at Anfield and on the second occasion to visit a prisoner in Walton Jail. I needed to interview him about similar offences to those which had led to his conviction and sentence. Visiting a football stadium and a prison doesn't really give a proper feel for a city as a whole. I had no connection to the place and no latent desire to live or work there.

I had been an Assistant Chief Constable in West Yorkshire Police for five years when, in April 1998, a new Chief Constable was appointed. It was Graham Moore, who was one of my friends in the service. We had been on a national development programme together in the early '80s and had kept in touch since. I was delighted when he got the job as I knew he would make a first-class Chief.

It became obvious within a couple of months, however, that friendships on a command team create more tension than harmony. By the summer of 1998 it was clear that I needed to move on. Graham had a long contract and it would be better for our relationship, and the force as a whole, if we went our separate professional ways.

I wanted to remain living in the north of England and, preferably, work in a metropolitan area. All my experience had been in inner-city policing.

An early advert appeared on the situations vacant pages of the *Police Review* – the professional organ for the police service – inviting applications for the post of Chief Constable at Merseyside. I thought about it but quickly rejected the idea.

I rejected the idea of submitting an application for one reason only. There was a Deputy Chief Constable in one of the Welsh forces who had previously worked in Merseyside and was considered a clear favourite for the vacancy back in his old force.

There was no other reason that I dismissed the idea of an application to Merseyside. It was, in many ways, an ideal fit for my domestic and professional circumstances. I didn't have in mind my Hillsborough tasking nine years previously. Those who now say that it should have been predominant do so with the benefit of hindsight and are influenced by the current and powerful narrative that surrounds Hillsborough. That didn't exist in 1998.

I had spent three months, as a Chief Inspector, working on a task group almost a decade previously. I had done nothing that I considered to be notable or particularly career-defining during those three months. I had done nothing meritworthy nor anything to suggest controversy. I certainly hadn't done anything to my cost or shame. Furthermore, my professional experience had, in the interim, been further developed in two different forces; three different ranks; and seven different roles.

During that nine-year interval no one had even hinted at any criticism of the post-disaster role that I had performed. I knew that Lord Justice Stuart-Smith had examined allegations about the process of statement emendation, but that had nothing to do with me. There was no obvious impediment, that I knew of, to my living and working in Merseyside if I chose to. Anyhow, this was irrelevant.

I had decided not to apply for the post because it was a job, I thought, with someone else's name on it.

At the final interviews, however, my predictions about Chief Officer appointments proved to be more fallible than I had imagined. The Merseyside Police Authority had interviewed six candidates and had chosen not to appoint any of them. The job was still open and the favourite, along with other competitors, was no longer in the running.

When the job was advertised again I sent for an application form and communicated with the Chief Executive of the Merseyside Police Authority, David Henshaw, to let him know that I was interested. The Chief Executive, and the application form rubric, could not have been more clear. Candidates were to use only the forms provided with no additional papers appended. Candidates were to stick rigidly to a limited word count and address only the nine competencies required of a Chief Constable. Candidates were instructed to draw on *recent* experiences to evidence the competency assessment which would be the first stage of the selection process.

I completed my application form in accordance with the instructions. I addressed the competencies that had been established by the Home Office as the core requirement for a Chief Constable. I drew on evidence exclusively from my recent experience as an Assistant Chief Constable and from no other part of my career. I complied with the word count guillotine. I submitted the form and copied it to Her Majesty's Inspector of Constabulary (HMIC), who would be required to submit an assessment of all candidates and who would be present as a professional adviser to the Police Authority at both shortlisting and final interview.

My application form, critics have pointed out after the fact, contains no mention of Hillsborough. That is true. It also contains no mention of my supervising the Independence Elections in Zimbabwe; or the exchange programme I undertook with the Metropolitan Police, working on the Vice Squad in Soho. It has nothing in it about setting up a new department to develop talent in an organisation; or about commanding football match operations; or about leading a team to take down the shebeens in north Sheffield, the illegal drinking dens and crack houses that blighted the city before our operation. The critics are right, the application form had no mention of Hillsborough ... but the HMIC assessment very clearly did.

The police senior appointments process was a highly regulated process. The Home Office set the rules in those days. A local Police Authority may appoint whomever they wished so long as a) the candidate had successfully completed the Strategic Command Course at the Bramshill Police Staff College, for which there was a competitive entry process, and b) they were approved by the Home Secretary as suitable for the post. Her Majesty's Inspector of Constabulary was the person who advised both the Home Secretary and the local Police Authority in their respective decisions.

The HMIC provided the Police Authority with his own assessment of all candidates and a brief history of their career to date. The third paragraph of mine read as follows:

> After university and promotion to Chief Inspector he was appointed to create a Career Development Department within the force and then had a part in a small team reporting to the Chief Constable in relation to the Hillsborough incident. Promoted Superintendent in 1989 he was posted to Traffic Department and then Sheffield City sub-division. He attended the Junior and Intermediate Command Courses where his performance was impressive.

That single paragraph dealt, succinctly, with about five years of my professional career. The HMIC's ten-paragraph report accompanied my application form and was available to everyone involved in the appointments process.

At shortlisting, the HMIC responsible for the north of England police region, Mr Dan Crompton, provided the Appointments Committee of the Police Authority with an even more compendious account: a single page for each candidate containing twelve bullet points. Bullet point number three on my page read: 'Member of a small enquiry team reporting to the Chief Constable on the Hillsborough Incident.'

The bullet point sheets were handed out to the short-listing committee as each candidate was discussed. The Chief Executive and the majority of the nine members of the Appointments Committee agree that this was done, that they had read the documents as each candidate was considered, and that they had seen and noted the Hillsborough reference. Two local councillors would later say that they had no knowledge of any documents being supplied by the HMIC and, if there were, they hadn't read them. They were embarrassed by the fallout that followed my appointment.

My own assumption that my work, post-disaster, was no impediment to an application to work in Merseyside seemed to be endorsed by the Appointments Committee, for I was duly shortlisted along with six other colleagues. No member asked the HMIC for any further information about my post-disaster tasking.

The seven candidates gathered in Liverpool on the evening of Sunday 11 October 1998. There was to be, what we called in the trade, an 'ordeal by meal' or 'trial by trifle'. It was the practice in the '90s to begin every selection process for Chief Officer posts with an 'informal' meal where the candidates rotated after every course to sit between two different members of the committee so that the appointing members could chat about anything they wished. All the official guff around this arrangement was that it was not a part of the selection process and that it was simply a means of breaking the ice. Anecdotal evidence indicated, however, that judgements were made about candidates during this informal process. Equal opportunities was an immature concept in the '90s.

The nine members of the Police Authority, two executive officers and the HMIC had, by the end of the evening, broken bread and engaged in small talk with each of the seven candidates. No one had asked me anything about Hillsborough, despite my connection having been brought to their attention.

There followed a two-day process during which every question asked of one candidate was asked of all. That may appear a rigid nod to fairness, but it was simply a Home Office guideline to prevent local appointers, inexperienced in HR matters, going off-piste in an embarrassing way. As the two days unfolded, I felt an increasingly positive reaction from the committee.

The final stage was a presentation on a professional topic, of the Authority's choosing, delivered in the Police Authority Chamber in full uniform. This was an exercise which enabled an assessment of the 'cut of the jib' of each candidate. An opportunity to see the candidates, who were still in contention, in the environment which was most familiar to the Authority.

We all then waited in an adjoining room for the white smoke to rise. After an hour had passed, David Henshaw, the Chief Executive, and Councillor Carol Gustafson, the Chair of the Police Authority, came into the room and invited me to rejoin the Appointments Committee next door. Mr Henshaw stayed behind to explain to the other applicants, collectively, that the Committee would be offering me the job.

I was thrilled. The more research that I had undertaken in preparation for the interview, the more I believed Merseyside Police to be a perfect fit for my experiences and my aspirations. After a little back-slapping with the Appointments Panel, I was taken off to have a medical, and then a photo shoot and, finally, a short private meeting with the Chair to agree press lines about the appointment and to discuss a start date.

It was about 5.30 p.m. on Tuesday 13 October that I got into my car at the Liverpool Hotel, where the candidates had spent the previous three days, and set off for home, which was on the other side of the Pennines. Forty-five minutes later, in driving rain and at the highest point of the M62 motorway, crossing the bleak Saddleworth Moor where Brady and Hindley had buried the bodies of their victims, the car phone rang. It was a brick-sized affair with a coiled lead that sat, imposingly, in the centre console. There was no hands-free facility, nor any legislation to preclude the phone being picked up.

It was a Merseyside Superintendent on the line. He courteously confirmed that we were not yet acquainted but that he needed to impart some news. 'First of all,' he said, 'may I offer you my congratulations and I look forward to working with you.' Nice start.

But then: 'Your appointment has caused a bit of a kerfuffle over here. Maria Eagle, a local MP, is on the warpath claiming that you have connections with the Hillsborough disaster. She's all over the media with it.'

A 'kerfuffle' was, I soon learned, a bit of an understatement. Maria Eagle had spoken in a debate in the House of Commons on 8 May 1998, when the House had received the Stuart-Smith Inquiry report. I was unaware of it. It was in that speech that she first made her accusation that South Yorkshire Police had appointed a team to orchestrate a black propaganda campaign and that the team had been so engaged in propaganda and historical revisionism for a number of years. Ms Eagle had noted a number of names on historic documents that she had read in the Commons Library which had been deposited there by Lord Justice Stuart-Smith. Bettison is not a common name and so news of my appointment in Merseyside had triggered an angry response from Ms Eagle and, thereafter, from others representing families' groups and justice campaigns.

The local interest in these allegations became intense. My name was mentioned in the *Liverpool Echo* in the majority of the daily editions over the weeks that followed my appointment. There was rarely anything new to say about Maria Eagle's general accusation made under parliamentary privilege. She did not repeat any of the invective outside of that privileged situation. Others, however, who weren't so concerned about avoiding defamatory comment, let rip. The thing that really kept the story running was an almost daily accretion of some fact or other from the Appointments Committee. Who knew what? Who asked what question?

Three members of the Police Authority resigned their positions – the two councillors who claimed not to have received the HMI's assessment and summary and, later, another, very honourable, councillor from Wirral, who wasn't even on the Appointments Committee. He resigned when it became clear that the Police Authority were going to confirm my appointment in spite of the controversy. This piecemeal fallout from the selection process helped fuel the running story.

There were some wild and wonderful headlines during this period, when more heat than light was being generated in Merseyside about my appointment. Amongst the cleverest, carried by the *Echo*, was: 'It's Time to Jettison Bettison'. A headline that could have graced any tabloid.

It may be difficult to imagine, in the aftermath of the national controversy created by the Hillsborough Panel

Report in 2012, that this 1998 precursor firestorm was contained locally. It was predominantly a story in Merseyside and the north-west, but it never caught fire nationally because there weren't any specific accusations that could be held up to the light. The dreadful irony is that the Hillsborough Panel Report unleashed a very similar non-specific whirlwind which, this time, went viral. And has stuck.

In the forty-eight hours that followed my appointment, I had two broad concerns. How should I respond to the misplaced accusations which were running in Merseyside so that I was able to do the job I was appointed to undertake? Secondly, how should I respond to the bereaved families, particularly those based in Merseyside, who would have been influenced and, understandably, distressed by the news reports? They were the most important constituents in my consideration. The first, broader, issue could only be addressed when I started my new job in Merseyside. I was a West Yorkshire Assistant Chief Constable, ninety miles away from Liverpool, with limited access to the local media there.

I had done nothing wrong and surely people would come to see that in the fullness of time. To have retreated from the flames would have been a mistake. It would have allowed the 'no smoke without fire' theory to be established. This was an unanticipated and unsubstantiated allegation that now had to be faced head-on. And faced down.

The bereaved families were another consideration altogether. I needed to speak with them directly at the earliest opportunity. They were owed an explanation.

I made the first of many overtures to the families' representatives, within forty-eight hours of my appointment, in a letter delivered to Maria Eagle. After a couple of paragraphs, in which I refute the idea of any impediment to my appointment and speak about my ambition for policing in Merseyside, I offered the following request:

> I am nevertheless aware of the depth of grief and anger felt by those bereaved in the Hillsborough disaster, and I know how much is focused upon South Yorkshire Police in general, and two or three senior officers in particular. I am prepared to answer questions in detail about my actions on 15 April 1989, and in the weeks and months that followed that fateful day. I would like the opportunity to meet with you and representatives of the families, privately, as soon as this can be arranged. I know that I shall be called upon to deal with questions in the media but, in the long term, I think the people who deserve answers are your constituents rather than the world at large. I am prepared to clear any time in my diary, including evenings and weekends. I do hope we can meet.

I closed the letter by quoting the *Liverpool Daily Post* editorial from that day, 15 October 1998. Sensing that Maria Eagle's non-specific accusation was unlikely to derail the appointment process, the editor had helpfully offered this conciliatory proposition: 'Mr Bettison's ... experience of the Hillsborough disaster should reinforce his empathy with Merseyside and its people not weaken it.' I told Ms Eagle that I wanted to be given the chance to demonstrate that potential in a meeting with the bereaved families.

Ms Eagle did not respond straight away, as it emerged, about the time she received my letter, that the Merseyside Police Authority announced that they would be meeting the Hillsborough Family Support Group and the Hillsborough Justice Campaign group on 2 November. The Police Authority would then immediately follow that up by holding a 'confirmation hearing' with me.

Both the Family Support Group and the Justice Campaign group, in the meantime, issued press statements, on different days, each calling upon the Authority to rescind the appointment. One might see how all of these announcements kept the local media pot boiling for weeks.

On Sunday 1 November, the day before the crunch meetings, I received a telephone call at my home from Councillor Carol Gustafson, the Police Authority Chair, to discuss the arrangements for Monday's meetings. Councillor Gustafson had, since the day of the appointment, been courteous and sympathetic. She was in a place where no politician ever wants to be, the target of negative public opinion, but she was made of strong stuff and had survived other personal and political crises in her life.

Councillor Gustafson and I would go on to have a hot and cold relationship professionally, but a fond respect for each other at a personal level until the day that she died, prematurely.

She had endured a hard life in her formative years and had dedicated herself to bringing up two children as a single parent against the odds. Arriving at local politics through the route of local union activism, she was an arch politician. Every incident that happened locally was either an opportunity or threat to her political survival and ambition. People were judged by her on the same basis. Away from the political environment, however, she had a heart of gold and an endearing vulnerability which she kept well hidden from political view.

The one trait of Councillor Gustafson that I found most frustrating, in her role as Police Authority Chair, is that she would try to please the last person she met. If we had worked through a strategy or a tricky policy on any policing matter, our agreement would only survive, in her mind, until someone spoke against it. At that point it was necessary to convince her all over again of the benefit and advantage of a particular direction.

This trait, with which I had not yet become fully acquainted, was barely disguised in our 1 November telephone conversation. I asked her if she intended to confirm my appointment the following day as I felt that the ambiguity was damaging to both me and the force. She gave me a very honest answer: 'I don't know, Norman, it depends on the numbers.' This was my first, or certainly most personal, encounter with the concept of the political calculus. Some politicians don't have intentions, they have positions that are either confirmed or altered by the whip once all the pros and cons have been counted and weighed.

David Henshaw, the Authority's Chief Executive, had written to Maria Eagle MP asking that she provide any evidence to support her allegation, made under parliamentary privilege, that I was or had been a member of a black propaganda unit. Such evidence was required to inform the Police Authority meeting with the campaign groups and their later meeting with me. No evidence was ever provided by Maria Eagle, then or since.

The meeting between the Police Authority and the campaign groups, to which I was not invited, was a fractious affair. The campaigners were not in a position, though, to provide any hard facts as to why I should be disqualified from being appointed. Sadly, they had come to an entrenched position based upon the widespread reporting of Ms Eagle's condemnation.

The meeting that immediately followed it was no less fractious. I gave a presentation which I stand by today. The Police Authority questioned me closely. There were political resignations in the air and a demonstration continuing outside. Notwithstanding, I was confirmed as Chief Constable of Merseyside Police and given the maximum term contract. My appointment was later approved by the Home Secretary who, at that time, had a power of veto in relation to the appointment of Chief Constables.

I wrote, again, to Maria Eagle on the following day, 3 November 1998:

> I pointed out to Police Authority members, in closed session last night, that my first instinct had been to contact the representatives of the families once I became aware of the allegations that were circulating about me following your comments in the House of Commons ... All I have ever wanted is the opportunity to put right the unfair comments that you have raised about my appointment. To clarify for you some obviously mistaken impression and to ease the concerns of the families ... I hope you still feel there might be some benefit to hearing what I have to say in answer to any questions that you have...

Maria Eagle's office rang to confirm that she would meet me.

On 9 November, one week before my starting date as Chief Constable of Merseyside, I drove to Liverpool specifically to meet Ms Eagle. She had been unable to gain support for the meeting from the Family Support Group that she represented but she saw me herself. At the end of the two-hour meeting, at which I answered any and every question that Ms Eagle posed, she suggested a joint press release. I agreed and the statement that she drafted and issued contained the following:

> Maria Eagle MP for Liverpool Garston and Chief Constable Designate Norman Bettison have had a constructive open discussion … Ms Eagle was impressed by Mr Bettison's willingness to be open … They both agreed that the families, above anyone else, have a right to know what happened following the tragedy. They hope that a meeting can be arranged as soon as practicable.

On 10 November, I wrote again to Ms Eagle imploring her to do whatever she could to facilitate a meeting, at any venue or time of her choosing, so that I might sit down with the families. 'It is important', I said, 'that they have the chance to see the whites of my eyes.'

On 12 November, four days before my start date, Ms Eagle wrote to me to say that the families had been informed of my willingness to meet and that 'they have procedures to go through before they can be in a position to meet you; but I am encouraged by their initial response'.

On 15 November, I was in town on the eve of my debut as Chief Constable of Merseyside Police and faced a press briefing. I reinforced my desire to meet the families at that conference. I repeated the plea in the media round that was arranged by Inspector Ray Galloway to coincide with my first two days in the job.

Conscious that Maria Eagle did not represent every bereaved family in Merseyside, I wrote to other Merseyside MPs on 17 November making a similar offer to that made to Ms Eagle. I would meet the Family Support Group representatives any time, any place, anywhere, with anyone.

On 26 November 1998, ten days into the job, and frustrated by my failed attempts to reach out via third parties, I wrote directly to the Chair and Secretary of the Hillsborough Family Support Group (HFSG), Trevor Hicks and Peter Joynes. I had the letters personally delivered to the HFSG offices at North John Street, Liverpool. I pointed out that there was, since Ms Eagle's intervention, a misconception about my role post Hillsborough. I said: 'I very much hope that you will allow me the opportunity to meet with you and explain the realities of those events.' I received neither an acknowledgement nor a response. It is perfectly understandable, given the claims of a trusted local Member of Parliament and the resulting media furore, that the people most hurt by the actions of South Yorkshire Police might feel reluctant to meet with me. I felt a compelling need, however, to try to explain and to address the hurt face to face.

At the time of my transfer to Merseyside Police, I was living in West Yorkshire. I became aware, early on in my Merseyside career, that Trevor Hicks, Chairman of the HFSG, owned a business which he managed from premises there. I wondered whether an informal meeting away from the febrile environment of Merseyside might be a better prospect. I therefore visited Mr Hicks's commercial headquarters in early 1999 alone and out of uniform. The receptionist confirmed that he was in his office but, when she checked with Mr Hicks, he was busy and he declined my offer to make a future appointment at a more convenient time.

I had often seen Mr Hicks at the Taylor Inquiry back in 1989. On one occasion I found myself sitting beside him in the body of the court. We exchanged inconsequential pleasantries about the weather or the progress of the inquiry. He may not have remembered it. I don't remember the detail of the exchange, just the feeling of being awed in the presence of a man who had lost both of his daughters in the most devastating of circumstances and who, in spite of that, managed to conduct himself with patience,

courtesy and dignity in dealing with the resultant bureaucracy. I hoped, in 1999, that I might get a chance to speak
again with that same Mr Hicks that I respected and who
had so impressed me. This time more substantively, about
spurious allegations surrounding my conduct in the aftermath of the disaster. The chance never came.

Within days of my visit to Mr Hicks's place of business,
however, I received a telephone call from Professor Phil
Scraton. Professor Scraton was based at Edge Hill College
close to Merseyside. As mentioned earlier, he headed up a
Liverpool City Council-funded programme called 'The Hillsborough Project', which had, since 1990, been researching
and investigating the causes of the disaster and its aftermath. He had already written two substantial books on the
issues from the perspective of the bereaved families and he
was in the process of publishing his third, which he had
titled *Hillsborough: The Truth*. Professor Scraton said that
he was in close contact with the support groups and, whilst
they were unwilling to meet me personally 'at this time', he
would very much like to. I agreed and we met in my office
in Canning Place, Liverpool, the headquarters of Merseyside
Police. I gave him several hours of my time. He took notes
and I answered all of his questions openly and honestly.

Professor Scraton and I continued to communicate and
correspond for some time afterwards. The tone was friendly
in that the letters are signed off as being from 'Norman'

and 'Phil'. In a letter to Professor Scraton on 24 March 1999, I repeated my long-held desire to meet representatives of the bereaved and asked that he do all that he could to aid that process.

On 19 April 1999, Professor Scraton wrote to me acknowledging his acceptance of the fact that, on the basis of his further research, there are no known links between my post-disaster role and the subsequent emendation of statements. 'I have made it clear [to journalists]', he said, 'that I wanted any story related to your appointment to be distanced from the [current] serialisation of my book. I have refused to supply any quote on the matter.' He said that he 'looked forward to meeting again and it goes without saying that I wish you every success both professionally and personally'. He signed off the letter 'Yours sincerely, Phil.'

Whilst this was an amicable exchange, Professor Scraton failed to deliver the one thing that I had asked him to do for me. He did not acknowledge or address my earlier request for his help in arranging a meeting with the families.

In that same letter, though, he set out a concern that he has repeated in more recent media interviews following the publication of the Hillsborough Panel Report: '[T]he word peripheral', he said, 'was used to describe your role post-Hillsborough. This appears to be contradicted by both the range and specifics of the tasks which you performed.'

I had talked with Maria Eagle for two hours about my post-disaster role. I spoke with Professor Scraton for longer. I have allocated two chapters of this book to describe the 'range and specifics of the tasks I performed'. That isn't a negligible degree of involvement. I only ever, to the best of my knowledge, used the word 'peripheral' in a very particular context. I said, in my recorded and published presentation to the Merseyside Police Authority at my confirmation hearing on 2 November 1998, that my Hillsborough role was peripheral *to the disaster itself*. I was being dubbed 'The Hillsborough Chief' in the local media and I intended, with that word, to convey the fact that I had no involvement with the planning or commanding of the policing operation on the fateful day.

As I became more established in my role as Chief Constable, the early controversy subsided, though it never disappeared altogether. I had demonstrated a willingness to be open and a preparedness to answer any residual questions about my connections to Hillsborough, and people seemed to accept my explanation.

I did not shy away from talking about Hillsborough if anyone was sufficiently inquisitive. A pertinent example involves the Bishop of Liverpool, the Right Reverend

James Jones, who went on to become the Chair of the Hillsborough Panel.

The Bishop and I had arrived in Liverpool about the same time. There were a group of us who were contemporaries in positions of leadership at the time of a positive shift in the confidence and fortunes of the City of Liverpool and many were out-of-towners. The council's Chief Executive and the Vice Chancellor of John Moores University were Yorkshiremen, like me. It was one of those propitious times when a number of individuals, with few cultural preconceptions or prejudices, come together and are able, collectively, to make a tangible difference. In this instance, to the fate of the city.

This collegiate focus was sustained and supported by a range of regular meetings. One of them was a church-led initiative. Founded by the Anglican Bishop of Liverpool, David Sheppard, and the Catholic Archbishop of Liverpool, Derek Worlock, who collaborated closely after the Liverpool riots of the 1980s, the Michaelmas Group met on Thursday mornings for breakfast. The membership included all the people with positions of power and authority in Liverpool. The agenda was driven by whatever was topical in the city. David Sheppard and Derek Worlock had reasoned that if something like a Michaelmas Group had existed then, the Toxteth Riots might have been averted. Their successors, Bishop James Jones and Archbishop

Patrick Kelly, continued the regular meetings. The Chief Constable was a core member and I attended regularly.

Around the tenth anniversary of the Hillsborough disaster in April 1999, which was a major event in the city, Bishop James asked me to speak at the Michaelmas breakfast meeting about the legacy of the disaster, and about what remained to be done.

I provided an objective, and also compassionate, analysis of the various judicial proceedings and scrutinies that had followed the disaster. There were people in the Michaelmas Group who had perspectives of their own, drawn from local experience, and it was a lively discussion chaired by the Bishop. I wrote to Bishop James on 18 May 1999, referring back to our discussion, and enclosed copies of the Taylor Inquiry reports and the Stuart-Smith Scrutiny Report which he had asked to borrow so that he could read further into the background of the disaster and its aftermath.

I repeated my, by now familiar, request to him and to the other movers and shakers at the Michaelmas Group. I asked them to please use their influence and contacts in helping to introduce me to the families' representatives for a face-to-face meeting. Nothing ever came of it.

The Bishop, in his later role as Chairman of the Hillsborough Panel, may have failed to recall my sympathetic third-party account of the Hillsborough legacy and my acknowledgement of the families' long struggle at his

Michaelmas Group meeting back in 1999. If he had, he might well have encouraged the Family Support Group representatives to meet me before they denounced me in 2012. He was in an ideal position to help.

———————

By the year 2000, I had been Chief Constable in Merseyside for two years and my strategic change programme was well advanced. Merseyside Police had previously benefited from an additional annual cash grant over and above their allocation based on a national formula. The additional grant was established after the Toxteth Riots of the early '80s and had never been rescinded. About the time that I took over, the Home Office had decided that all forces should live on their formula grant alone.

Apart from the Metropolitan Police, which has national and international responsibilities, all forces were required to move, gradually, towards the formula allocation. Some had an under-provision and were grateful for the change to the funding arrangements. Most inner-city forces, and Merseyside in particular, had a historic over-provision and needed, over three years, to reduce spending to the formula allocation. That meant three years of stripping out costs.

Merseyside was, traditionally, a very centralist and top-heavy force. That could not be sustained in light of the budgetary cuts. I therefore used the budget correction as the tipping point, or internal crisis, to facilitate a cultural transformation in Merseyside. We shifted the vast majority of our resources away from headquarters and divisions and into self-determining neighbourhood teams. This was a policing style that suited the urban 'villages' of Merseyside very well.

It was a popular change programme with police officers, partners on the ground and, most importantly, with the Merseyside public. It was very successful in building local resilience and a real community focus. Along with similar experiments around that time, in Leicestershire and Surrey, it was the genesis for the Neighbourhood Policing Strategy that was to spread throughout the country in the first decade of the twenty-first century. The strategy has now started to come apart in the face of severe austerity cuts, which have, ironically, driven resources back to the centre in each force.

My tenure was progressing well. There was no residual campaigning against my appointment. I was seen, generally, as a power for good on Merseyside. My various attempts to gain an audience with the Hillsborough families, however, went unanswered.

To the best of my knowledge I made only two personal connections with families directly affected by the disaster and neither occasion lent itself to dialogue. The first was at a school event on the Wirral. I was regularly invited, in my professional role, to give prizes and speeches at schools, colleges and the three universities in Liverpool. Early in my tenure, I was told that one of the schoolgirls who would be involved in a presentation at a Wirral school had lost a family member in the disaster. I sent word to the headmaster, immediately, to offer to withdraw if my presence was likely to be upsetting for the girl, or for her family who would be there to support her. I was told that such action would not be necessary. I was never told which of the girls that I met that evening was the one directly affected by the disaster, nor which were her parents in the audience.

The second direct connection was with a very courteous host at a retired police officers' function. This ex-police Inspector had a son who had been at Hillsborough on that fateful afternoon and had been in respiratory arrest for long enough to have caused permanent neurological damage. We often talk about the ninety-six in hushed tones, but we don't bring to mind, as often as we should, those whose lives have been permanently scarred by the injuries sustained at Hillsborough. We remember the bereaved but are perhaps not as thoughtful about the carers who also live with the impact of that terrible day each waking moment. It was one such carer who sat next to me at this reunion lunch and he was hospitable and generous in ensuring that I had everything I needed. It was only afterwards that my staff officer, Martin Hill, asked me if I knew that my luncheon host was a father who had caring responsibilities for a badly injured son. I had no idea – he had never mentioned it. Martin told me that my host preferred not to talk about Hillsborough in order to keep his emotions in check. I am pleased that I did not impose upon that grief by forcing a conversation.

Aside from these two chance meetings, the topic of Hillsborough, after my fiery baptism on Merseyside, was a relatively dormant issue. In August 2000, and in the wake of the collapse of the criminal trial of David Duckenfield, when the jury failed to reach a verdict on manslaughter charges, there was just one further salvo aimed in my direction.

Interviewed by local media in the aftermath of the Duckenfield trial, Trevor Hicks was asked what the next steps would be for the Hillsborough Family Support Group. Amongst the declared manifesto, Mr Hicks said that the group would be renewing their call for my resignation. That item became the headline in the *Echo* and the *Daily Post* on 12 August 2000.

I therefore wrote to Mr Hicks on 16 August as follows:

> It is a matter of grave disappointment to me that
> the circumstances surrounding my involvement
> in the aftermath of the Hillsborough disaster are still

clouded by misconception and misinterpretation ...
I believe it is imperative that a meeting, proposed by
me back in 1998, be held so that you and the families'
representatives can put your concerns to me directly.

I had the letter hand-delivered by a police officer who had
worked alongside the Family Support Group in making
arrangements for their public events. I was delighted to
receive a response, faxed to me at 10.19 p.m. the same
day. It was from Mr Hicks and the header showed that it
had been sent from his home. He told me that there would
be a families meeting on Sunday 20 August 2000 and that
my letter and request to meet would be on the agenda. He
promised to 'revert after the meeting to advise what, if anything, we are prepared to do in respect of a meeting etc.'

Whilst it was not an overly positive response, it was the
first direct communication from the Family Support Group
in two years and I seized upon it. I wrote, rather effusively in
retrospect, to Mr Hicks on the morning of 17 August:

I was delighted to find your fax waiting for me this
morning. I note the time that it was sent and thank you
for burning the midnight oil to respond. This is the
first time that you or the Families Support Group have
communicated directly with me ... I am really grateful. I look forward very much to hearing from you

again after the families meeting on Sunday 20 August, I am sincere in my desire to meet.

I never did hear from Mr Hicks or the Family Support
Group. I was, however, able to read their decision in the
Liverpool Echo on Monday 21 August 2000 under the
headline 'Hillsborough Snub for Bettison'. 'Members of
the Hillsborough Families Support Group', the article read,
'unanimously rejected Mr Bettison's call for face-to-face
talks to end the controversy surrounding his role in the
aftermath of the 1989 disaster.'

That was the last word from those who represent the
Family Support Group. It was their unanimous decision.
It was delivered via the media in spite of my personal correspondence. Their campaign against me would not be
raised again for another twelve years.

I left Merseyside Police in November 2004, after six
happy and successful years at the helm. My fixed-term contract had only twelve months to run and I was offered a job
in the private sector as Chief Executive of an organisation
delivering training to UK and international police forces.

It would be easy to misunderstand the relationship that I
enjoyed with Merseyside if viewed only through a post-hoc,
Hillsborough-centric, lens. Some people, and institutions,
have striven to create a false picture that I was an unwel-
come and insensitive interloper who fought, for six years

whilst Chief of Merseyside, to cling on to his job in the face of fierce opposition.

The *Liverpool Daily Post*, sadly no longer with us, was the sister paper to the *Liverpool Echo*. They were published on the same presses with a great deal of common copy material; the *Post* with a broadsheet tone in the morning, the *Echo*, unashamedly tabloid, in the evening. In 2004, Alastair Machray was editor of the *Daily Post*. He is now the editor of the *Liverpool Echo*, which, since the Hillsborough Panel Report in 2012, has consistently denounced me. In 2004, when news of my appointment to Centrex was first announced, Mr Machray's *Daily Post* carried the following editorial:

BETTISON A HARD ACT TO FOLLOW

The appointment of Merseyside Chief Constable Norman Bettison in 1998 was controversial in the extreme. He arrived from the South Yorkshire force held bitterly to account by so many in our region for its policing of the Hillsborough disaster nine years earlier; and there was a great deal of anger and protest around the decision to appoint him.

But it is a mark of the excellent contribution that he has made here that his departure will be marked with deep regret by many across the region.

He has forced through many changes within the Merseyside force, not all of them universally welcomed by his staff. He has never flinched from taking difficult decisions, particularly when it came to getting more officers on to the front line with initiatives like his community policing policy. A hands-on, assertive individual, he swiftly won over most of his critics with his dynamic and charismatic leadership style.

Neither was he to be found wanting when it came to fighting the corner of this region in the fight for greater funding. His leaked memo to government, setting out the unique problems Merseyside faced in tackling organised crime, pulled no punches in stating the special case for extra money for his force.

In his final months on Merseyside, he promises us a last big push in his war against anti-social behaviour. On his past form we can be confident that he will be as good as his word.

The Police Authority took a lot of criticism for choosing Norman Bettison and deserves a great deal of credit for having the courage of its convictions and being proved right in the long run. We hope and trust that it will prove just as astute and single minded in its choice of a successor to carry on the good work.

I love Liverpool. It is the world in one city and the friendliest, most sociable place I have ever lived. I thoroughly enjoyed my time both as a resident and as Merseyside's Chief Constable. If my six years there, and my regular appearances in the media, caused occasional reminders of pain to those who had suffered the most since the terrible disaster at Hillsborough, I am genuinely sorry. I acknowledged that unintended consequence of my appointment in my valedictory interview with the *Daily Post*, which carried the above editorial.

I sought, during my time in Merseyside, to build a bridge. But I could never gain the permission of the people who held the title to the ground that it was to be built upon.

CHAPTER 7

AN INDEPENDENT VIEW

15 April 2009 – 12 September 2012

There has been a memorial service on every anniversary of the disaster. The commitment to this act of remembrance for the departed, and demonstration of support for the living, has never diminished. The crowds have grown each year. At the twentieth anniversary, on 15 April 2009, there were 37,000 people gathered at Anfield. Just reflect on that for a moment: twenty years after a tragic loss of life, over 30,000 people still turn out, on a working day, to remember those lives that were lost and to reinforce their unity in their memory.

It was another fine spring day on 15 April 2009. The crowd were addressed, and thanked, by Trevor Hicks, Chairman, and later President, of the Hillsborough Family Support Group. An ecumenical service of remembrance was led by the Bishop of Liverpool the Right Reverend James Jones. Then, on this occasion, there was a guest speaker.

Trevor Hicks invited Andy Burnham MP, then Secretary of State for Culture, Media and Sport, to the platform. Born in Aintree, Liverpool, Mr Burnham retained family links in the city. He is an Evertonian, but that does not preclude attendance at the memorial service. Liverpool is a village and the blue and red distinctions only ever matter for two hours every Saturday. He hadn't been invited because of his place of birth; he wasn't there because Everton's ground is next door; nor because he shared a football passion with many of the congregation. He was there because he was a minister of the government of the day. He was Secretary of State for Sport and all governments, since 1989, have been urged to understand the pain and the anguish felt amongst the community that gathers each year to remember the ninety-six.

Andy Burnham had written a speech of standard content. It invoked the name, and the condolences, of the then Prime Minister Gordon Brown. It was a speech designed to connect with the football fan assumed to reside within everyone at Anfield that day. Ultimately, it was a speech that offered what the families had become used to, and tired of; tea and sympathy.

Mr Burnham was only fifty-three seconds into his speech when he mentioned the Prime Minister. 'The Prime Minister has asked us to think at this time…' Andy Burnham was born in Liverpool – he might have been expected to understand the likely response to political platitudes.

Roy Dixon, a grandfather from Childwall, a pleasant suburb of Liverpool, had heard enough after fifty-three seconds. Speaking afterwards, Mr Dixon said: 'We were fobbed off for years and years and I didn't want to just hear a politician going on. It was like a red rag to a bull to me.' Roy Dixon shouted, at the top of his voice, the words 'WHAT ABOUT JUSTICE?!' Those words echoed around the amphitheatre like the cries of the bereaved families in the Hillsborough gymnasium.

As one, the 37,000-strong crowd rose to their feet and, spontaneously, began to sing, in the style of 'Go West' by the band Village People:

> Jus-tice for the ninety-six
> Jus-tice for the ninety-six
> Jus-tice for the ninety-six
> Jus-tice for the ninety-six

More than 30,000 people sang those five words repeatedly in a demonstration of solidarity for one minute and sixteen seconds. That must have seemed an awfully long time to Andy Burnham standing at the microphone, and for the Bishop of Liverpool sitting on the stage immediately to his right. An outpouring of common suffering that no condolences of the Prime Minister was likely to salve.

It is remarkable that Andy Burnham, who was visibly shaken, continued with his prepared speech. It was incongruous to pick up exactly at the point where he had been interrupted, but he did. 'The Prime Minister has asked us to think at this time about the families with these words...' He was shocked and didn't know, at that moment, what he should do or say in the face of such suffering and anger. He later put aside his notes and spoke about his personal connections with the city and the people of Merseyside. That helped.

It is to Mr Burnham's credit that he summoned the courage to go from Anfield to the town hall in Liverpool where there was a reception for the bereaved families after the service. He there began to ask about what a government, his government, might do to begin to address the accumulated and collective emotional reaction that he had just witnessed.

He was told. The shopping list had been available for years. Top of the list was a request for the disclosure of everything that might be known about the events of the day and, perhaps more importantly, about the legal and political procedures that had failed the families for twenty years. Next, a review of the material that might have supported or influenced those procedures and a scrutiny of the processes and oversight involved. Finally, because of the families' mistrust of the state which is perceived to have failed them at every turn, the first two tasks should not be undertaken by a government department or the legal establishment.

As an aside, it is remarkable how, in the twenty-first century, 'the establishment' is a concept that has become expanded and demonised. The term now seems to imply not only the aristocracy and people with political power or controlling authority in the state, but any public servant and anyone who is bound, financially, to the state. As just one example, after several failed attempts to identify someone of sufficient eminence and skill to command the confidence of victims of historical abuse, the Home Secretary had to look to New Zealand to find someone to chair the ongoing child sex abuse inquiry. Literally the other side of the world. No one with the appropriate skill set in this country could seem to shake off the establishment tag. It is a worrying development if any public appointment struggles to enjoy public trust and confidence.

This trend will have two fundamental consequences.

Firstly, an underlying cynicism about the determination of any issue on behalf of the state. This will lead to the holding of inquiries about inquiries. Secondly, there is a danger that any scrutiny in the name of the state becomes wedded to the popular narrative. Inquiries, where the starting point is to confirm what the public seem to think or fear, are themselves a frightening prospect. Senator McCarthy led just such an inquiry in 1950s America when the US population was terrified by the perceived threat and influence of Communism. I am not sure how this ground is going to be recovered, but there needs to be a public debate about the constitution of public inquiries outside of the frequent controversy of actually trying to establish one.

Andy Burnham, after leaving behind the 37,000 voices at Anfield, listened carefully at the town hall reception to proposals about how he should respond to them. I cannot know how formed were Mr Burnham's ideas about what the government response should be by the time he left Liverpool on 15 April 2009. What followed, however, was precisely what had been called for by Professor Scraton in his book, *No Last Rights: The Denial of Justice and the Promotion of Myth in the Aftermath of the Hillsborough Disaster* – the second of three publications which document his research about the Hillsborough disaster.

In *No Last Rights*, published in 1995, Professor Scraton recommended that

- Inquiries should be staffed and administered by representatives from a wide cross section of independent agencies, drawing on academic research.
- There should be full disclosure to all interested parties/persons of all the evidence gathered in the course of investigations by the police or other agencies.

These two fundamental tenets, recommended fourteen years previously by Professor Scraton, underpin the creation of the Hillsborough Panel.

Mr Burnham attended a Cabinet meeting chaired by Gordon Brown on 16 April 2009. He recounted his experiences of the previous day at Anfield and Liverpool Town Hall and suggested getting parliamentary support for a further review of the Hillsborough disaster. The Prime Minister agreed and asked Cabinet to 'get behind Andy'. Following a proposal put to the House, Home Secretary Alan Johnson met the Hillsborough Family Support Group later that year to consult with them about the creation and make-up of a panel to undertake the review.

Home Office officials contacted Med Hughes, the Chief Constable of South Yorkshire Police in 2009, about disclosure of the vast archive which had been carefully retained by the force for twenty years. Med Hughes welcomed the initiative; he considered that the force had nothing to hide and that public scrutiny, leading to a better understanding, would be beneficial. He also saw the practical advantage of handing over to a third party an archive which occupied warehouse-sized storage space on force premises. He was insistent that, after preserving the material for two decades, its new keepers should look after it in a responsible fashion. He was reassured by Christine Gifford, a member of the Advisory Council on National Records and Archives, and Sarah Tyacke, former Chief Executive of the Public Record Office of the United Kingdom, who guaranteed that the archive would be maintained in its complete and comprehensive state.

Med Hughes went further than just an undertaking to disclose the Hillsborough archive. His further initiative will have important consequences for all lawyers in the future. In the Stuart-Smith Scrutiny Report of Hillsborough, conducted in 1997, it was found that the emendation of police officers' accounts appeared to have been initiated not by the police, but by those who were legally representing the force. Med Hughes therefore volunteered to waive legal privilege on all documents, including all communications between lawyers and his predecessors.

There was no obligation to do so. Legal privilege is a historic, and fundamental, right, enshrined in common law and statute to protect the private consultations between any client and their legal adviser. There are good public interest reasons for this, alongside other protected communications such as professional disclosures received by doctors or priests. Med Hughes sought to present South Yorkshire Police as being completely open and transparent in what was likely to be a significant public scrutiny. It meant that the present-day incarnation of the Hammond Suddards Law firm, which had also scrupulously maintained an archive of Hillsborough material, were obliged to disclose every last document.

If this aspect of the work of the Hillsborough Panel has not already been noted in every law firm across the country already, I suspect the penny will drop soon. This precedent means that any public inquiry into historic events, and I predict there will be more, will see pressure applied to follow the Hillsborough line with a demand for disclosure of otherwise legally privileged material. To withhold anything now on the basis of legal privilege, after the Hillsborough Panel have broken new ground, would be to look evasive. My prediction is that there will be less written down by lawyers in future.

Let me emphasise the point about the openness and transparency of South Yorkshire Police and Hammond Suddards LLP. These are the very institutions which have, according to popular myth, undertaken a criminal conspiracy to suppress the truth and replace it with a false version of events for twenty years. They had, in fact, retained every scrap of paper; every note and minute from every meeting; and every fax and record of telephone communications. Nothing had been shredded. No crucial document that was collated by the Wain team in 1989 was misplaced by anyone representing those organisations. The current keeper of these meticulous records was about to put them, voluntarily, into the public domain. The Hillsborough Panel, the government and the Independent Police Complaints Commission have all praised the contemporary management of South Yorkshire Police for their voluntary provision of this treasure trove of material. Quite rightly. But what about the previous managements that have stored it, catalogued it and protected it for twenty years?

There are many documents, disclosed to me by those investigating alleged wrong doing, that have got my handwritten notes in the margins. There are documents that are uniquely mine, such as a report of a visit to the House of Commons in November 1989 to show a video to a small group of MPs assembled by one of their number. It is the only copy in existence and the only written reference to such meeting. Does anyone seriously suggest that if I had been misconducting myself on that visit that I would have committed the fact to writing? That, after my post-disaster work was over, I would have handed all my personally annotated documents into an archive; and that a deceitful police force would have catalogued and kept all those documents for two decades? As my own counsel was to suggest, sardonically, when I appeared before the recent inquest: 'If you were a black propagandist, Sir Norman, you weren't a very good one.'

With the positive support of the Chief Constable of South Yorkshire Police, the Home Secretary announced, in December 2009, the formal creation of an independent panel to review the Hillsborough disaster, whose remit would be to:

- Oversee full public disclosure of relevant government and local information within the constraints of a disclosure protocol.
- Consult with the Hillsborough families to ensure that the views of those most affected by the tragedy are taken into account.
- Manage the process of public disclosure, ensuring that it takes place initially to the Hillsborough families and other involved parties, in an agreed manner and within a reasonable timescale, before information is made widely available.
- Prepare options for establishing an archive of Hillsborough documentation.
- Produce a report explaining the work of the panel. The panel's report should also illustrate how the information disclosed adds to public understanding of the tragedy and its aftermath.

The independent panel were therefore expected to put the Hillsborough families at the centre of the process. Quite right, as it is they who have felt excluded from so many of the processes that have fallen out of the disaster. They have become used to having had things done *to* them rather than *with* them. They were treated shabbily by strangers in a foreign town in the hours after the tragedy; abused and defamed by a popular national newspaper; denied the opportunity at the initial inquest to learn all that they could about the last moments in the life of their loved ones; kept at arm's length and, they felt, patronised by previous scrutinies, such as that of Lord Justice Stuart-Smith.

They would be at the very heart of this new review and it would be undertaken by some of the people who had supported them on their long and, thus far, fruitless journey. When the Home Secretary announced the constitution of the panel on 26 January 2010, its foremost member was Professor Phil Scraton. Professor Scraton would lead the group that would be responsible for research amongst the disclosed material and write the subsequent report. A key member of his sub group would be Katy Jones, who had been the principal researcher on the production team of Jimmy McGovern's drama-documentary *Hillsborough*, which told the story of the tragedy through the eyes of three bereaved families. Mr McGovern's powerful polemic had exposed the hurt and the injustice felt by the families.

The public outcry that ensued led, directly, to the setting up of the Stuart-Smith review of Hillsborough in 1997.

Professor Scraton was very well known to the families because he had already written the seminal texts on the subject of the Hillsborough disaster, which, collectively, documented the families' long struggle. Amongst countless academic journal articles and media features on the subject of the Hillsborough disaster, Professor Scraton had published the following major works: *Hillsborough and After: The Liverpool Experience* (1990), *No Last Rights: The Denial of Justice and the Promotion of Myth in the Aftermath of the Hillsborough Disaster* (1995) and *Hillsborough: The Truth* (1999).

This latter book has been described by the deputy editor of the *Liverpool Echo* as 'widely accepted as the definitive account of the disaster and its aftermath'.

This prompts a question which I shall need to follow up immediately thereafter with my personal endorsement of this panel and praise for the product of its labours: the question is about how the panel might accurately be described as independent.

That the panel was independent of government is irrefutable. They were independent, too, of all of the institutions that had let the families down so badly over twenty years. They were therefore the most appropriate people to carry out this task. They did a fantastic job in raising precisely the concerns and questions that the Hillsborough families deserve an answer to. And I applaud the panel in that endeavour.

The principal members were not, though, independent of any prior judgement in relation to the issues under review. Before they began their reading and research they were not agnostic about the causes of the disaster and, more particularly, about events that followed in the aftermath. Professor Scraton had already written the 'definitive account of the disaster and its aftermath' and had reached the conclusion that there had been a conspiracy in South Yorkshire Police to suppress the truth.

Mr Burnham had spoken with Professor Scraton at Liverpool Town Hall on the day of the twentieth anniversary memorial service. The day that the minister was formulating his plan for an independent review of all that was known about Hillsborough, and he was keen to have Professor Scraton on board. Mr Burnham has recently recounted the conversation that took place that day to Kevin Sampson who has published a book called *Hillsborough Voices*:

> Phil Scraton came up … and was asking, 'what do you
> think disclosure could achieve?' And I said, 'Well if all
> we achieve is a report that has the Stationery Office's
> official crest on it and it's basically the facts as laid out

in your book, with a government wrapper around it, that alone would be worth doing. Because those are the facts – we know those are the facts – but not many other people do.'

That conversation, if accurately recalled by the then Secretary of State for Culture, Media and Sport, describes an unusual approach to independence.

There is a well-known and universal phenomenon, understood by psychologists, called the Einstellung effect. Roughly translated from German it means 'single state of mind'. It is the idea that we humans, no matter how wise or professionally disciplined we may be, are likely to fall into the habit of viewing novel stimuli as fitting a model that we already have in our minds about the way the world is or the way that it operates. There are very good reasons why our prehistoric forefathers would be wired to quickly compute stimuli against an experiential context. It might save them from being attacked by predators or deter them from eating poisonous berries. It is a natural instinct that, in our contemporary affairs, we must guard against and be watchful for.

Judges and thoughtful police officers are always wary of one particular aspect of the Einstellung effect. It is called confirmatory bias. This describes the danger of going into any inquiry or investigation with a search for the evidence that confirms our initial hypothesis. If we do this, then we are in danger of overlooking evidence that may in fact count against that hypothesis. Senior Detectives talk of 'following the evidence, not the suspect' to remind themselves, and their subordinates, of the need for vigilance. Even then, cops can succumb to this human frailty, and some initial responses to the terrible disaster at Hillsborough may well be a poignant case in point. But so too can medics, judges and even academics.

One example might help to illustrate the ever-present danger of confirmatory bias. Professor Scraton's long-held view is that the intention of Chief Superintendent Terry Wain was to obtain, from police officers, their comment and opinion about the behaviour of fans so that a case could be built against them. He expresses this view at page 191 of his 1999 publication *Hillsborough: The Truth*.

The panel's report, which Professor Scraton also wrote, picks up the same theme and references a document which was found during their research. It is an account of a police officer, Sergeant Wright, whose report about the disaster follows a template that includes a request to provide information about 'the mood of the fans'. The conclusion drawn by Professor Scraton in his earlier book thus seems to be corroborated by this discovery in the work of the panel.

Whilst noting the significance of Sergeant Wright's document in supporting this earlier hypothesis, the panel have, throughout their three years of research, overlooked another document in the name of PC Illingworth. PC Illingworth, in providing his account of the day, was working to a template too. Only this one does not ask about 'the fans' at all. This one asks instead for the officer's comment and opinion about the management of the policing operation, and PC Illingworth gives a critical account.

How widely circulated these different templates were is not easy to tell. It is not hard to find some officers' accounts that follow the 'Wright' template and some that follow the 'Illingworth' version. It may indeed be the case that there are more than these two templates yet to be found in the archive through painstaking and objective analysis.

I was asked at the Coroner's Inquest if I had any idea how it came to be that Mr Wain had issued an open-ended and innocuous template to guide completion of self-prepared accounts and that it had been variously updated and revised by others. I said that I was sure that a police force was not the only organisation that was vulnerable to Chinese whispers. There was no email in 1989, no online cut-and-paste facility and no version controls on documents. It is likely, in the haste to get the job done, that various couriers have noted down differently what they might have heard Mr Wain ask for, or what they themselves thought was relevant.

It seems clear to me, on any fair and objective reading

of the Illingworth document, that there wasn't a well-orchestrated strategy to demand damning testimony about Liverpool fans. PC Illingworth was crucially placed at the fence of Pen 4 as the disaster unfolded and might have been a priority witness if this was the intention. It is a pity that the document with his name on was not afforded a similar prominence by the panel as that given to the one bearing Sergeant Wright's name. It is a pity, too, that the IPCC seemed to have also overlooked it. I was served with Sergeant Wright's document and asked searching questions about its genesis and purpose. I was not served with PC Illingworth's, nor asked a single question about that.

The Panel Report quotes heavily from Lord Justice Taylor's Report. Although it was produced within sixteen weeks of the disaster, the Taylor Report was seen, until the more recent inquest conducted by Lord Justice Goldring, as the most definitive account of the causes of the disaster.

Some of the quoted passages are not accurately transcribed by the panel, however, and could, inadvertently, give a mistaken impression. For instance, the panel (p. 43 of their report) quote Lord Justice Taylor as saying that 'The police had initiated a vilification campaign' in the immediate aftermath of the disaster. In fact, Lord Justice Taylor does not use those words at all. Taylor did express the view (para. 257 of his interim report) that he was appalled by the early press reports, such as those in the *Sun* newspaper,

and condemned the press and those individual police officers that were present at the match who were said to have
contributed to that false picture. But nowhere in his reports
does he assert or imply that this was a 'police campaign
of vilification'.

Furthermore, Taylor specifically pointed out in that
very same paragraph of his interim report that the Chief
Constable, Peter Wright, had made an immediate, and
dignified, statement disassociating himself and his force
from those grave accounts in the press. In their direct quo-
tation of the condemnatory paragraph from the Taylor
Report, the panel have, inexplicably, omitted that crucial
contextual sentence.

There may be other errors of transcription, examples of
confirmatory bias and omission of contra evidence to be
discovered in the Panel Report. But such detail takes nothing away from the achievements of the panel. They have
done a remarkable job of reviewing 450,000 pages. The
review has produced what had been missing for twenty-
three years. A formally commissioned account written
from the perspective of those who have been bereaved and
injured by the disaster, and who have been insulted and
fobbed off by a number of processes and institutions since.
It poses questions that must now be addressed by those
institutions and the reinstatement of new inquests was one
of the long overdue outcomes. The members of the panel

can be justifiably proud of their work and their legacy. It is because of them that Margaret Aspinall can now, finally, collect the death certificate for her son James, who was lost in the disaster. She swore that she would never collect it whilst ever it was said that he died as a result of an 'accident'.

During my enforced sabbatical I have reread a wonderful little book, written by the Right Reverend Nicholas Frayling, retired Dean of Chichester. He was Rector of Liverpool Parish Church when I worked and lived in the city. He gave me a copy of *Pardon and Peace*, which he had written in 1996, two years before the Northern Ireland Peace Agreement was secured. The prophetic book sets out the conditions that he believed were necessary, in Ireland, in order to establish a basis for lasting peace. I turned to it again, more recently, with the thought that it might provide some inspiration about the basis for the reconciliation that is still necessary around the issue of Hillsborough. He could have been describing the justification for a Hillsborough Panel, thirteen years before its conception, in the following words.

> Many people believe that history should be set aside
> – 'there's too much of it' – and we should move on.
> I realise too that there is no such thing as history,
> there are only events which, in the fullness of time,

become overlaid with myth and culturally determined interpretation.

But if we are to repay the wrong, or to heal the wounds, then it is absolutely essential that we revisit past events and, with as much objectivity as we can muster, interrogate the historical records. Only thus can we begin to understand, and to pray and work with intelligence rather than mere emotion.

The interrogation of the historical records by the Hillsborough Panel has influenced thinking and action in relation to the Hillsborough disaster. It has changed perceptions permanently. It was written to achieve that very purpose. There is no shame in that. Any author is like an offending player in the off-side rule. The late, great Bill Shankly once said: 'If a player is not interfering with play then he shouldn't be on the pitch.' Similarly, if a writer doesn't set out to influence the thoughts of others, then they're wasting someone else's ink.

The Hillsborough Panel Report makes no allegations of wrongdoing by any person. The Panel Chairman was explicit about its role in the press conference called to publish the report. 'We are not an inquiry,' Bishop James Jones said. 'People have not given evidence or been questioned. Our job has simply been to oversee the maximum possible disclosure of all the documents and to write a report that adds to public understanding. Our terms of reference don't allow us to make any recommendations.'

Those who receive the report, therefore, ought to be clear about its status, and open-minded about its content. Deborah Glass, Deputy Chair of the IPCC, described it publicly as definitive when criticising me for mentioning something which couldn't be found in its pages. It may be authoritative, but it is not definitive. It covers the ground, without pretending to be complete. It raises concerns rather than seeking to provide remedies. It is not a papal bull, immune to any question or challenge by mere mortals. And what no report, or book, can ever lay claim to is a monopoly of the truth. Even if an author asserts it on their title page.

Politicians, campaigners and many in the press have, however, seized upon it as a gospel testifying to a criminal conspiracy that had suppressed the truth for a quarter of a century. I was the only person named in the report that remained alive and who was still serving as a police officer. The last man standing, so to speak. I had also been a public figure in Merseyside and had risen to the rank of Chief Constable. I immediately became the poster boy for conspiracy theorists ... and the whipping boy for revenge.

David Aaronovitch wrote a thoughtful opinion piece in *The Times* in April 2015, not about me, or Hillsborough, although it could have been. He was railing against the modern rise, particularly online, of a 'we believe you' movement which seeks to redress the perceived imbalance against victims by an automatic acceptance of any allegation made by, or on behalf of, the victim. It would be almost acceptable, he said, from a campaigner, but catastrophic if it comes from a journalist (or a regulator): 'This is the politicisation of truth – in which partisans instrumentalise the lives of others to support their own view. And when we judge people to be guilty not for what they have actually done, but for what we think they represent, then we are all in big trouble.'

If David Aaronovitch is right about this recent trend in British society, then, not for the first or last time in the witch hunt that was to develop, I seem to have found myself to be in the wrong place at the wrong time.

CHAPTER 8

THE HUE
AND CRY

12–14 September 2012

Eight months after the hue and cry had begun, my mobile phone rang at 9.58 p.m. on Monday 20 May 2013. I am in the habit of resting the phone on the curved arm of the sofa whilst watching television in my sitting room at home. The vibration of the incoming call tipped the phone onto the floor and I scrambled to retrieve it.

I had just watched a BBC *Panorama* documentary

and the credits were still rolling. The episode was called 'Hillsborough: How They Buried the Truth'. I had declined several invitations to appear on the programme. After all, I was then living by the maxim, suggested to me by a wise counsellor when my troubles had first begun: 'Always remember that a scapegoat is someone to be talked about, not listened to.'

My reluctance to take part had not stopped the researchers from finding and using 1989 archive footage of me walking into the Taylor Inquiry wearing a Columbo-style mac and a Tom Selleck moustache (in my defence I should say that both were fashionable back in the day). The producers had also included images of me briefing police officers in the Hillsborough gymnasium before a 1991 football match. This was an event that post-dated the disaster by two years but, never mind, the edited and undated film helped to create an impression of me as a key figure responsible for the policing of football at Hillsborough, and responsible, too, for the force response to the disaster. That implication was bolstered by the appearance in the programme of ex-Superintendent Clive Davis, who offered an account of a briefing, given by Chief Superintendent Wain, forty-four hours after the disaster, during which Mr Wain is alleged to have said that our job was to fit up the Liverpool fans.

Mr Davis told the *Panorama* viewers that I was at that

meeting. I have dealt with his allegation already. I attended no such briefing. It is interesting that Mr Davis gave this account to television producers before speaking to the regulatory body that had begun an investigation seven months before the *Panorama* programme was aired.

The *Panorama* presenter mentioned my name, liberally, in the first quarter of the programme but, as the narrative was built, and conclusions were drawn, my name and image no longer appeared. I can be sure of that because, naturally, I was watching the documentary more intently than most viewers would have been.

The telephone caller after the broadcast was John Harding, who was then my solicitor – a man of concise communication even when compared with others in a profession where time equals money. If, instead of law, he had gone into medicine, John would be good at surgery but hopeless at bedside manner. Without any greeting or preamble, he said: 'They seem pretty sure that you've done something, they're just not sure what.' After a perfunctory word of consolation, which always seemed an afterthought to John's professional counsel, he hung up.

It had come to this. There existed a narrative about a significant historical event and, like all folklore narratives, it was simple and relatively one-dimensional. It had been fashioned and honed over the years. And now I found myself at the heart of that narrative. The tragedy at Hillsborough revealed a failure of policing. That is true. I agree with that. It was Lord Justice Taylor's conclusion drawn within sixteen weeks of the disaster. Furthermore, so the popular narrative runs, there has been a conspiracy involving the police and others which has sought to cover up the true causes of the disaster for a quarter of a century. And, moreover, I am now presumed to be one of its chief architects. It must be true, because we all saw it tonight on *Panorama*.

Eight months earlier, I had no inkling that it might come to this. On Wednesday 12 September 2012, the Hillsborough Panel, after three years of research, were due to publish their report. I had known the publication date for several weeks. I had provided a brief summary of my post-disaster role at the invitation of the South Yorkshire Police team, which would be receiving and responding to the report. They were preparing to address issues that might arise from the report and had raised a question about my role in case they were asked. I was keen to learn, but not concerned about, the result of this significant review.

I travelled from home in Yorkshire to London by an early train that day. It was a dull autumn morning and I had used the journey time to read my papers for two meetings that I was due to attend. I had been Chief Constable of West Yorkshire Police, the third largest provincial force, for six years; a Chief Constable since I joined Merseyside in 1998; and a member of the Association of Chief Police Officers (ACPO) for nineteen years. I was a Vice President of ACPO, elected by its membership. I was involved in a lot of national policy-making and was often in London for meetings with colleagues or government.

On this autumn morning, I was due first at the Headquarters of the British Transport Police in Camden to take part in ACPO Cabinet. This is a collective of Chief Officers who individually, on behalf of the Association, provide a national lead on various aspects of policing policy. The idea behind Cabinet is that a relatively small number of active members will produce national policy that can be subsequently endorsed by the full Council of Chief Constables. In theory, Cabinet was meant to take the posturing and small-p politics out of operational policy-making. In practice, the heads of the locally independent forces still voiced a range of views when called upon to make a collective decision. One of the roles of the ACPO President and Vice Presidents was to recognise where controversy and equivocation might arise and to try, through bilateral conversations, to reach consensus.

Sir Hugh Orde, the Association's President in 2012, chaired the Cabinet meeting that morning. I remember it as a meeting that was typical of its kind. A huge agenda where individual colleagues, who may have done a considerable amount of work on a policy area, would present their proposals to Cabinet. Cabinet would give its thumbs up or thumbs down before the proposal could be put to the forty-three independently minded Chief Constables for sign-off. We worked our way through the topics in front of us although it often struck me, at Cabinet and ACPO Council meetings, that we would sometimes spend a disproportionate amount of time on the trivial versus the more significant topics. Association business, as in politics, was often about the art of the possible.

Just before noon, as the agenda was diminishing, my phone had vibrated with an incoming text message. It was from Oliver Cattermole, the head of press and communications for ACPO. It said: 'Your name has just been mentioned at the Hillsborough Independent Panel press conference. Thought you'd want to know.'

This did not ring any alarm bells, but it was still a surprise. I texted back: 'In what context?' The instant reply: 'In response to a question from an *FT* journalist about your role post Hillsborough.' I couldn't understand the *Financial Times* point of reference. I knew of one or two campaigning journalists who had pursued a Hillsborough narrative for many years. I came close to meeting one of them, David Conn of *The Guardian*, in the run-up to the publication of the panel's report. In the end, my Chief Constable colleague at South Yorkshire, Med Hughes, had agreed that, as the current head of the organisation that had been subject of criticism over the years, he should be the one to respond to Mr Conn and other journalists who were tracking the work of the Hillsborough Panel. But the *Financial Times* link was out of left field. I texted back to Oliver: 'What did they say about me?' and, by return: 'Nothing substantive. He was a member of a team post disaster etc.'

I cannot say that I felt relaxed. The publication of the Hillsborough Panel's report, after three years' deliberation, was likely to attract much publicity. I had not envisaged that my name would be implicated at the time of publication. I still bore the metaphoric scars from the controversy over my appointment in Merseyside and I could see that some of those embers might be fanned into an odd flame. But, at that moment, lunchtime on Wednesday 12 September 2012, I was still relatively unperturbed.

An old friend, a district judge, would email me four days later to highlight my naivety. After I had made some injudicious public comments about my own recollection of the disaster and its aftermath, her email grabbed me by the throat.

'What are you doing?!' she demanded. Didn't I realise that this is likely to become the biggest test of police and judicial integrity ever seen in this country? The politicians had already released the hounds. She advised me to cease making public comments and get myself the best legal representation that I could find. Apart from an immediate exchange of emails, in which I thanked her for her frank assessment and advice, I didn't hear from her again.

Lots of other acquaintances in the professions, in politics, in journalism and even some in the police service, adopted a similar radio silence. My address book now reveals a clear distinction between friendship and acquaintance. By lunchtime on Wednesday 12 September 2012, it seems that I had become toxic. I was unaware of that transition.

When the ACPO Cabinet agenda was cleared, it was time to make my way across town to my next meeting. I led for the police service on the development and implementation of strategy and policy around preventing extremism and radicalisation. I was due to chair the quarterly meeting of cross-government representatives at the Department for Business, Innovation and Skills (BIS) in Victoria Street, next door to Westminster Abbey. There would be, around that table, representatives from education, health, prisons, local government and security services as well as police leaders who held counter-terrorism portfolios. I could not know, as I travelled from Camden, that this would be the last ACPO meeting I would ever chair.

I had hitched a lift with another Chief Constable who had been at Cabinet and who also had a subsequent meeting elsewhere in Westminster. Alfred Hitchcock was the Chief of Bedfordshire. He led for ACPO on youth offending which gave him his place at Cabinet. Alf had a lovely line when making public presentations. Right at the outset he would break the ice by saying: 'I know that you all have three questions. The answers are, "yes", "no" and "girls".' A theatrical pause and then, 'Yes, my name really is Alfred Hitchcock. No, I am not named after the famous film director. My father was an Alfred, as was my grandfather. And finally, I won't be passing the name onto my kids as I only have girls.'

When travelling through London's busy traffic alongside Alf, I received an increasing number of text messages. It became apparent that, after the Hillsborough Panel had given their press conference at which my name arose courtesy of the *Financial Times*, I had then been highlighted again by the President of the Hillsborough Family Support Group, Trevor Hicks. The support group, which had campaigned about Hillsborough for twenty-three years, and which had been very closely involved in the work of the Hillsborough Panel, were given a platform to speak to the press representatives who were assembled in Liverpool Cathedral to receive the panel's report.

I do not know whether Mr Hicks had always intended to turn the spotlight on me in the post-publication phase or whether he was prompted by the earlier *Financial Times* question. Whatever the case, it ended up with Mr Hicks naming me, and only me as far as I can see from the transcript of his comments, as a person at the heart of a police cover-up, what he called a 'dirty tricks campaign'.

Mr Hicks began his indictment with what he must have intended to be a humorous aside. 'The lawyers have advised me to be careful what I say here. However, I intend to ignore it (audience laughter).' Having implicated me in his assertion that the Hillsborough Panel Report vindicated the longstanding claims of the campaigning group that there was a conspiracy to cover up the truth about Hillsborough, he said that 'Bettison, if he has anything about him, he will, I think the term is, consider his position'. And then: 'If he is anything of a man he will now stand down and go and scurry up a drainpipe somewhere (more audience laughter).'

I didn't know the detail of this press conference when cocooned in Alf Hitchcock's car, I just knew that my phone was hot. My own press office in West Yorkshire were on to me. Oliver Cattermole, at ACPO head office, was telling me about national media interest in my position. Kind souls were informing me that they had heard my name on early news reports from the Liverpool Cathedral launch and hoped that all was well. I told Alf what was going on to excuse the fact that I was a distracted passenger who should have been chatting gracefully to his transport provider. Alf, who formerly lived in the north-west and had witnessed my arrival as Merseyside Chief back in 1998, said that it sounded like my Merseyside baptism all over again. He suggested that I shouldn't worry about it... But I was starting to.

I arrived at the meeting room at BIS with five minutes to spare. There was coffee and a Danish pastry available and I was ready for both. In the legion of government representatives who sat around my quarterly Prevent Strategy group meeting there was no need for anyone from the Department for Business, Innovation and Skills, but they have the best suite of meeting and conference rooms of any government department so we always booked our meetings there.

I made the best job I could of chairing my final Prevent Strategy meeting. I had my phone beside me on the table, which became a distraction. I could not resist, from time to time, checking the growing number of messages about people who suddenly, and unexpectedly, wanted to hear my thoughts about Hillsborough. My instruction to Nigel Swift in the West Yorkshire Police press office and Oliver Cattermole at ACPO was that I had no comment to make and to refer everyone to South Yorkshire Police, where the relatively new Chief Constable, David Crompton, my former deputy at West Yorkshire, would be handling any media enquiries. That seemed a sensible position to adopt. I wish I had stuck to it.

I remember that one of the items on the Prevent Strategy Group agenda was an update on the Channel Programme from its lead, Craig Denholm, Deputy Chief Constable of Surrey. Channel is a scheme, with a line of separate government funding from the Home Office, to which the police and other government agencies can refer individuals who demonstrate a vulnerability to radicalisation. Under the auspices of Channel, Craig's team would identify appropriate interventions that might prevent someone from developing into a fully-fledged home-grown terrorist. Channel, which I had nurtured from its early trials, had become a key part of the national response to the growth of extremism. It is even more relevant today with the pull of Islamic State and other global terror groups.

By September 2012, I recall that we had passed a significant number of interventions mark and Craig was updating on progress. Firstly, to report that Channel seemed to be effective because, in its formative years, there had been not a single Channel client who had gone on to commit a terrorism-related offence. Secondly, we were striving to get Education and Health to see the benefits of the programme and to encourage more referrals from teachers and mental health practitioners who were in the front line of witnessing a shift to radicalism amongst individuals in their respective client groups. In the early days their practitioners were reluctant to be seen to be profiling their flock.

I rehearse this episode in what was, by now, the closing act of my forty-year career to remind myself that there is more to my policing history than Hillsborough.

I boarded the train at King's Cross to travel home. I was due into Wakefield just after 8 p.m. I had earlier rung my staff officer, Sam Millar, and asked her to put a copy of the Hillsborough Panel's report in my car – I left a spare key in the office. She told me that it was 395 pages and so I asked her to highlight the report for me wherever I was mentioned by name or wherever the work of the so-called Wain team was discussed. I reminded her of my media position – all enquiries to be passed to the press office in South Yorkshire.

I sat, confused, on the train. I didn't know how I had ended up in the position of being a lightning rod for the anger about Hillsborough and I didn't, at that stage, know what had been said about me by Mr Hicks in his rhetorical remarks. Nor, perhaps more importantly, by the Hillsborough Panel in their formal report. I would come to learn these things later and also, with the benefit of hindsight, work out for myself why I was in the crosshairs. On that journey through the darkening evening, when offices were closed and my staff were off duty, I was alone with my thoughts. I did the *Times* Sudoku puzzles and I remember thinking it a bizarre activity in which to be engaged whilst in the eye of the storm. Without access to the internet, I just could not think of anything more productive to do.

I had rung ahead to Gillian, my wife, to warn her of the interest in our name and to let her know that I had a night of reading ahead of me. I told her that I would eat on the train. The phone rang at about 6.30 p.m. It was Nigel Swift, the head of West Yorkshire Police's press office. Apparently, staff from the *Yorkshire Post*, the biggest circulation newspaper local to us, had been ringing constantly during the afternoon. First of all, asking for, and now demanding, a comment from me.

My relationship with the *Yorkshire Post* and other local papers had always been transparent and clear. I would seek to use the medium of the newspapers to promote the work of a police force and a public service of which I was proud. I did not expect them to print everything that we hoped, nor in a fashion that we wished. In fostering this relationship, I wrote regular op-cd feature articles on issues of current concern. I tried to inject an element of controversy in my writing, such as when I wrote about the 'Health and Safety Taliban' getting in the way of the emergency service ethos or the 'Drinking to Oblivion Culture' that was prevalent in our cities. Right up until 12 September 2012, I like to think that I had a good relationship with the *Yorkshire Post*. I was on friendly terms with its editor, Peter Charlton, and with Tom Richmond, who, as well as being deputy editor, was also its business editor and racing correspondent.

It was not an overly cosy relationship, and no amount

of bonhomie or exchanged tips for the Grand National could corrupt our respective positions. I had said to both Peter Charlton and Tom Richmond that if the *Yorkshire Post* ever caught West Yorkshire Police with its metaphorical pants down then they should report it. And they often did! In the pre-Leveson days, local Chiefs and local editors could be trusted to manage the boundaries of what each of them recognised as a symbiotic relationship.

Nigel Swift told me that the *Yorkshire Post* was furious about the fact that I had pulled down the shutters. He had fended off the junior reporters but now faced the wrath of the relatively newly appointed, and London-based, political editor, who was threatening all kinds of story lines in the face of my reluctance to comment. Nigel told me that there had been an editorial meeting at the *Post* and that Tom Richmond had been deputed to ring me personally. I was to expect his call. I perhaps shouldn't have taken it.

The deputy editor was as angry as I had ever witnessed. His colleagues hadn't appreciated the stonewalling throughout the day. He pointed out that Trevor Hicks, who had lost two daughters at Hillsborough, and who deservedly had the world's sympathy, had named me as implicated in a conspiracy to blame fans for causing the deaths and thus suppressing the truth that the police were to blame for the disaster. (Remember that I had not, in fact, heard precisely what Mr Hicks had said at this stage.) He went on to say that he believed it was in my best interests to make some sort of comment – any comment – rather than continue with my ostrich-like position. He said two things that caused me to reflect. Firstly, he said that the media would crucify me without some countervailing response. Secondly, he pointed out that this was an allegation about me personally, not about me as Chief Constable of West Yorkshire Police, and I therefore had to respond. I told him that I would reflect overnight. The deadlines for the morning editions were closing. I can remember saying that I wouldn't be 'railroaded', which, even as I said it, struck me as ironic given that I was sitting in a packed train carriage.

I did reflect overnight, after reading the Hillsborough Panel Report from cover to cover and, ultimately, I decided to say something. Tom Richmond's first point – likely crucifixion at the hands of the press – was probably correct. But four years' careful reflection has led me to conclude that his second point should have had no positive influence on my decision whatsoever. The fact that this firestorm surrounded me personally, rather than my job title, should have caused me to be even more circumspect in making any public statement. If people ask: 'What have you learned from your ordeal?', this is one feature: don't fuel the fire when you're tied to the stake.

Actually, what I also know on reflection is that it would not have made an iota of difference to the premature ending of my career. The hue and cry was out, the pitchforks and burning torches would still have turned up at my draw-bridge even if I had remained firmly, and silently, locked inside my castle.

I settled down at home to read the Hillsborough Panel Report. I was helped by Sam Millar's highlighting. My name is mentioned nineteen times in five different sections of the report. There is a sub-chapter heading with my name in the title. But nowhere within the 395 pages does the report accuse me of any wrongdoing.

I texted the Chief Executive and solicitor of the West Yorkshire Police Authority, Fraser Sampson, who would later become an influential actor in my departure from the force. I asked him if he had had chance to read the Hillsborough report. He texted me at 11.17 p.m. that night to tell me that he had the report and was going through it. He texted again at 6.39 a.m. the following day to say that he couldn't find any cause for concern within it.

I crawled into bed at about 3 a.m. content in the certain knowledge that I had done nothing that I was ashamed of twenty-three years previously, but also satisfied because there were no direct accusations about me, or about my role, in the authoritative report that had been published the previous day. The report was written, arguably, in a leading style, and for anyone who already had a prejudice about the police role, post disaster, there were references that allowed them to infer all kinds of mischief. But there was no direct criticism and no smoking gun. As I went up to bed I was undecided about whether or not I should make any media comment.

On Thursday 13 September 2012, I had booked the day as annual leave, so too with the Friday, Saturday and Sunday. A Chief Constable's diary requires about three months' notice to take a four-day break. I did not absent myself because of the furore, less still did I book leave in connection with the publication date of the Hillsborough report. I have a keen interest in historic motor racing and the mid-September weekend is the date of the historic revival meeting at Goodwood in Sussex, probably the premier event in the annual historic racing calendar. I had been due to meet friends for a weekend at leisure.

After only three hours sleep, I awoke to the sound of what I took to be drizzling rain. I had never noticed before that the sound of whispering voices in the silent darkness sounds exactly like light rain. My house has a perimeter boundary wall. My bedroom is configured so that the open window of the en-suite bathroom permits the only view beyond the boundary and onto the access road to the house. Whilst visiting the bathroom about 6.30 a.m., I came to the view that it wasn't rain I could hear but voices. I cracked open the bathroom window and saw, in the dawn light, a gaggle of four men dressed in dark and waterproof outerwear and three had got expensive-looking cameras around their necks. They were journalists and photographers whispering acknowledgements to each other as they gathered outside my front gate. There were two 4x4 vehicles parked on the access road and they seemed to be encamped.

I woke Gillian to tell her the news. The first implication was that our early departure for Sussex was off. I immediately saw the consequences of being seen to drive off in my car after putting weekend luggage in the boot. The second implication was how to get rid of these people, who, whilst doing their job professionally and in the name of public interest, can be more than a little intrusive.

Upon checking with my office, I learned that there were a larger number of 4x4s and men with cameras at my headquarters. I was asked whether someone from the office should go out to tell the pack that I was not expected in that morning because I was on leave. I suggested not as I didn't want the number outside my home to double. These others were OK where they were, twelve miles away from my front door.

I was constantly turning over in my mind the words of Tom Richmond from the night before. I decided that I would put out a media statement. Having reached that decision I perhaps should have given it much more thought and taken advice. I was on annual leave; my bags were packed and in the hall; I had done nothing that I needed to defend; and the Hillsborough Panel Report was not critical of me. What had I to lose? The clock was ticking.

I picked up the phone to my PA, Helena Wyles, when I knew she was in the office. After exchanging pleasantries and hearing of her own confrontation with the press and photographers outside Headquarters, I asked her to take dictation over the phone. Helena's shorthand is excellent and, after years of working together, I know the steady pace of dictation that leads, efficiently, to a finished typed product.

The statement, made without notes or preparation (another learning point), flowed. It would do, of course, because the core of the statement was basically what I had been saying to every enquirer or bar room companion over the years since the disaster. If they became aware of my personal knowledge of Hillsborough, they either asked my opinion about causation or, more often than not, expressed their own homespun view about the cause of one of the greatest peacetime tragedies that this country has ever witnessed. It is a general rule, much broader than the issue of the Hillsborough disaster, that people's opinions aren't necessarily influenced by knowledge and facts. I have confronted countless notions that 'it was caused by Liverpool fans turning up late and drunk and forcing their way into the ground. What option did the police have?' Such commentators often back up their analysis with the reported experience of a friend, or a friend of a friend, who lived in the area or was passing through and saw it for themselves. And I have always offered a similar considered response.

Given Tom Richmond's interpretation of Trevor Hicks's remarks, that I was somehow perceived as being in the camp of the trenchant fan accusers, I thought my tried and tested, even-handed response would do here. I spoke the words without stumbling. I had practised them for twenty-three years and knew them by heart. And Helena typed them up as follows:

> The more we learn about events, the more we may understand. I sat through every single day of the Taylor Inquiry, in the summer of 1989. I learned so much. Taylor was right in saying that the disaster was caused, mainly, through a lack of police control. Fans' behaviour, to the extent that it was relevant at all, made the job of the police, in the crush outside Leppings Lane turnstiles, harder than it needed to be. But it didn't cause the disaster any more than the sunny day that encouraged people to linger outside the stadium as kick-off approached. I held those views then, I hold them now. I have never, since hearing the Taylor evidence unfold, offered any other interpretation in public or private.
>
> It is against that backcloth that any documents with my name attached, out of the 400,000 revealed,

must be seen. For example, the reference to preparation for the contributions hearing was to position South Yorkshire Police's liability against the Football Club, the stadium engineers and the council, which issued a defective safety certificate. It was NOT to apportion any blame whatsoever to the fans.

In the absence of all the facts, I was called upon to resign fourteen years ago, when I became the Chief Constable of Merseyside. I really welcome the disclosure of all the facts that can be known about the Hillsborough tragedy because I have absolutely nothing to hide. I read the 395-page report from cover to cover last night and that remains my position. The panel, in my view, has produced a piece of work that will stand the test of time and scrutiny. Whilst not wishing to become a conducting rod for all the genuine and justified hurt and anguish, I would invite anyone to do the same as me and read the document and the papers online.

They document, in detail, my personal actions in respect of the Hillsborough tragedy, which were, in summary, as follows: I purchased a ticket and was an off-duty spectator at the match. As soon as I realised the unfolding tragedy, I put myself on duty, giving immediate assistance behind the South Stand. I later set up a receiving centre, at a local police station, for supporters who had become separated from friends and family.

In 1989, I was a Chief Inspector in a non-operational role at Headquarters. Four days after the disaster (and after all the vile newspaper coverage had been written), I was one of several officers pulled together by the then Deputy Chief Constable, Peter Hays [*sic*], to support him in piecing together what had taken place at the event.

By that time, the Chief Constable, Peter Wright, had handed over the formal investigation of the tragedy to an independent police force, West Midlands Police. It was West Midlands Police that presented evidence before the Taylor Inquiry. The South Yorkshire Deputy Chief Constable's team, under the leadership of Chief Superintendent Wain, was a parallel activity to inform Chief Officers of facts rather than rely on the speculation rampant at that time. Another team was later created, to work with the solicitors who were representing South Yorkshire Police at the Taylor Inquiry, to vet statements from South Yorkshire Police Officers that were intended to be presented to the Inquiry. I was not a member of that team. I never altered a statement nor asked for one to be altered. Two South Yorkshire Police teams have been conflated in the minds of some commentators. I subsequently

sat through each day of the Taylor Inquiry, briefing
the South Yorkshire Chief Constable and Deputy
Chief Constable on a regular basis. These briefings
acknowledged and accepted the responsibility of the
force in the disaster. The evidence was overwhelming. Shortly after the conclusion of the Taylor Inquiry,
I was posted to other duties. I had nothing further
to do with the subsequent Coroner's Inquests and
proceedings, other than occasional advice because
of my knowledge of the evidence presented to the
Taylor Inquiry.

We never did get away to Sussex that day. The reporters
and photographers hung around until mid-afternoon, at
which point their number had grown to more than half
a dozen, including folk with television cameras as well as
those with long-lens SLRs. I stayed indoors and made lots
of telephone calls.

Amongst the calls was one made to the Chair of my
Police Authority, Councillor Mark Burns-Williamson.
The Police Authority was my collective boss. Each provincial police force, and its Chief Constable, was answerable to
a seventeen-member committee of councillors and selected
independent local people. The Police Authorities across the
country were due to be phased out by dint of new legislation and replaced, within a few weeks, by a single, elected

Police and Crime Commissioner (PCC) for each force area. Cllr Burns-Williamson was favourite to win the vote. The looming election was an unspoken context to everything that we did as a force in the run-up to November 2012. Whilst it was important that we weren't seen to favour one candidate over another, Mark did expect the force and its Chief Constable to be aware of the implications of any hint of embarrassment for the outgoing Authority of which he was Chairman.

That was in my mind when I spoke with the Chair on Thursday 13 September. He was sympathetic, particularly when I recounted the story of the gathered pack outside my house. He told me that the Authority had already received a number of questions and complaints about my alleged conduct. I asked him how the Authority would be responding. He told me that they would play it long and perhaps meet the following week to decide on a response. I told him that I had made a statement to the press.

The Police Authority, through the office of Fraser Sampson, the Chief Executive and solicitor, would later – much later – criticise me for not sharing my press statement with them before publication. I wouldn't seek to cavil about whether I should have done – it was a raging storm and they became caught up in it too. In my defence, I would only say that Mr Hicks had mentioned me by name, not by job title, and the press pack were at my door and not at the steps

of the Police Authority. This was a personal matter unconnected with the force and its accountability structure.

Whatever happened to our relationship subsequently,
I am sure that when we spoke on Thursday 13 September,
there was no tension between me and my political master.
However, as the politics developed, so did the tension.

I had said my twopenneth. The pack had retreated. My
Chairman appeared to be supportive and his executive and
legal adviser, Fraser Sampson, agreed with my assessment
of the Hillsborough Report. I was now free to go on my
weekend break the following day. Or so I thought.

At 6.30 a.m. on Friday morning I awoke to the same
sound of 'drizzling rain'. I looked out of the bathroom window to find fewer people but now TV cameras to the fore.
I cursed myself for not having packed the car the night
before and secreted it somewhere. I went out to confront
the reporters. I made a Faustian pact with Lucy Manning
of ITN, who was the most prominent journalist present. If
I gave a 'drive away' interview through the window of my
car, would she and the other reporters go away and leave
my family in peace? She was able to say yes without consulting anybody else. They set up and chose the spot where
the interview would take place. I walked out in uniform
and got into the car with a nod to the cameras. I stopped
at the agreed spot, and wound down the window to Ms
Manning. It was all going so well until her first question.

She said that I continued to blame the fans for the disaster, and asked what I had to say to the families of those who lost their lives at Hillsborough who are outraged by that slur. The camera detects my chin hitting the floor. I was not blaming the fans for the disaster, I was saying the opposite. Hadn't she read my statement?!

I had not seen the Granada News programme, which was broadcast in Liverpool and the north-west region on Thursday night. On that programme, in the light of my media statement that day, Margaret Aspinall, who had taken over the role of Chair of the Hillsborough Family Support Group from Trevor Hicks, had condemned me. It wouldn't be the last time. It was she who had interpreted my statement as 'continuing to blame the fans for the disaster'. Her claim and my counter claim made for good telly. By agreeing to an ad hoc interview with Lucy Manning, I had stepped into a self-dug hole.

I always believed I could respond positively to the media even when the most critical finger was being pointed at my force. I had been doing it, day-in, day-out, for nineteen years since becoming a Chief Officer. Furthermore, I had served my Chief Officer apprenticeship under two great communicators. First, Richard Wells, the Chief of South Yorkshire Police post disaster, who was articulate and charismatic. I learned from him that saying sorry or being prepared to explain the context of any decision or action was not a sign of weakness. Mr Wells had publicly expressed remorse, numerous times, on behalf of his force for its failure to care for the young lives lost at Hillsborough as it should have done.

I later went as Assistant Chief Constable to West Yorkshire Police, in the early '90s, where I worked with Keith Hellawell, who was the Chief. He had a televisual magnetism. One of his great communication skills was an ability to express personal opinions about the knottiest of social issues in such a way that caused people to think not that he necessarily had the answers, but that he cared deeply about trying to find them. Having sat by these two mentors, I had developed the confidence to put myself forward to be accountable to the public, at any time and for any occasion that demanded it.

I remember, for example, an impromptu press conference in 2008 on the steps of Dewsbury Police Station, when the place was besieged by the world's press, who were growing restless about my force's apparent failure to find the missing school girl, Shannon Matthews. The pack was baying for police blood. What I couldn't tell them was that we were looking very closely at the actions of Shannon's mother behind the scenes.

I was also there to satisfy the media appetite in the aftermath of that investigation, once we had discovered Shannon's whereabouts and arrested her mother and uncle in relation to her abduction. It was important to praise the investigating officers and also to publicly thank 'our friends in the media' for their 'invaluable assistance and patient support'. Media appearances became familiar and comfortable.

I hadn't yet realised, however, that the crucial difference, identified by Tom Richmond on the Wednesday evening, is that media handling is much more straightforward when the issue is about your organisation. You can deliver a line; an explanation; sometimes an apology; and, less frequently, an admonishment, and then you can walk away. Go home, leave the organisation behind, and take off your uniform or suit. For only the second time in my professional life this was personal. There is no walking away or second chance to explain. One has to take account of the fact that any words spoken will be set against a prejudicial backdrop and therefore run the risk of driving, rather than diminishing, the story. For a seasoned communicator, I had never felt so misunderstood.

The penny dropped, finally, that there was literally nothing I could say on my own account that would make my current situation better and the strong possibility that anything I said, even if I believed it to be the truth, would make that situation worse. I had worked that out before the email from my district judge pal, and before I received the wise advice that scapegoats are created to be talked about not listened to.

On Thursday 13 September 2012, I made my last public statement about Hillsborough until now. I dictated it over the phone that morning whilst a passenger in the car driven by my wife, en route to our shortened weekend in Sussex. It was only ten lines long and it was expressed in language that could not be misinterpreted or misrepresented. Ironically, its purpose is generally misunderstood, although I don't mind. It is referred to widely in the press as 'Bettison's apology for continuing to blame the fans'. If it serves that purpose for anyone who was genuinely upset by reading or, more likely, hearing an account about my previous comments, then so be it. I am pleased.

It was intended, though, as a clarification and reinforcement of my core message in the previous text. The core message was that South Yorkshire Police, and others who had a crowd safety responsibility at Hillsborough, were to blame for the disaster. I was expressing regret not for mentioning the fans in my statement, for I did so only to absolve them from blame, but for the misunderstanding that has been an additional burden for some of the bereaved families to bear for a quarter of a century. Their apparent belief that I, and others who have a connection to South Yorkshire Police, continue to shrink from the truth.

Prior to this book, these were my last words on the causes of the disaster. I stand by them.

Let me speak very clearly. The fans of Liverpool Football Club were in no way to blame for the disaster that unfolded at Hillsborough on 15 April 1989. I formed this clear view on hearing all the evidence that was presented to the Taylor Inquiry, having sat through every day from its beginning, just four weeks after the tragedy, to its conclusion. The evidence was overwhelming. The police failed to control the situation, which ultimately led to the tragic deaths of ninety-six entirely innocent people. I can be no plainer than that and I am sorry if my earlier statement, intended to convey the same message, has caused further upset. My role was never to besmirch the fans. I did not do that. I am deeply sorry that impression and slight has lingered for twenty-three years.

I usually like to drive but I was content, that day, to be driven by Gillian all the way to our hotel on the Sussex/Surrey border. It was in a village called Chiddingfold, which suffered, in 2012, from being a mobile phone blackspot. I received no calls once we had arrived at about 5 p.m. I watched no news on TV. We met our friends but there was no laughter. I sat and ruminated. I went to bed at ten. I was tired but did not sleep.

My natural inclination, as a strategist and as someone with forty years' operational experience, was to try to figure some way out of this terrible bind that I was in. It was surely just a question of formulating the right plan.

I hadn't yet received the district judge's email, which was to arrive a couple of days later, which highlighted the political target on my back and which I seemed to have inadvertently, and clumsily, overpainted in even brighter colours. I hadn't yet realised what I now know and which I am strangely at peace with: there are some forces in life that create just too great a current to swim against. The skill is in recognising them, conserving one's energy, and allowing the current to take you to a point where a foothold is once again possible. That night I was staring at an unfamiliar painted wardrobe in an unfamiliar hotel room weighing up several different options that might lift the uncomfortable finger of suspicion from me. I didn't yet realise that I was still swimming against the tide.

CHAPTER 9

IT'S NOT PERSONAL, IT'S JUST POLITICS

15–24 October 2012

As soon as I began to hear traffic on the busy A283 that passed beneath the hotel bedroom window, I got up and showered. If I had slept at all it was only fitfully. I felt numb but the shower was invigorating. I went downstairs alone to find breakfast and to get away from the feeling of being locked in an unfamiliar hotel room with only my locked-in and circular thoughts. I was surprised to discover the Saturday newspapers were already laid out on the bar beside the dining room. I easily found prominent stories in three of them that named me and a couple that carried my photograph. The *Daily Mail* had a double-page spread with a banner headline over my image that read: 'The Masters of Cover-Up'.

It must be a common experience for celebrities to sense the gaze of recognition from strangers even when engaged in pastimes away from their public performances. I guess that feels OK so long as the recognition arises from a positive or neutral predisposition. I wasn't used to that phenomenon at all. It seemed, this weekend, as though everyone I met had already read the papers and recognised the guy from room six – *You know, the one who was responsible for the Hillsborough disaster…*

I have discovered three truths, over these last few years, about media impact, particularly in the context of newspaper reports. Firstly, people hardly attend to anything unless it affects them personally or they identify a connection with the story. Secondly, people quickly forget a lot of what they read. Life is fast and the media output is vast these days. People don't have the time or the motivation to remember. So far, so good for anyone who may wish to assert their right to be forgotten. The downside of this imperfect attention and memory is that the fragments that do stick in people's remembrances are generally simplistic and exaggerated

– probably as a justification for choosing to commit something to memory at all in this booming, buzzing world. Thirdly, therefore, where the media have been critical and, for me, since 12 September 2012, that has been a recurrent theme, then people tend to exaggerate the reason there might be for any criticism.

A good friend of mine, an athlete, was jogging with her running partner sometime after this initial firestorm. Her pal, who is described as intelligent and well-read, said: 'Your friend Norman Bettison is in a spot of bother, eh?'

My friend asked: 'Why, what do you think he's supposed to have done?'

'Well, he was the Chief Constable when all those people were killed at Hillsborough?' she replied.

'That was twenty odd years ago,' she countered. 'How old do you think he is?' and carried on jogging.

The young owner of the hotel brought me a pot of tea and I knew that he had seen the papers. He stared a little more intently than is normal or comfortable for the purpose of breakfast service. Of course it might just have been my paranoia for I have had to learn, since this time, to temper my reaction to being stared at. I had already decided on my course of action before the waiter's stare; before I had seen the newspaper headlines; before I had even come downstairs. I had certainly resolved my next step before I tested it on the first of my friends to join me at the breakfast table.

Vincent is a commercial lawyer. He listens carefully. He is wise and gives only considered responses. Furthermore, he is prepared to disagree, diplomatically, and will give his reasons why. He is always worth listening to. I told him that I had decided to seek to refer myself to the regulatory body that investigates the conduct of police officers. I couldn't do it unilaterally, as my disciplinary authority was the West Yorkshire Police Authority, but I would ask for their permission to do so on Monday. I shared with Vincent the fact that my Chairman had told me that the Authority were playing it long and would meet next week to determine any action. I needed to do something more immediately to address the current trial, and judgement, by media.

Vincent thought it a sensible option, pointing out that MPs do that all the time, though I was seeking neither his advice nor approbation on this occasion.

After breakfast, Gillian and I headed for Goodwood. I had not been able to get a phone signal since arriving in Chiddingfold and the same was true that morning. I was driving, so, with no hands-free facility in a 45-year-old car, I asked Gillian to keep checking for a signal on my phone so that I could pick up any messages.

We were just outside Chiddingfold, beyond the golf course, at around 9.50 a.m., when the phone rang for the first time since 4.49 p.m. the previous day. The caller had been trying for some time, apparently, to get through. It was Elaine Shinkfield, office manager at the West Yorkshire Police Authority, who, through my wife as call handler, asked that I get in touch as soon as possible with Fraser Sampson, the Chief Executive and solicitor to the Authority. At 9.56 a.m., I found a driveway to safely pull off the road and made that call. I had intended that Fraser would be my point of contact on Monday morning to advance my plan to refer myself for formal investigation. I had done nothing wrong twenty-three years ago and I wished to encourage an appropriate and independent third party to get to work as quickly as possible to confirm that. Although this was Saturday morning, I saw no problem in having that conversation now.

At 9.57, I began a call that would last eleven minutes and twenty-six seconds. I told Fraser that I wished to obtain the permission of the Police Authority to refer myself for investigation. He told me that an extraordinary committee had been convened for 11 a.m. that morning to consider the storm which was raging, and that was why he had been trying to contact me. I asked him whether, in his opinion, they would take a decision to refer me to the IPCC that morning. It is typical of Mr Sampson's tendency to keep his cards very close to his chest that he gave me an equivocal, and lawyerly, answer. They may do, he said, but on the other hand they may take stock of the situation and arrange to meet as planned later next week to decide on a course of action.

On that basis I asked him to put my proposal to the committee; that they give me permission to refer myself to the IPCC today, and that we coordinate press statements thereafter. He said he would do that and let me know. He did say that he wasn't optimistic that they would go along with that proposition.

One might imagine that the Chief Executive to the Police Authority; a lawyer; a man who had written the seminal text book on police disciplinary procedures, might have demurred if he thought for one moment that I was suggesting anything underhand or even inappropriate. One might think that he would refuse to convey that message and perhaps chide me for even suggesting it. He made no such attempt to dissuade or discourage. After the Police Authority's extraordinary meeting, at 12.46 p.m., he sent me a text. It read: 'Norman – sorry just off phone with MBW [Authority Chairman, who wasn't at the meeting]. Members were unanimous in all aspects and weren't impressed with the suggestion at all. Mark [Chairman] should be calling v. soon'.

I found out from a Police Authority press release that the extraordinary committee had decided to refer me to the IPCC themselves. That was fine, that is what I wanted. They didn't do that until Tuesday. Whilst I had been proposing to make the referral that afternoon, the decision in principle and the method and timing of the referral are the prerogative of the Police Authority.

So, by mid-afternoon on Saturday 15 September 2012, I knew that I would be referred to the independent regulatory body that investigates police wrongdoing. There were no conduct matters disclosed by the Hillsborough Panel Report and so the only thing that the Police Authority could refer were matters of public complaint that had repeated Mr Hicks's broad assertions that I was a member of a dirty tricks campaign. There were public complaints, too, that had been received by the Police Authority following my press statements over the previous two days.

Reflecting on the way the Saturday had panned out, I was content. I had risen with the idea of self-referral. That proposal had been put, on my behalf and without hesitation, by the Police Authority's Chief Executive. The Special Committee had rejected the proposal and instead taken the decision to use their discretion to refer what matters they could to the IPCC. I accepted their authority to do so and welcomed the eventual outcome.

That should have been an end to that particular matter and I genuinely believed that it was. Three weeks later, when the political mood had turned against me and I was resisting attempts by my Police Authority to unseat me, Mr Sampson recommended to the Police Authority that a further indictment should be added to my charge sheet. His legal advice to the Police Authority was that my suggestion, on 15 September, to refer myself to the appropriate regulatory body, may well have amounted to 'an attempt to influence improperly the decision making processes of the West Yorkshire Police Authority'. Mr Sampson wrote to me on 11 October 2012 to formally notify me that this would be the position adopted by the Police Authority and that this further matter had been referred to the IPCC for investigation.

Mr Sampson had broken off personal communication with me some days prior to this letter. If, however, we had still been talking, I might have asked, mischievously, if he was also being referred for aiding and abetting my 'interference'. As it was, there were so many other slings and arrows flying in my direction at that time that I adopted an attitude of 'throw it on the cart with the rest'.

I was staggered when, after stepping down from my post on 24 October 2012, the IPCC declared that they intended to continue to investigate the so-called 'interference', which they described as a 'serious matter'. It wasn't. Ninety-six people dying at a football stadium is a very serious matter. Allegations of corruption and cover-up are serious matters. My eleven-minute telephone conversation with the Chief Executive and solicitor of my Police Authority in the midst of a media feeding frenzy was not serious, although I had misjudged how it might be turned against me.

What I had certainly misjudged is the appetite amongst some, following a hue and cry, to run the quarry to ground by any means possible. The tone of the IPCC press announcement about how they intended to set about the task of responding to the public concern about the contents of the Hillsborough Panel Report would leave me in no doubt about their desire in that regard. But that would be later on. There was still some water to flow under the West Yorkshire Police Authority bridge before then.

———————

It is hardly a novel observation to point out that some politicians don't always reach judgements or initiate action from a purely moral basis. Their position on a particular issue is occasionally taken on pragmatic or propitious grounds. The politically expedient thing to do may sometimes emerge slowly. Little weights of public opinion are added to the scale one by one until a sharp and urgent correction is required to restore the political stability.

On 13 September 2012, the day after the publication of the panel report, I know that I had the genuine sympathy of Councillor Mark Burns-Williamson, the Chairman of my Police Authority. He had been briefed that there was nothing in the report that indicated any wrongdoing on my part. He had heard of Mr Hicks's personal attack but that wasn't creating any wash on his own political shore. He was a Labour councillor in Wakefield, elected on a comfortable majority. We had worked together closely for six years. He had asked me to stay on as Chief Constable at the end of my five-year contract in January 2012 and had given his full support to my serving a further three years' extension that would have enabled me to bridge the old political machinery – the Police Authority – with the new – the Elected Police and Crime Commissioner. As the favourite to win that election, he wanted the organisational constancy that I could offer.

He knew Gillian, my wife, through work-based social events and I had gotten to know his partner, Caroline. He naturally felt for both of us, and our family, when I told him of the press siege at home.

Cllr Burns-Williamson continued to have regular conversations with me. On 15 September, when I told him that I had spoken with Fraser Sampson about self-referral, and later that day when he rang to confirm that the special committee, in which he had played no part, had decided to refer me themselves. On 17 September, we talked about an already-scheduled Police Authority meeting that would take place on Friday 21st. Cllr Burns-Williamson invited me to address the current controversy after the completion of normal business. It would be, he said, 'below the line', which means that it would not be the subject of public report.

I hadn't asked for confidentiality, he wanted it for political reasons – to keep a lid on it. Throughout the first nine days, the politically expedient thing to do, for a local politician, was to carry on and hope the heat subsided.

When there is a full Police Authority gathering, the members meet in camera and without any record, before the meeting proper. This pre-meeting is an opportunity for the Chairman to influence the vote before any debate. I have often, tongue in cheek, said to my Authority, following a quick and unanimous decision in the formal session, that I appear not to have been at the right meeting that day.

Police Authority meetings are rarely the subject of television coverage but there were at least three networks represented with cameras and reporters at the meeting on the 21st. I just had time to hear a local news broadcast before I had to leave for the meeting. Cllr Burns-Williamson had spoken to reporters on his way in to the pre-meeting. He had given me the 'football manager's endorsement' – the one that seems always to be followed by the chop. Asked about my position, Cllr Burns-Williamson said that, at this time, the Authority had confidence in the Chief Constable to continue to lead West Yorkshire Police. I know Mark Burns-Williamson, and his political approach to controversy, sufficiently well to be sure that he believed that was the case going into the pre-meeting. He wouldn't have said it otherwise.

I was surrounded by the press pack on my way to join the Police Authority after their pre-meeting and felt emboldened by Cllr Burns-Williamson's comments. When asked by the waiting reporters whether I would be resigning that afternoon, I replied that I was meeting my Police Authority and that, as far as I was concerned, it was business as usual. I wasn't the first and I won't be the last to misread the 'football manager's endorsement'.

The Authority meeting proper was standard fare. A little more frosty than usual I thought, but with the press being well represented in the public gallery there could be lots of reasons for the unusual dynamic. I gave the quarterly report on three aspects of force monitoring that were important to the Authority. Firstly, the austerity squeeze was well under way in 2012 and I reported £63 million savings projected for the financial year. Secondly, I was pleased to report that cost-cutting was not affecting performance, with reductions in crime in the overwhelming majority of categories. Thirdly, the force undertakes a monthly survey of public satisfaction and confidence monitored on a neighbourhood-by-neighbourhood basis. I reported at this meeting, which was to be my last after nineteen years as a Chief Officer, that public confidence had never been higher in West Yorkshire. This was timely given the attempts by Mr Sampson over the following weeks to lever me out of my post on the grounds of force ineffectiveness.

After the normal meeting, there was a break for coffee whilst press and public were cleared for the below-the-line discussions. I stayed put, looking for some feedback from the pre-meeting from either the Chairman or the Chief Executive, who were both sitting, as always, to my immediate right. I would normally expect some clue about the prevailing mood of the members. I received none that day, which was telling in itself. Then the members began to file back into the room.

Looking around the room, there were sixteen of the seventeen members present. I had people's attention but it seemed to me as though there was anger reflected in a few eyes. Perhaps, I told myself, it was because of today's public spectacle. Nobody would have enjoyed running the press gauntlet. In other eyes, particularly those of the independent members, I thought I could detect a kind of sadness. The sort of look the condemned man might get from the more compassionate members of the hanging party.

I delivered my prepared account. I spoke for twenty minutes about the history, and the previous 'fallout', arising from my involvement in the Hillsborough disaster. I used four props: the Taylor Report; the Hillsborough Panel Report; press headlines from the last week alongside the press headlines from November 1998, when I was appointed Chief in Merseyside; and finally my recent press statements. I was keen to read my press statements in full on the basis that most of the members would not have seen them directly and might have been influenced by the mis-reporting of them.

There were two or three questions from members. None were substantive. I can only recall one from Councillor Ken Smith, who asked whether I had taken anyone's advice before issuing my press statement on the previous Thursday. I remember it because the point that he was making was obvious and intended to embarrass. I don't think it mat-tered to him what my answer was.

I left at about 12.45 p.m. to allow members to meet pri-vately. I knew that there was a mood running against me but, as with all things political, the outcome would depend upon how the numbers fell.

I had a call at about 1.45 p.m. from the Chairman. He wanted to meet me at the Authority offices but suggested that I come at 4 p.m., when the press would have left. I wasn't surprised by the agenda at 4 p.m., but I was a little surprised by the immediate leap to a conclusion. In the first words uttered at the meeting, Councillor Burns-Williamson asked that I step aside because of the controversy. If I did so, he said, he would be willing to say what a wonder-ful job I'd done as Chief in West Yorkshire. I said that I had no intention of stepping aside just a week after I had been called upon to 'scurry up the nearest drainpipe'. I needed to submit myself to investigation in order to clear my name. That is why I had sought immediate and self-referral to the statutory body that could achieve that. Mr Burns-Williamson asked me to reflect on the impact on the force, on the Police Authority and on the staff at the Police Authority HQ, for whom, he told me without intended irony, it had been a difficult day.

I suggested that, if the Authority thought my position was untenable, they should suspend me pending a full investigation. The Chairman responded that any investigation was likely to take a long time and that the Authority wouldn't countenance an extensive period of limbo.

There then followed a cameo that gave an insight into the Authority's earlier private discussions. Councillor Burns-Williamson (Labour) had asked his Deputy Chairman, Councillor Les Carter (Conservative), to be with him when he delivered the Authority's edict. Sensing a standoff between me and the Chairman, Councillor Carter proffered: 'Can't you see how this will impact on the PCC elections, Norman?' (Which was honest.) To which the Chairman responded: 'Les, we agreed that we weren't going to mention the elections.' (Which was probably also accurate.) Councillor Carter just couldn't help himself. The forthcoming election was the elephant in the room.

One wonderful aspect of the old seventeen-strong, cross-party Authority was that party politics were usually left at the door. In West Yorkshire and, surprisingly, also in

Merseyside, characters of different political persuasions would create strong alliances to achieve the mutual aims of the Police Authority. Here, on 21 September 2012, these strange political bedfellows had a common concern that unexpected controversy should not interfere with the Chairman's subsequent bid for power.

I asked that Fraser Sampson, as someone who understood employment law as well as Realpolitik, should join us. I told the three of them that I had no intention of stepping aside until there had been an independent investigation of my post-disaster involvement. Resignation would allow the narrative to run that I had escaped the bullets in an act of cowardice. That is precisely what I wanted to avoid. I wanted, instead, to face any accusation. I left them to reflect.

Whenever a Chief Police Officer hits choppy water with his or her Police Authority, there is a buddy system, within ACPO, whereby one of the Association members will act as 'friend' and go-between. It has been found, over the years, to provide the best chance of calming troubled waters. If that fails, then the 'friend' continues to be a sounding board for the colleague in the eye of the storm. I had identified a 'friend' as soon as the hue and cry reached fever pitch the previous weekend. Craig Mackey, the Deputy Commissioner of the Metropolis, is well versed in police disciplinary procedures. He is also a thoroughly decent fellow who tends to make more friends than enemies and has form for finding win/win solutions in tricky situations.

I told Craig that, whilst I had put the onus back onto the Police Authority at the Friday afternoon meeting, I nevertheless understood the significance of the conversation that I had just had. A Chief Constable, like any Chief Executive, relies for his or her authority on the confidence of their staff – the dressing room, so to speak – and also the confidence of their Authority or Board.

It seemed, from the conversation that I had just had, that I could no longer count on the latter. I was a lame duck from that point. I asked Mr Mackey to negotiate on my behalf an agreement to retire at the end of an IPCC investigation. I would be prepared to commit to it now. I thought that an IPCC investigation, of my role at least, was possible within a ten-month timeframe. So my opening gambit was a preparedness to go at the end of the investigation, or August 2013, whichever was the sooner.

I took a call on Sunday 23 September from Her Majesty's Inspector of Constabulary (HMIC) Roger Baker. Fraser Sampson had contacted him, presumably to try to enlist his help in encouraging me out of the door. Mr Baker was too wise to offer direct encouragement but he did tell me that Fraser Sampson had retained the services of John Beggs QC to help them find a legal means of unseating me. Roger Baker assured me that he had reinforced the need for the Authority to be sure that there was a prima facie case against me and that there was a public interest consideration if they wished to suspend or dismiss me. He said that they hadn't approached it in that strategic way. Some members had simply turned against me on Friday and they were now resolved to get me out. It was left to the Chief Executive, Mr Sampson, to find the means.

On the Monday, Craig Mackey put my retirement plan to Mr Sampson. His response was that they were now well advanced along the avenue of requiring my resignation on the grounds of force ineffectiveness. This was bizarre. Section 11 of the Police Act 1996 had introduced a measure to enable a local Police Authority, in conjunction with the Home Secretary, to get rid of an underperforming Chief. It was a measure that had never been used because one could see, immediately, from the legislation, that there must have been a path that led to that nuclear option. Poor performance; written appraisal; intervention; no improvement are the kinds of steps one would expect to see. Each step presenting an exit route for the failing Chief. I, on the other hand, had on the previous Friday posted the best results the force had seen in recent times against a 15 per cent reduction in budget.

Craig Mackey was assured, by Mr Sampson, that the Home Secretary's private office were in support of the Section 11 route and that John Beggs QC was advising on process.

Coincidentally, John Beggs is currently the counsel to David Duckenfield and will have recently forced every nerve and sinew in representing his client's interests. Here, according to Mr Sampson's account, he was advising on my professional demise. The symbol of the legal profession is, appropriately, blind justice.

I wasn't moved by the threat of Section 11 proceedings. The likelihood of success in using novel legislation in a case where inefficiency and ineffectiveness could easily be disproved struck me as evidence of an Authority overreaching itself. It was, however, a clear indication of the degree of determination to get rid of me.

At 3.45 p.m. on Tuesday 25 September 2012, I took a call from the Chairman. It was a meandering conversation. He first of all hoped that I was OK. He then read out a resolution, prepared by Fraser Sampson, that indicated a lack of confidence in my ability to continue to lead the force. A resolution intended, he said, to be put before the full Authority. He then said that he hoped not to go down the formal route and that this informal channel was open and that I could speak to him at any time about stepping down. I asked about my offer, through Craig Mackey, to go at the conclusion of an investigation or August at the latest. 'Members think that is too long,' he said. 'They are thinking about a more immediate date.' He concluded the conversation by telling me that he wanted my response in

seven days, but it wasn't clear to what part of his conversation I was meant to respond.

At 4.30 p.m., I had a call from the HMIC, Mr Baker.
He had been told that the Authority had now initiated the
Section 11 procedure and the earlier call from the Chair
was the trigger. I told him that I hadn't understood the
call in that way. Mr Baker went off to speak with Fraser
Sampson and called again to report that Mr Sampson was
frustrated that the Chairman appeared to have gone off
script. I was told to expect a formal copy of the resolution,
which duly arrived from Mr Sampson by email at 5.34 p.m.
But no grounds for the no confidence resolution. I chased
up with Mr Mackey and Mr Baker. They told me that
Mr Sampson would be working up the grounds that night.
I wondered aloud with each of them about whether it
might not have been better for the grounds to have preceded the resolution.

I never did get those grounds. Section 11 was a flight
of fancy that got airborne, briefly, somewhere between
Fraser Sampson and John Beggs QC. The members of the
Authority just knew that they wanted shot of me, they
didn't really care how. That could be left to the lawyers.

The next day saw the staff in the press office at the
Authority briefing against me to my own press officer,
Nigel Swift. Whilst I trusted Nigel implicitly, the resolu-
tion of no confidence was likely to become the talk of the

force and, thereafter, as sure as night follows day, the press would have it. Things were coming to a head. Perhaps that was Mr Sampson's strategy all along.

I had my last-ever conversation with Mr Sampson at 1.50 p.m. on Thursday 27 September 2012. It was precipitated by my message to him, following up on the resolution that he had sent to me two days previously. I told him that I was not prepared to respond until a) I had seen the grounds that would support a vote of no confidence and, then b) I had an opportunity to consult a lawyer. We were sparring, nothing more.

He rang, unexpectedly, to acknowledge receipt. I was on leave at home that day and he rang me to say that he had just called at my office and wanted me to know that it had been an intended welfare visit. A unique event in my fourteen years' experience as Chief Constable. He told me that the grounds 'weren't quite finished yet' but that he would discuss service of them with Craig Mackey. As I say, the grounds never arrived. Mr Sampson and I would never have need to speak to each other again.

The following day I saw Cllr Burns-Williamson at a neutral venue: the Cedar Court Hotel at Wakefield. In spite of the Chairman having the bullets to fire, I realised that it would be others who were providing them and loading for him. Mark Burns-Williamson would be uncomfortable; we had been friends. He would, by now though, be reconciled to the fact that my dispatch was necessary on the grounds of political expediency. As a politician, he would have seen the guillotine in operation many times. Although we were, to all intents, locked in a fight to the finish, I knew I could discuss alternative options to Section 11 dismissal which might better achieve his politically expedient ambition.

I told him that I saw the Section 11 procedure as a device and it wouldn't achieve its intended purpose. We might all get damaged in the process. I did understand, however, that as a candidate in the forthcoming PCC election, he might well need a political resolution to what had become the 'Bettison problem'.

I offered to announce, forthwith, my retirement in May. Firstly, it would give the incoming PCC, on the first day after the election in November, an opportunity to advertise for a Chief Constable. It generally takes six months from advert to appointment. Secondly, it would give the IPCC a fighting chance to fulfil their investigation into my conduct. I remained anxious to end a forty-year police career with my integrity intact.

The alternative, I warned him, was a dirty fight over Section 11. I left him to think about that whilst I went off to pay for the coffee and biscuits.

He warmed to the idea of an early announcement of retirement pre-dating the PCC elections and promised to work on Authority members with a view to agreeing on my suggested way forward. He was to be at the Labour Party conference at Manchester throughout the following week, which was vital to his political future as West Yorkshire's elected PCC, but he would sound out his fellow members from there. As we parted he assured me, in the detached way that politicians do, that this situation wasn't what he wanted. It wasn't personal, it was just politics.

Craig Mackey served on Fraser Sampson a formal notice setting out my offer and on Thursday 4 October 2012 it was put before the Authority. At 2.40 p.m. that day, the Chairman rang to say that, with one abstention, the Authority had accepted the compromise but they wished the retirement date to be 31 March 2013. I asked for time to consider that and made a call to Craig Mackey as my ACPO 'friend' and confidante. Whilst connected to Craig, my Deputy, John Parkinson, informed me that the press office had received word from the *Yorkshire Post* that a councillor on the Police Authority had briefed them that the Authority had met and were unanimous that I should resign following a vote of no confidence. That was the story they intended to run the following day. I therefore decided to announce my retirement that evening, to take effect from 31 March 2013. I knew that would be a bigger story than the leak.

I spoke with the Chairman before issuing my public statement. I told him that I was appalled by the leak, knowing that he would be too. I undertook to send him a copy of my retirement announcement and he undertook to speak to the local media about his reluctant acceptance of it. I saw him on TV that night and heard him the next morning on BBC Radio Leeds. I hope he was being sincere when he expressed his disappointment that it had come to this and praised my record whilst Chief. The same Chief that was threatened a few days previously with Section 11 requirement to resign on the grounds of being ineffective. Still, it wasn't personal.

The news of my retirement was welcomed in many quarters. Trevor Hicks, on behalf of the Hillsborough families, told the press that 'this is the first of the new scalps, his will be the first of many'.

On 5 October 2012, I wrote to the Independent Police Complaints Commission to confirm that it was my intention to retire on 31 March 2013 and asked that they now expedite any investigation so that it could be completed before that date. If an investigation is completed to the point of finding prima facie evidence of gross misconduct, then a stop can be put on retirement until the officer has faced disciplinary proceedings. I was always confident that it would never come to that and so I gave the regulatory body the earliest notice of my intentions and copied that letter widely, including to the Home Office and the HMIC. I still, at this time, believed that there might be a swift and fair process undertaken by an independent regulator. I had never been down this road before and, now that I have, I realise that my expectations of the IPCC, on both fronts, were set too high.

Taking stock on the evening of 5 October 2012, I reflected on three frenetic weeks since the Hillsborough Panel had published their report. Three weeks since Trevor Hicks had implied that I was at the heart of a criminal conspiracy. Three weeks in which my professional career had come to be hanging by a thread. I seriously entertained the thought, on 5 October, that I might still retire, honourably, in six months' time. I was foolish to think that.

By late October, the IPCC had made clear their intentions and had reinforced the view that there was some merit in the swirling allegations of a criminal conspiracy to cover up the truth about Hillsborough. Given that mine was the only name in the public domain, it bolstered the prejudgement about my alleged involvement. Notwithstanding this development, I was still working my lengthy notice period and genuinely hoped that the IPCC might, during that time, get to the bottom of these historic and unspecific accusations. The *Yorkshire Post* had published an excoriating editorial about me following the IPCC announcement, but I had survived it. The media attacks were becoming fewer and further between. In the absence of new facts there was only so much vitriol that could be expended on one person.

The media can always find fresh targets. It was, though, only the lull before the next storm.

I had been aware that there was to be a debate in the House of Commons on 22 October 2012 about the Hillsborough Panel Report. The report had been commissioned by Parliament in 2009 and it was necessary for it to be formally received by the House.

I anticipated that politicians would want to be seen to be rallying to the call for justice. Indeed, the majority of speakers in the debate included in their address a variation on the theme of 'Now we have the truth. Justice must follow.' It was a theme set by the Home Secretary in opening the debate and echoed by most other contributors. What I hadn't anticipated is that I might be singled out and named in the debate. After all, I had been identified as a 'suspect' by the IPCC and they had begun a criminal investigation. If, as a result of the attendant publicity, any Member of Parliament had been approached with any testimony concerning me they would surely pass it on to the IPCC for formal investigation. I was naive to believe that might be the case.

Alec Shelbrooke MP (Conservative), Member for Elmet and Rothwell in West Yorkshire, was the first to have a nibble. Interrupting the shadow Home Secretary's address, Mr Shelbrooke asked: 'I am sure that the Right Honourable Lady, a fellow West Yorkshire MP, shares my concerns that the Chief Constable of West Yorkshire is being investigated by the IPCC ... Does she agree that in order for the public to have faith in the investigation, he should be suspended?'

Yvette Cooper MP (Labour), Member for Pontefract and Castleford, was too wily to be caught out like that and straight batted the questioner, who, she had probably deduced, was making a party political point. The Labour-led Police Authority had chosen not to suspend me. Mr Shelbrooke, as a local Conservative MP, had condemned that decision in the pages of the *Yorkshire Post*.

Mr Shelbrooke was soon joined by Derek Twigg (Labour), Member for Halton near Merseyside. Mr Twigg told the harrowing story about the recent death of Eddie Spearritt, a constituent, who was seriously injured at Hillsborough and who lost his son Adam in the disaster. Mr Spearritt Snr had passed away before he could learn the truth from the Hillsborough Panel. Mr Twigg told the Home Secretary and the House that the Spearritt family are now concerned about the position of Norman Bettison, which needs the closest scrutiny.

Sensing the early mood in the fevered debate, and the mention of my name on a couple of occasions, John Pugh (Lib Dem), Member for Southport, Merseyside, tried to rein in the witch finders. I had met John Pugh during my time as Chief Constable in Merseyside and, as I did with several of the local MPs, I had explained carefully and truthfully what my role was after the disaster. Mr Pugh struck a conciliatory tone in the debate.

> I do not believe that the world is peopled by saints and sinners, there are many shades of grey, and I dare say that some in South Yorkshire Police were doing the right thing. Many of us will have met a lot of people involved. I think, for example, of Norman Bettison, then Chief Constable for Merseyside, with whom many of us are acquainted ... Everyone needs a fair hearing, and there has to be a huge moral gulf between someone putting a gloss on the actions of their police force, and [the act of] incriminating others. That has to be reflected in any subsequent judgement.

Keith Vaz MP (Labour), Member for Leicester East, who was not traditionally known as a friend of the police service, also tried to encourage the suspension of judgement.

> The Honourable Member for Elmet and Rothwell [Alec Shelbrooke] mentioned Norman Bettison earlier ... we should give the IPCC the opportunity to make a judgement on Norman Bettison's case. I know what the families feel, and I have heard what he [Shelbrooke] has said today.

The interventions by John Pugh and Keith Vaz did not mollify Mr Shelbrooke. He came back into the debate and made a wild accusation that questions had been recently raised about me applying pressure on people, as Chief Constable, to cause them to change their statements. He said that, whether guilty or innocent, I should now be suspended and not be allowed to retire in six months' time.

Frankly, I wouldn't have minded suspension. Once a Chief Constable has been suspended, his or her authority is compromised and it is difficult, perhaps impossible, to return to duty and regain that authority. Nevertheless, suspension would have introduced some time constraints on the IPCC to complete their investigation, which has now been running for more than four years.

Some MPs wanted to go further than suspension. Rosie Cooper (Labour), Member for West Lancashire, told the House that many of her constituents would applaud *any* action taken against Sir Norman Bettison for his role in Hillsborough and, for starters, called for my knighthood to be summarily removed.

The naivety in believing that I might retire from a forty-year career after an objective and thorough investigation by the IPCC was to become apparent at 7.26 p.m. on the evening of the Commons debate. At this precise time, Maria Eagle MP (Labour), member for Garston and Halewood, was called by the Deputy Speaker. Building upon a general proposition – the by-now widely accepted fact that there was indeed a cover-up and a black operations campaign in South Yorkshire Police after the disaster – she contributed the following: 'Those who ordered and orchestrated that campaign have had many years of impunity to enjoy their burgeoning careers.'

I could see where this theme was leading but, even then, I could not contemplate the viciousness of the attack that was to follow: 'One of the people that I named, in 1998, as being involved in orchestrating it is Sir Norman Bettison ... I should make it clear that he has always denied involvement in the black propaganda campaign in public. However, I have a letter...'

Ms Eagle showed the letter for dramatic effect. I had no inkling of what it might contain. I could not imagine how devastating it would be.

> It is from John Barry, who will swear a statement to the effect that in 1989 Norman Bettison said to him: 'We are trying to concoct a story that all Liverpool fans were drunk and we were afraid that they were going to break down the gates ... so we decided to open them...' So what Sir Norman denies in public he boasts about in private conversation.

John who? was my first response. I couldn't place the name

but I would soon know what he looked like. Immediately after the Commons debate, and long before he gave his sworn testimony to the IPCC, John Barry did a round of media interviews, including with BBC News, ITN News, *The Guardian*, the *Daily Mirror* etc. He and Maria Eagle's office had orchestrated a campaign. Ironic really. She would use parliamentary privilege to air the accusation on the floor of the House. Mr Barry was to follow it up with a retelling of the accusation on carefully selected media platforms. I was outflanked and skewered.

Of course, I was given the opportunity, after all of these media stories had been aired or printed, to say something in response. Another thing that I have learned in this long ordeal is that a response just keeps a story running. A response, two days after the original story, simply gives a newspaper the opportunity to re-hash the original allegation. My response to outrageous allegations would, from now on, be through the formal process of investigation, and through the courts if necessary, not through the media.

The thread by which my career hung was unlikely to hold the added weight of this sensational accusation. I thought it sensible to pause for twenty-four hours, however, to test how the local winds were blowing. I did not have to wait that long. The *Yorkshire Post*, on the day following the debate, was condemnatory. A new apparent 'fact' – a recent letter supposedly recounting a 23-year-old conversation

– and a local MP on the warpath (Alec Shelbrooke) was a boost for the editorial besiegement, which had been running out of steam. My fortune was finally read, however, a few hours later still.

The fates had conspired to restore my name at the centre of the most prominent local news story on the very day that the four candidates for the forthcoming election for Police and Crime Commissioner were to have a live debate on BBC *Look North*, a local television news programme. The key issue in the televised debate became the question, put to each candidate, of what they would do about the 'problem of the Chief Constable'. Three out of the four candidates said that they would, if elected, use their new, arbitrary powers as PCC to suspend me and to require my resignation with immediate effect. Councillor Andrew Marchington, the Lib Dem candidate, was in the minority. He was the only one who said that he would want to consider all the evidence as well as the popular demands.

Mark Burns-Williamson, the outgoing Police Authority Chairman, was asked about the Authority's prior acceptance of my retirement with six months' notice. He said that, as a result of the Parliamentary Debate and the new disclosure, he believed it was the wrong decision. He was one of the three who declared their commitment to an early execution if elected to power.

I didn't really need my trusted deputy, John Parkinson,

to drive the twenty-odd miles to my home that night to convince me that my course was run. I know he was only seeking to help. I had already realised that any professional and political support was exhausted. I told John to prepare to take over the command of the force – it would be in good hands. I then contacted my ACPO 'friend', Craig Mackey, that night, and asked him to convey to Fraser Sampson my intention to retire within the statutory notice period. I was prepared, at the discretion of the Police Authority, to work out that short notice or leave immediately. Either way, I was not intending to leave the decision about my future at the whim of an incoming PCC.

I knew which option Mr Sampson would support, though I only learned of the Authority's formal decision by way of their press release. At 12.45 p.m. on Wednesday 24 October 2012, I received a telephone call from Oliver Cattermole, the ACPO press officer, to tell me that BBC online and several Twitter feeds were carrying the story of my immediate 'resignation'. That wasn't a word that either I or Craig Mackey had used, but it was a word chosen by Fraser Sampson because he considered it the most accurate legal definition of my offer to retire forthwith. I did not have the stomach to argue the appropriateness of that description, reports of my sudden resignation were simply the crowning insult.

It was forty years, two months and three days since I had

first walked into the Sheffield and Rotherham Constabulary Training Department, which was on the first floor, above the Black Swan public house on Snig Hill, Sheffield. Sergeant Don Jackson had welcomed me and around a dozen other teenagers into the police family. He told us on the first day that there were three things the service expected from us at all times: our commitment, in the face of many challenges; courtesy, in the face of abuse and distrust; and integrity. That, he said, is like one's virginity: once it's gone it's gone. He told us that we followed a proud and distinguished line of police officers and that, every day we were out on patrol, we represented not just ourselves but the service as a whole.

It was a powerful induction which made an impression on me that lasted for four decades. I had never lost sight of Sergeant Jackson's three precepts despite the way that I relinquished my vocation in 2012.

CHAPTER 10

IN THE SHADOW
OF SALEM

12 October 2012 – present day

T
he Independent Police Complaints Commission
(IPCC) is the statutory body that has a responsibility to investigate allegations of wrongdoing that
are made in relation to the police. I had sought permission,
within seventy-two hours of the publication of the Hillsborough Panel Report, to refer myself to the commission for
urgent investigation. That permission was declined by my

Police Authority, the body to which I was accountable, who decided that they would make a formal referral themselves. I had duly written to the IPCC on two separate occasions, welcoming their attention and seeking an early resolution of the referred matters. That was more than four years ago.

The IPCC is the latest in a succession of regulatory bodies created to oversee matters of complaint against the police. The first was the Police Complaints Board (PCB), established in 1977. The PCB had only a reviewing function following the local investigation of complaints by any police force.

Lord Scarman, in his report about lessons from the Brixton Riots in 1981, suggested that the PCB lacked independence and teeth. It was eventually replaced, in 1985, by the Police Complaints Authority (PCA). The PCA gained new powers of oversight and executive decision-making in relation to complaints and their disposal. Nevertheless, the system continued to struggle to attract public support.

The inquiry into the murder of Stephen Lawrence in 1999 found that confidence in the police amongst ethnic minority communities remained worryingly low, particularly around the way that their complaints were dealt with. That inquiry recommended a new regulator with the resources and powers to carry out their own investigations. The pressure group Liberty echoed that call and, following a public consultation exercise, the government created the IPCC as part of the Police Reform Act 2002.

The commission has, over the years, accreted to itself greater and wider powers through legislation and statutory guidance. They now have the wherewithal to decide how a complaint is to be investigated: either by a police force under their active management or by their own staff acting as an independent and self-contained investigatory force. They have the powers of arrest, detention and search. They have the power to recommend criminal prosecution in conjunction with the CPS. They have the power to direct disciplinary bodies to hear cases where the matters under investigation don't reach the criminal threshold. They have the power to determine the severity level for such hearings. These are awesome powers which put the IPCC on a par with the police forces that they oversee. It does, in my recent experience at the hands of the IPCC, beg the time-honoured question: 'Who will guard the guards?'

The IPCC has fought the same battle as its predecessor bodies, to convince a sceptical public that it can offer true independence. They have pledged, and reiterated, over many years, a commitment to put the complainant at the heart of every investigation.

It is a laudable aim of any investigator. I endeavoured, in my own investigations, to consider the needs and the interests of the complainant throughout the investigation. It is the compassionate and fair thing to do. It would be entirely wrong, however, to go so far as to allow those particular and sometimes partisan interests to interfere with a professional and objective search for the truth.

The IPCC have not been short of high-profile incidents that have warranted their attention in recent years. The death of Ian Tomlinson after contact with the Metropolitan Police; the shooting dead of Mark Duggan by police firearms officers; and the complaints of police inactivity, or worse, in relation to the sexual grooming of young girls in Rotherham are cases in point. It is the Hillsborough issues, though, that have represented a kind of high noon for the commission.

After the publication of the Hillsborough Panel's report, which made no allegations of wrongdoing against any individual or institution, there quickly developed a narrative in the press and Parliament which crystallised into a very serious allegation indeed. That South Yorkshire Police, from the very top of the organisation, had fashioned a criminal conspiracy to cover up the true causes of the Hillsborough disaster and to put the blame, instead, onto the Liverpool football fans. A conspiracy, it is alleged, that has been maintained for two decades.

These are not complaints about the errant actions of individual operational officers. If the narrative were true then it raises concerns about a corruption at the dark heart of policing. If the IPCC have any purpose at all, it is surely to locate and eradicate a canker such as this, and to be seen to be doing so with a single-minded resolve. The public would expect no less of the commission. It is easy to see how Hillsborough might, justifiably, become their crusade.

Within weeks of the publication of the panel's report, the narrative of corruption and conspiracy was sufficiently well-established in the public consciousness that a prominent politician such as Andy Burnham MP could appear on *Any Questions?* on Radio 4 and simply assert that the evidence of the scale of the cover-up by South Yorkshire Police is truly shocking and that it raises questions about the foundation of police integrity in this country. He has, more recently, invoking parliamentary privilege, accused the South Yorkshire Police force – over many years – of being 'rotten to the core'. The Prime Minister, Theresa May, in a speech to the National Conference of the Police Federation whilst Home Secretary, listed Hillsborough amongst contemporary 'scandals' in policing. No one has been in a position to rebut this political rhetoric. No one has attempted to disagree with this view. It is a view so commonly held that anyone challenging the narrative risks isolation or accusations about their own integrity.

So there has been no counter narrative from the Association of Chief Police Officers; from the College of Policing; from any free-thinking journalist; nor from the current hierarchy of South Yorkshire Police, who seemed keen at one point to establish their historical distance from the pogrom that was under way. Despite that strategic position, the most recent Chief Constable of South Yorkshire Police, David Crompton, has himself been swept from office in the wake of the Hillsborough outrage. It is difficult to discern whether he is accused of any misconduct at all. Nevertheless, he is suspended from office by the arbitrary decision of a Police and Crime Commissioner who claims that public confidence in the force demands he be replaced following the recent proceedings and verdict of the Coroner's Court.

People who have run the risk of being tarred with the same accusative brush have either kept their heads down or, worse, got behind the witch hunt themselves.

Typical of its type is a feature article, written for *The Times* in September 2012, within forty-eight hours of the publication of the Hillsborough Panel Report, by Lord Blair of Boughton. Ian Blair was a contemporary of mine in policing. He left the service in 2008, having been criticised, as Metropolitan Police Commissioner, for his handling of the Jean Charles de Menezes shooting and his lack of openness in the aftermath. He seems to have been rehabilitated as a crossbench peer and eminent arbiter on matters of policing integrity. 'Hillsborough', said Lord Blair,

> appears to be the most egregious example of deliberate dissimulation in the history of British Policing ...

> The shadows of this apparently disgraceful behaviour
> will long lie over the police service as a whole ... This
> attempt to re-write history has echoes of the colonial
> cover-up of brutality by British forces under Dyer at
> Amritsar or against the Mau Mau in Kenya.

I'm sure you will get the picture. In order to avoid being swallowed up by the narrative around police corruption arising from Hillsborough, it has been necessary for commentators on policing matters to expose their wounds and add increasingly rhetorical layers of condemnation to the baseline accusations.

No one, around the time of the Hillsborough Panel Report, said that it might be better to await the outcome of an objective investigation. Not even the body that was charged with a responsibility for that investigation.

On 12 October 2012, exactly one month after the publication of the panel's report, Deborah Glass, Deputy Chair of the IPCC, published a document called 'Decision in Response to the Report of the Hillsborough Independent Panel'. Paying tribute to the tenacity of the Hillsborough families' long campaign for the truth, Ms Glass acknowledged, and pledged to respond to, their eagerness, now, to see justice after so many years of denial.

This language was on all fours with the stated commitment of the commission to put the complainant at the heart of their investigation. But, in appearing to promise 'Justice after so many years of denial', that seemed like over-promising at the start of a supposedly objective process.

At paragraph thirteen of her report, Ms Glass does point out to the careful reader that the Hillsborough Panel has made no direct allegations against any individual or institution. Yet, in the very next paragraph, she states, unequivocally, that there are potential criminal issues disclosed by the report concerning allegations about what happened after the disaster, including that evidence was fabricated and misinformation was spread in an attempt to avoid blame. She even spelled out what the criminal charges might amount to before an investigative stone was turned. It all added up to the image of a commission setting about a serious task with a concluded sense of purpose.

Whatever my own assessment of Deborah Glass's commentary on the Hillsborough Panel Report, and her subsequent televised press conference to launch the investigation, it was clear what message the press and public had taken away. The *Yorkshire Post* published the following account:

> Yorkshire's most senior police Chief may face criminal charges after the biggest ever investigation into British Policing was launched yesterday. The Independent Police Complaints Commission said the actions of

> Sir Norman Bettison … could amount to pervert-
> ing the course of justice, an offence which carries life
> imprisonment. The IPCC said it has identified a large
> number of potential criminal and misconduct offences
> and will now work alongside the Crown Prosecution
> Service to bring those responsible to justice.

Having seen Deborah Glass's televised press conference and read the reports and editorial comment in the *Yorkshire Post*, the recently retired Honorary Recorder of Bradford, His Honour Judge James Stewart, was moved to write to the newspaper. The letter, published in the *Yorkshire Post* on 22 October, pointed out that Ms Glass's injudicious remarks and the resultant reporting of them meant that it was 'doubtful whether Sir Norman Bettison, if subsequently charged with any offence, could be subject to a fair trial'. He concluded: 'I don't know the truth of the situation any more than anyone else. However, it does strike me that the coverage thus far has lacked balance. I always thought that, in this country, a man was presumed innocent until proven guilty.'

Ms Glass's comments, when launching the IPCC investigation into matters pertaining to Hillsborough, might be thought to demonstrate, in the view of the learned judge, an apparent bias in advance of any investigation having taken place. Her approach is by no means unique. We seem to live in an era where all kinds of institutions strive to be instantly popular; demonstrate they are on trend; and seek to avoid any immediate public criticism falling on themselves. They say things that are presumed to be popular in the short term without considering the longer-term implications.

A striking example of this tendency was demonstrated, a little more recently, by Detective Superintendent Kenny McDonald of the Metropolitan Police. Mr McDonald was in charge of the Met's Operation Midland, the investigation into the alleged paedophile activity of named, high-profile individuals. In a television interview, at the very outset of the investigation, Mr McDonald pre-empted the outcome by stating that the evidence of a key witness and accuser was both 'credible and true'.

There are some contemporary popular campaigns, such as those around historical sexual abuse, where the narrative has become so deeply ingrained that even seasoned investigators are drawn towards a kind of newspeak. They intone platitudes such as 'the victim must always be believed' – a phrase which may serve as a useful motto for the twenty-first century in overcoming past cultural barriers, but is hardly an immutable investigative rule.

Campaigners can be forgiven for asserting the claim to new expectations in investigative processes. But if easy rhetoric, such as 'the victim must always be believed', becomes the guiding principle for journalists and regulators then we are, as David Aaronovitch has said, 'all in big trouble'.

From my experience of criminal investigation over four decades, I would say that a responsible investigator is always better served by keeping and demonstrating an open mind and following the evidence in a professional manner. That approach has served us well since the Judges' Rules were set out, in 1912, as a guide for investigators.

That open-minded approach was not apparent at the start of the IPCC Hillsborough investigation. The formal public launch and press conference seemed to be shaped as much by popular attitudes as it was by prima facie evidence.

Following Ms Glass's breathless response to the Hillsborough Panel Report (*The Guardian* called it 'dizzying'), the pace and focus of the investigation has since been more pedestrian and unstructured than I could have ever imagined.

I had written to the IPCC on 5 October 2012, welcoming their scrutiny and again, later that month when ousted by my Police Authority, to say that, notwithstanding, I remained committed to assisting their investigation. I did not hear anything further from the IPCC until 15 February 2014, seventeen months after being so publicly identified by the commission as a central suspect in a criminal conspiracy. The IPCC wrote setting out their terms of reference for the investigation and stating that they wished to interview me, under criminal caution and in accordance with the Police and Criminal Evidence Act, at 10 a.m. on Tuesday 11 March 2014. They told me that there might be documents disclosed to me prior to the interview. The letter also added that if I failed to attend voluntarily then consideration would be given to arresting me to complete the interview. That was an unnecessary and gratuitous threat given my communications in 2012 that I was not only willing, but anxious to get this thing resolved.

There was indeed pre-interview disclosure – a mountain of it, and more has been served subsequently. The disclosed documents currently fill four lever-arch folders.

The material divides into four broad categories: firstly, anticipated documents, drawn from the 450,000 that were available to the Hillsborough Panel, and referenced against my name in their report; second, material unfamiliar to me that was held by Hammond Suddards solicitors who represented South Yorkshire Police after the disaster; third, documents that have nothing to do with the Hillsborough aftermath at all, such as my application form for the job of Chief Constable with Merseyside Police; and fourth, material that has little or nothing to do with me at all.

Some of the first items on the disclosure list, which were loosely organised in a chronological order, were press photographs of senior officers briefing Margaret Thatcher, then Prime Minister, the day after the Hillsborough disaster.

This confirmed, in my mind, that the IPCC had truly 'put the complainant at the heart of the investigation' as they proudly and frequently boast.

The Hillsborough Panel had not so much as hinted that I was in any way involved in briefing senior politicians in the immediate aftermath of the disaster. This is, though, one of the odd myths that was created, when controversy surrounded my appointment to Merseyside, that I was responsible for briefing and misleading the Prime Minister about the disaster. Like most myths it was not clear where the notion had come from.

Analysing the disclosed documents, it was obvious what the investigative lines were going to be at interview. I therefore prepared a fourteen-page statement addressing all of the relevant issues. I intended to hand the statement to the interviewers whom I met on 11 March 2014.

The interview was conducted at the IPCC offices in Sale, Greater Manchester. I attended with my solicitor Nick Holroyd. The first thing we did was to hand over my fourteen-page voluntary statement and video tapes from 1989 that were likely to be of use to the investigators. The interview was tape-recorded and I was given the criminal caution in order to make me aware that anything that I said or failed to respond to, in this context, could be used in a court of law. I understood the dance moves but had always led in the past. It was uncomfortable adjusting to the submissive role but it was important to assist the investigation.

The interview was discursive and, on this first day, lasted for almost five hours with a break for lunch. I was content that the issues that were put to me were adequately addressed by my voluntary statement. Wherever an issue came up that had not been subject to prior disclosure, I prepared a further written response and handed it to the investigators. There have been five in total.

I was asked to return for interview on a further three occasions over the succeeding months. I agreed on all occasions, always meeting the diary availability of the investigators. The three subsequent interviews each took place at the IPCC regional office in Wakefield.

I attended on 17 April, 3 June and 4 June 2014. The total time spent in interview was over twenty hours. I remain content that I have addressed, by way of formal written response, all of the issues that were put to me at interview.

Towards the end of the last interview, held on 4 June 2014, the IPCC investigator, Sharon Dalton, formally served upon me a statement by John Barry. I was acutely aware of John Barry's allegation about comments that he claims I had made to him in 1989. It had been publicised by Maria Eagle MP in the House of Commons during a debate on the Hillsborough Panel Report in October 2012. John Barry had then done a round of media interviews where he repeated the allegation that, in 1989, I had told him that my job was to concoct a story to put the blame for the disaster on the Liverpool fans. It was the final straw that cost me my livelihood. Here was an opportunity to see his statement about that alleged conversation for the first time.

The IPCC's disclosure of Mr Barry's statement was curious for a number of reasons. First of all, the statement had not been taken from Mr Barry until February 2014, a full sixteen months after he had made his serious allegation in the most public fashion. Second, and notwithstanding this inordinate delay in taking a statement, it was available for disclosure along with other papers that the IPCC had sent to me in March 2014 and yet they had chosen to hold this back. Third, in response to a question from my solicitor on 3 June Sharon Dalton had said that every relevant document that was available for disclosure had been disclosed. Yet, twenty-four hours later, there was this fresh disclosure of a statement taken months prior. Fourth, and most curiously of all, the investigators stated that they did not want to ask me any questions about Mr Barry's allegation and, in the time that remained in interview that day, they were as good as their word.

That has remained the position of the IPCC until the present day. They have never asked for my response to Mr Barry's allegation that he first raised publicly four years ago and which he regularly repeats in the media. From a professional investigator's point of view, I cannot understand why not. Any objective search for the truth would surely seek to establish the veracity of Mr Barry's crucial account.

After an IPCC investigation of twenty months, and after twenty-odd hours of being interviewed, this seemed an inappropriate place to leave the potentially devastating and therefore critical testimony of Mr Barry.

I wanted the opportunity to rebut his allegation. I asked my solicitor, Nick Holroyd, to write to the IPCC immediately after that last day of interview. He did so and stated that his client was keen to deal with any other outstanding matters, including the Barry statement, and offered dates in July 2014 for further interview. The IPCC responded on 26 June 2014 to say that they now intended to trace and take statements from others on the MBA course that was shared, in 1989, by me and Mr Barry. The email indicated an intention to convene a further interview thereafter. I was pleased to learn of those intentions. Whilst it would be difficult for anyone to accurately remember conversations and events from twenty-five years ago, I hoped that some would remember my enforced absence from the programme at the very time Mr Barry was alleging that I had made a confession to being involved in a criminal conspiracy. It was important that the IPCC investigators track down those potential witnesses and any documentary evidence, such as a course register.

I heard nothing more about this crucial line of investigation. There was no disclosure of further material and no suggestion of another interview date. In fact, there was no communication at all. The IPCC were not interested, and have strangely remained uninterested, in my account.

Nine months later, I was summoned to appear at the Coroner's Inquest to give evidence and be examined about my involvement in the post-disaster procedures and evidence-gathering. The Coroner, Lord Justice Goldring, had ruled that Mr Barry should also be called at the same time as me so that his testimony could be heard by the jury.

It was obvious to me that this disputed evidence would form the centrepiece of my court appearance. It would receive wide publicity, yet again, two years after Mr Barry had first made his allegation. I was therefore keen to establish what other evidence had been obtained by the IPCC investigators, who had promised, nine months earlier, to pursue this avenue.

My legal counsel, Paul Greaney QC, wrote to the IPCC on 23 March 2015 to enquire, pointing out that both Mr Barry and I were due to give evidence within weeks. He listed the reasons why it was fair and proper to disclose beforehand what evidence had been discovered. He seemed just as astonished as I was to receive a letter in response which confirmed that 'no further witness statements have yet been obtained from those who attended the same MBA course as your client'. The IPCC indicated that the line of investigation remained live and that '[w]e will notify you of the outcome in due course'.

Mr Greaney wrote what can only be described as a stern letter to point out, once again, the unfair position that this would put me in when giving evidence alongside Mr Barry at the inquest. He sent the letter electronically on 7 April 2015 to the head of the Hillsborough investigation at the IPCC, encouraging, even at that late stage, urgent enquiries with fellow students, and administrators, on the MBA course.

Mr Mahaffey, the head of the investigation, responded electronically at close of business on 28 April, three weeks after the urgent request for action from my lawyer and less than two days before Mr Barry and I were due to step into the witness box at the inquest. Mr Mahaffey said:

> We have been aware of the allegations of Mr Barry since Maria Eagle raised them in Parliament (October 2012). Lines of enquiry which related to this issue were progressed as far as possible given resource constraints but were not made an absolute priority. Had the Coroner requested that we prioritise them, we would have done so. No such request has been received.

I do realise that there is only so much that can be achieved by 220 staff in relation to the complex set of issues surrounding the Hillsborough disaster. Nevertheless, I would have thought that the widely published allegation that someone openly boasted that he was engaged in a criminal conspiracy to shift the blame for the disaster onto the Liverpool fans might have warranted some kind of priority within the intervening two and a half years. At the very least, the memories of those who would have evidence in relation to this serious allegation might be subject to further deterioration or influence during that interval.

When I received my summons to give evidence at the Coroner's Inquest, I was asked about my dates of availability in April. I was as helpful as I could be in response. I was available throughout the month but did warn the Coroner's team that my youngest step-daughter was to be married from home on the bank holiday weekend of 2 May and so, if there was a likelihood of being part heard at the end of the month then I would prefer to start my evidence after the bank holiday weekend. I was assured that I would definitely not be part heard at the end of the month and the first dates that were provided to me were in mid-April 2015.

I've been around the court process long enough to realise that listing does not always run smoothly and wasn't surprised when those dates slipped. The dates kept slipping, sometimes in order to accommodate other witnesses who had availability difficulties. The job of a court listing officer must sometimes feel like three-dimensional chess.

The court date eventually slipped to 28 April, four days before the wedding weekend. I was reassured that those approving the listing arrangements were alive to my personal circumstances and they remained confident that I would be fully heard before the weekend.

To cut a long story short, I eventually gave evidence over four days beginning on Thursday 30 April 2015. Two days before the wedding weekend and two days after it. This arrangement which I had been trying to avoid meant that the newspapers, on the day that guests began to arrive for the wedding, contained the rehashed allegations of John Barry. Furthermore, as I was part heard, I was prohibited from discussing the evidence with anyone.

The courthouse had been described to me by my lawyer who had sat in from time to time. Even so, I was seriously impressed by the set up. The witness box faced the jury and three images were simultaneously transmitted to more than a dozen television screens strategically hung from the ceiling so that everyone present had an easy view. The images were a close-up of the face of the witness answering questions; a simultaneous transcript of the questions and answers given; and, where relevant, a copy of the document under discussion. It was the most technologically efficient courtroom I had ever encountered.

There were public galleries at either ends of the cavernous room with seating for 150–200 people. The galleries were full on day two of my evidence, when cross examination was due to begin, but less packed on the other three days. The galleries enclosed the pit of the court, which had four quadrants, the witness box and the jury box opposite each other across the narrower plane of the room, the Coroner to the right of the witness and the left of the jury. Opposite him were four or five rows of counsel. I counted sixty-seven barristers on the list representing nineteen interested parties to the proceedings. The legal teams representing the bereaved families dominated the first two rows – there were thirty-two barristers arranged in four separate teams, which represented different groups of families.

This was an imposing parade of legal horsepower. When considering that the court sat, in this fashion, for around 300 days over a two-year period, it can no longer be said that the ninety-six people at the heart of the inquisition failed to get the respect and attention they were due. Finally, after twenty-seven years of waiting, this was a thorough process that has at long last provided the challenge, and answers, that the families of the ninety-six were looking for, and deserved.

My own cameo contribution to the coronial proceedings had nothing to do with providing answers about the cause or circumstances of deaths of any of those individuals.

Even though I was on hand in 1989 and had something to say. That wasn't why I was invited to appear.

I wasn't summoned, either, because there was any suspicion that I had some responsibility or accountability for those deaths. I hadn't been involved in the planning or the command of the fateful police operation.

I was there, at the Warrington Court for four days, because I had become a symbol of something that had been mythologised over a quarter of a century. Some people genuinely believe that there had been a conspiracy within South Yorkshire Police that started as soon as the disaster occurred. A conspiracy to deflect the blame away from the force and place it instead on the fans. I had, through fate and circumstance, become the most recognised name whenever this tale of conspiracy was retold.

I was there to be tested. I was 'on trial'.

In the inquisitorial procedure adopted by this court I was first of all examined by counsel to the inquest Jonathan Hough QC. I was told by my own counsel that he would 'play with a straight bat' but had an obligation to identify and ask all the searching questions that any interested party might have about my actions and motivations. That is the way that it transpired.

I was then cross-examined by two of the counsel representing the different families groups, Peter Wilcock QC and Mark George QC. The final examination was by my own counsel, Paul Greaney QC. His role was to ensure, on my behalf, that the jury had a broad understanding of the evidence I could give.

This thorough and comprehensive interrogation under oath was transcribed and runs to 282 pages. The transcript can be easily found online and is therefore in the public domain. It is a permanent record of my responses to any questions that have been raised about my integrity and it addresses some of the myths that have been created around my name.

Twelve months had passed since the IPCC had last made contact. And so, in June 2015, after I had been tested so thoroughly at the Coroner's Court, my solicitor, Nick Holroyd, wrote to the IPCC. He asked that they take the opportunity to review the sworn evidence that I had given over four days at Warrington. He also asked that the commission review my status as a 'suspect', which is how they had described me as long ago as October 2012. Within hours of receiving the enquiry, Mr Mahaffey, the head of the Hillsborough investigation, responded. He did not indicate whether he had, in fact, taken the opportunity to review the 282 pages of transcribed evidence, but said:

> Sir Norman Bettison's status to the IPCC remains
> that of suspect. It is our intention to further inter-
> view your client and I would hope that this process

can be completed before the end of August. I have copied in Sharon Dalton [the person who conducted the previous interviews] ... to make the necessary arrangements.

I heard nothing more from the IPCC after this communication. There was no further interview, as promised, before the end of August 2015. It was in September 2015, therefore, that I decided I ought to write my own account. I had information to add to the Hillsborough narrative and the IPCC did not appear to be interested in hearing it.

Following a further prompt from my solicitor in June 2016, in which he sought to know the timetable for the long-promised further interview, the IPCC wrote to apologise for the passage of twelve more months in which there had been neither contact nor update from anyone on the investigating team. It seems that there had been a change of senior investigator since Mr Mahaffey's assurance about an impending interview and there was no longer, in the mind of the new head of investigation, an intention to interview me further at this time. It was this revelation that caused me to decide that my account should be published. That, and the fact that three other books about the disaster were published in the summer, each asserting, confidently, that the existence of a police cover-up had now been firmly established.

This book might be the only way in which my own account of the Hillsborough aftermath will ever be heard. By the Crown Prosecution Service as well as by the public.

———————

There is an old saying: 'It never rains but it pours.' There is nothing quite like notoriety for attracting other, unexpected and undeserved, opprobrium.

So far, over the last few chapters, I have described how it has felt to be caught up in a witch hunt. That has been in the context of what I have come to call 'the main event' – i.e. the accusation that I conspired with others to cover up the true causes of the Hillsborough disaster. Once my name became attached to this allegation, it opened the floodgates to other slings and arrows of outrageous fortune.

As in a biological context where a toxic agent depletes the immune system, so it follows in a social context. I have been a cop for forty years, a very senior one for nineteen. I have been trusted and lauded. I have never been accused of any wrongdoing. My integrity credit rating has been high.

What this credit worthiness ensures, in a contemporary social setting, is that one's motives are not often questioned. If ever they are, at times of controversy, then others seem prepared to stand up to support, explain or sometimes defend one's actions.

It has been fascinating for me, as a psychologist, to experience what happens once a toxic virus is introduced into an existing, stable social environment.

The popular narrative has insinuated that a police force acted abominably a quarter of a century ago. I was a member of that police force and employed on the relevant project. Ergo, I am abominable. A virus of suspicion and loathing quickly spreads.

It is easy to see how medieval crowds could be inspired into a mob armed with torches and pitchforks. The modern-day equivalence is the internet with its trolls and bloggers.

Most of the social immune system crumbles at this point. Family stay true. Indeed, relationships become stronger in adversity. A few friends, some unexpected, stand up to the accusers, but their punches don't land. Most others adopt a position of self-preservation, a perfectly natural and instinctive behaviour that has served organisms well throughout evolution.

A lot of friends have remained close in a spirit of silent scepticism about the popular narrative. They matter to me. A few, wary of the taint, have avoided me.

With a depleted immunity people can say anything they wish about you, cast all manner of aspersions, and there is no available countervailing response. There is always the retreat to defending one's own corner at every verse end, but remember the learned lesson from a previous chapter

– no one wants to hear from a scapegoat. Only an ability to take a longer-term perspective can fend off a debilitating sense of persecution.

The first thing to find its way through the lowered defences was the narrow and self-contained IPCC investigation into my conversation with Fraser Sampson, the Police Authority Chief Executive, about my proposal to refer myself to an appropriate investigative body at the start of the hue and cry. Having agreed to put the proposal, on my behalf, Mr Sampson later chose to interpret my request as an attempt to improperly influence the Police Authority.

Deborah Glass, the Deputy Chair of the IPCC, at the time of responding to those demanding my head, said that my proposal to self-refer was a serious matter of concern and chose to deploy scarce and valuable resources to investigate it. I am still baffled by that response.

This was not a criminal matter and there could be no sanction against me, but I agreed to be interviewed. The investigator had completed his task by mid-December 2012. It was quite straightforward. Fraser Sampson and I were more or less agreed on the facts. The real question was about my motivation.

The investigator, Steve Reynolds, reached the conclusion that my conversation with Mr Sampson had not amounted to gross misconduct. That view was shared by Moir Stewart, the Director of Investigations at IPCC Headquarters. He wrote an email to Deborah Glass, the Deputy Chair of the IPCC, when he became aware of an intention to amend the findings, to caution her against changing Mr Reynolds's conclusion and linking this standalone investigation to the wider Hillsborough allegations that had recently arrived on her desk.

> Deborah,
>
> As Steve states we met with Helen and David and, having considered the evidence, did not feel it stacked up to gross misconduct. I am not sure we can use the wider context of Hillsborough. The H investigation has not yet started and so we only have allegations against Bettison – not findings. To then use these against him in this case seems premature. The Panel's Report is just that and not an investigation and Bettison was not interviewed.

Notwithstanding the conclusions of the investigator, and the advice of her Director of Investigations, Ms Glass had her Headquarters staff rewrite the investigator's 'final' report. Which is ironic really, given the nature of the most serious of the allegations against South Yorkshire Police from twenty-seven years ago that she was about to begin to investigate.

This altered report was published in March 2013, three months after the investigator had concluded his task. Ms Glass had consulted lawyers representing the Hillsborough Family Support Group before publication, although why that was necessary, or even appropriate, I cannot fathom.

The foreword to her report, in my opinion, serves to illuminate a prejudicial view and it ignores the advice from her Director of Investigations:

> The Hillsborough disaster and its aftermath have become synonymous in the public consciousness with allegations of police attempts to cover up the truth, manipulate messages and deflect blame. Sir Norman is facing investigation into allegations that he played a key part in this ... Given the effect that those allegations have had on the public perception of him and policing generally, his attempt to manipulate and manage the perception of the referral of complaints about him is particularly concerning.

Ms Glass concluded, in direct opposition to the investigator's original report, that the IPCC *did* find a case to answer for gross misconduct, discreditable conduct and abuse of position in making that eleven-minute call to Fraser Sampson. She further concluded that my action, in seeking the permission of my Authority to self-refer, would so undermine my position as Chief Constable as to have made it untenable. If a disciplinary panel were able to consider these matters (they couldn't as I was no longer employed) then, her report states, dismissal would be justified as an appropriate sanction.

Of course, the report which was sent out to the media, with an accompanying statement from Ms Glass saying that it was now 'for the public to judge him', had the anticipated effect. A headline and editorial in *The Times* stated, categorically, that the IPCC had concluded that I had behaved disgracefully and would have been sacked if I hadn't gotten out from under. The editorial, drawing on what they saw as 'IPCC coda' in Ms Glass's foreword, deduced that retiring had been a despicable act of cowardice on my part. A perception that I had been desperately trying to avoid by fighting to remain in post until after the IPCC had concluded their more substantive investigation.

A BBC2 documentary on Hillsborough broadcast the following week had no time to change the programme but added a closing statement which informed the viewer that an IPCC investigation into my post-disaster work had found a case to answer for discreditable conduct. Obviously written by an under-pressure programme editor who had no time to read what the report was actually about but had picked up, from the foreword, Ms Glass's gratuitous link to the broader Hillsborough allegations.

Whilst the IPCC are entitled to decide that there is a case to answer in any matter of complaint, they are not entitled to decide how the case would have been disposed of in lieu of a proper hearing. Ms Glass had concluded that dismissal would have been the appropriate sanction. Even the IPCC Chair, Dame Anne Owers, advised against this approach. In an email sent on the day before publication, she told Deborah Glass: 'We should not have prejudged the outcome of a hearing.' But it was too late, the report was already out for consultation with the lawyers of the Hillsborough families and it couldn't be changed.

Shortly after this report was published, the commission, in an unconnected case, was rebuked in the Court of Appeal for doing precisely what Deborah Glass had done on this occasion. Lord Justice Beatson, in that case, reminded the IPCC that they had no power to be both judge and jury as well as investigator.

I obtained legal advice that indicated a fair chance of success in having the report overturned at Judicial Review, but it would be a pyrrhic victory. The report had encouraged loose newspaper reports that damaged my reputation. But, as that was already fish-and-chip paper, why risk a considerable financial outlay to simply achieve the rewriting of a report that would be republished and reported upon all over again? It is sometimes wiser to turn the other cheek.

Next up on the list of associated indictments arose from

a rather bizarre convergence of fates. Another public outrage about historical police events had been triggered,
single-handedly, by an ex-Metropolitan Police undercover
officer called Peter Francis. Interviewed for a Channel 4
documentary, Mr Francis alleged that he was tasked by
his Metropolitan Police bosses to infiltrate those close to
the Stephen Lawrence Campaign for Justice, including
Stephen's family, in the aftermath of Stephen's murder in
the 1990s. It was a claim intended to shock. I watched the
Channel 4 programme as it was broadcast, in the summer
of 2013, and saw no connection to anything in my own
professional orbit or knowledge. I was surprised, later, to
read that Mr Francis, having made such a shocking allegation on television, was not prepared to furnish any details
of his alleged tasking to those undertaking a proper investigation of his claims.

Notwithstanding Mr Francis's reticence to be more specific in his accusations, his disclosures on the Channel 4
programme created public indignation at a level similar to
that achieved by the Hillsborough cover-up story. He even,
in the Channel 4 interview, referenced Hillsborough as a
comparable example of police corruption. There is now
a judicial inquiry, under Lord Justice Pitchford, examining
the historic role, tactics and conduct of police undercover
units. It will run and run.

None of this affected me, or so I thought. Just one of the

actions that was initiated by Theresa May, the then Home Secretary, in the light of Mr Francis's disclosure, was to call for all forces to search their records for any undercover work undertaken in relation to the Stephen Lawrence Campaign for Justice and the Macpherson Inquiry into his murder.

When West Yorkshire Police checked their Special Branch records, they found that a Special Branch officer (not an undercover officer) had notified me, in 1998, about the antecedents of a man who was due to attend a public meeting in Bradford chaired by Lord Justice Macpherson. I was at that time Assistant Chief Constable in West Yorkshire Police with a specific responsibility for policing in Bradford, which was still recovering from a recent history of riots and violent disturbances.

Lord Justice Macpherson had concluded his London-based hearings into the murder of Stephen Lawrence by late 1998 and embarked on a tour of UK cities with a significant ethnic mix to learn about local police and community relationships and to test out, in the provinces, his inquiry's emerging recommendations for London. Such public meetings in these strife-torn cities in the 1990s were potential flash points. Hence the briefing up to me as the ACC responsible for tranquillity in Bradford. It was nothing to do with Stephen Lawrence, his family or the campaign in his name. Less still was it anything to do with undercover policing.

Here again, however, there was no preparedness on the part of anyone looking at these documents to attach a benign interpretation to the motivation behind them or even to suspend judgement. Some ex-colleagues of mine were overly cautious given the toxicity around my name and raised the documents, without context, with the Police and Crime Commissioner's office.

They were subsequently referred to the IPCC by Mark Burns-Williamson, by now West Yorkshire Police's elected Police and Crime Commissioner. He could have simply forwarded them with a short media comment if he wished to be seen to be open and transparent. He chose instead to issue a two-page press statement and appear on the local evening news to declare that

> documents discovered by West Yorkshire Police raise significant concerns over the role of Sir Norman Bettison at the time he was Assistant Chief Constable of West Yorkshire Police in 1998 ... [These] may suggest an attempt to intervene in the course of a public inquiry and influence the manner in which the testimony of a witness was received.

This press statement was made, yet again, before any investigative stone had been turned. It enabled the newspapers to have a field day. They probably couldn't believe their luck in having one individual linked to two causes célèbre. The *Daily Mirror* of 4 July 2013 was a particularly brash example. An unflattering photograph of me on its front page alongside a photo of Stephen Lawrence and the all-upper-case headline 'Hillsborough Cop in Lawrence Smear Probe – Shamed Chief faces new claims over murdered Stephen's family'.

Notice how 'Shamed Chief' and, elsewhere, 'Disgraced Chief' were beginning to become terms of common currency wherever newspapers referred to me. All part of the branding exercise in advance of any test of the allegations from the 'main event'.

Following the direction of the Home Secretary for forces to search 1990s records for any evidence of undercover policing around the Stephen Lawrence family, there were at least three referrals to the IPCC. Greater Manchester and South Yorkshire as well as West Yorkshire each referred documentation around Special Branch work in advance of public meetings in their force areas. The IPCC acknowledged all three, handed two back to the forces concerned for local investigation, but kept one for independent investigation by the commission itself. There was therefore more newspaper coverage about their decision to elevate only the investigation about me.

It was nine months later, following a thorough investigation, that the IPCC reported no connection between the

West Yorkshire documents and the Stephen Lawrence family, or campaign group. The investigation also found that there was no case to answer by anyone involved in the making or the receiving of the intelligence reports. There was no attendant press statement from the West Yorkshire Police and Crime Commissioner. There was little in the way of any report that this apparently sensational connection between Hillsborough and Stephen Lawrence had, in fact, been a bit of a damp squib.

Along the way, during my four years in purgatory, numerous allegations have been raised that I may have conspired with others to pervert the course of justice in all manner of proceedings. There was a particularly nasty historical aspersion cast about the integrity of my father. My dad, the most honest man I have known, sold a small amount of platinum swarf in 1987, which he had cleared out of my deceased grandfather's workshop. Grandad had collected the filings in an old snuff tin and I was with my father when he sold it for about £100 at a reputable precious metal dealer. The precious metal dealer had a protocol with the local police to report all sales from private individuals. My father's possession was enquired into and the inquiry was immediately closed. End of story.

A vindictive former police officer, himself sacked for dishonesty and sent to prison, recalled the incident from 1987, and when my face and name began to appear in the media more recently, he shared the story, perhaps in an embellished way, with his local MP, John Mann. Mr Mann is often to be seen on television expressing outrage about this, that or the other issue. In December 2014, it was he who presented to Scotland Yard, in the full glare of publicity, a list of twenty-two names, thirteen of them former government ministers, who were accused of being child abusers.

On this particular occasion, Mr Mann was outraged by the suggestion of a cover-up by South Yorkshire Police in 1987 following an investigation into the father of the man now accused of covering up the blame for the Hillsborough disaster. He followed up his television interview with a letter to South Yorkshire Police and the IPCC demanding that they re-investigate the thirty-year-old matter. My father, by the way, had been dead for twenty years.

Even the IPCC, on this occasion, could not see any merit in taking this further. South Yorkshire Police, on the other hand, found themselves in a tricky bind. Mr Mann's accusations were of a historic South Yorkshire Police cover-up and so, in the current climate, they did not want to be seen to ignore the complaint, however farfetched. Particularly as it came from an MP.

South Yorkshire Police asked Derbyshire Police to investigate the matter, which they did with scrupulous attention, diverting valuable resources from the protection of the people of Derbyshire. The investigators, over a number of months, traced and interviewed fifty-one witnesses. They recommended that there were no offences disclosed from their investigation.

South Yorkshire Police, fearful of any backlash, still felt unable to accept that recommendation and close down the investigation on their own authority. They sent all the papers to the CPS asking that they instead make the final decision on the matter. The head of CPS for South and West Yorkshire was an acquaintance of mine after our years of working in partnership to reform the criminal justice system locally. He therefore sent the file to another CPS region for independent review.

Eventually, seventeen months after John Mann's misplaced allegation, and lots of newspaper reports linking me with 'another man' accused of the theft of a 'large quantity of high value platinum wire', the CPS disclosed that no further action would be taken. They added, for the purpose of clarity, that '[a]n essential legal element of the offences alleged is that the prosecution must be able to show that the goods in question were in fact stolen. There is insufficient evidence to establish this.'

The *Yorkshire Post* reported the outcome fairly but added a footnote to their report: 'The former Chief Constable is still under investigation by the IPCC over Hillsborough and also the public inquiry into the murder of Stephen Lawrence.' I was not to be let off the hook.

Perhaps the most bizarre additional indictment that I have gathered along the way is a recorded allegation that I conspired to cover up a historical murder. It has sometimes felt over the last four years, that Salem, like Blake's Jerusalem, is being built in England's green and pleasant land.

The bare bones of this particular charge are as follows. A man died at Airedale Hospital in West Yorkshire in the early 2000s. In 2004, a nurse from that same hospital was charged with the murders of a number of patients by the method of opiate overdose. Airedale Hospital Trust paid out significant sums in compensation to affected families. Thereafter, the son of the man who had previously died asked West Yorkshire Police to examine his father's death in case of foul play. They did and concluded that the death could not be connected to the other murders. The son complained about the competence and integrity of the West Yorkshire Police investigation and challenged its conclusion. West Yorkshire Police asked Greater Manchester Police to review their investigation. Greater Manchester came to the same conclusion, that the death of the complainant's father was not linked to the other murders.

Now, all of that activity took place whilst I was Chief Constable in Merseyside, and I had no knowledge of, let alone involvement in, any of the decisions. I returned to West Yorkshire Police in 2007 and the complainant continued to be dissatisfied about the outcome of all the actions recounted above. I was unaware of his dissatisfaction and had no personal knowledge of his letters, which he continued to write to the force and the Police Authority.

After the hue and cry over the Hillsborough matters, and my subsequent departure from my post, the said complainant wrote again to the West Yorkshire Police and Crime Commissioner. He set out a simple logic in his letter: 'as Bettison lied about Hillsborough, well its more probable than not that he lied regarding my father's murder at Airedale Trust'.

The West Yorkshire Police and Crime Commissioner couldn't accept that simple leap of logic and his office wrote back to assure the complainant that I wasn't even in the force at the time of the alleged actions to deny his father's murder. They told him, therefore, that they would not be recording or investigating his complaint. Said complainant wrote to the IPCC appealing the West Yorkshire Police and Crime Commissioner's decision to not record or investigate his complaint.

The IPCC accepted the Police and Crime Commissioner's conclusion about my not being present in the force at the relevant times and therefore it was unlikely that the complaint could be upheld. They did not agree, however, with the decision not to record the complaint. There was nothing on the face of the complaint that made the alleged behaviour impossible. They instructed the Police and Crime Commissioner to accept the complaint as being true, record the matter as a formal complaint and only then decide what level of investigation it warranted.

The office of the West Yorkshire Police and Crime Commissioner wrote to tell me of the recording of this matter, which will stand out in my 'complaints file' that is maintained, even in retirement. A complaint that I was part of a criminal conspiracy to cover up the cause of death of a gentleman who passed away at Airedale Hospital. The Police and Crime Commissioner told me in the same letter that he had taken the pragmatic decision not to investigate the matter further.

In this same period, a man complained to the Police and Crime Commissioner that, some years previously, I had colluded with junior officers to cover up an allegation of racial discrimination. Another tried to convince the Commissioner that I and my successor Chief had jointly failed to properly investigate his complaint of torture, thereby failing to meet our obligations under the Articles of the European Court of Human Rights. In all fairness, the Commissioner's office did reject these and other similar overtures.

In Merseyside, an Inspector who had been disciplined by me a decade earlier also saw the opportunity in raising an allegation that I had engaged in a criminal conspiracy. She alleged that I might have conspired with a member of the judiciary to ensure that her disciplinary sanction was upheld at a subsequent Appeal Court hearing. The judge who chaired that appeal was the Lord Chief Justice, Igor Judge. The Merseyside Police and Crime Commissioner's Office did not inform me of the allegation but asked the Chief Constable of Lincolnshire Police to conduct an investigation. The former Lord Chief Justice remembered the case and was able quickly to dispel any suspicion that I had ever sought to influence his decision-making.

Having had little experience of being complained of over forty years, I was suddenly attracting public complaints in great number and exotic scope. I have heard celebrities involved in historical allegations of sexual crimes complain about the use of 'fly paper' tactics by investigators; i.e. if one creates enough publicity and notoriety around an individual it will attract more complaints. I can confirm that the 'fly paper' phenomenon does exist.

The internet provides a great platform for generating and marshalling apparent public outrage. The appearance of the depth and breadth of outrage intimidates politicians and public institutions. A recent example is the move to have Rhodes's statue removed from Oriel College, Oxford. An e-petition is relatively easy to garner. It can be done from a back bedroom without a great deal of effort on anyone's part. The so-called protestors don't have to leave their house and only have to click one button. Rod Liddle had a humorous tilt at this contemporary craze in the *Sunday Times*:

> It's not the signing of e-petitions that matters. It's the response to them. It's the sight of authorities trembling in their corduroys and deciding that the mob – a very small mob, all things considered – should rule.
>
> It is not democracy to let these click-happy clowns decide policy, or even provoke a response. When a petition garners ten million signatories, maybe the government or public authority should think again. But even that is less than a sixth of our population. Better to ignore them altogether.

Rod Liddle's amusing slant does, however, raise a serious question. Have we developed, as a society, a sufficiently mature response to a relatively new trend? An immediate reaction may not be the most appropriate way to respond to a cluster click in the longer term. The cluster click, like most of the content of social media, may represent an ephemeral and transient blip. A response, such as removing a 105-year-old statue, is permanent.

During my four years in the wilderness, there have been

all manner of e-petitions raised to have summary things done to me: to have me dismissed in the early days; to have my public sector pension withheld; to have my several honours revoked; and to have my honorary links to various universities withdrawn. Only one has, thus far, been successful and I am disappointed – not for the loss of an Honorary Fellowship, which my school teacher stepdaughter describes as a pretend qualification – but for the fact that universities can be so easily swayed these days. The traditional bastions of liberal free thought and expression seem actually to be terrified, in the twenty-first century, of doing anything that might lead to controversy or a loss of revenue. Mine is not the only case recently where vice chancellors and provosts have quaked at the sight of an e-petition.

The elected Mayor of Liverpool put his name to a call to have me stripped of my Honorary Fellowship that I was proud to have been granted by Liverpool John Moores University. The citation, that was read out to a packed graduation ceremony in 2004, highlighted my contributions to the City of Liverpool during my time there as Chief.

But now Mayor Joe Anderson wanted it taken away. It was a populist position for him to adopt. The *Liverpool Echo* got behind the putsch and so too did Liverpool FC fanzines and the JMU Union. Professor John Ashton, a medic who had been at Hillsborough and tended to the dead and dying, and who was also an Honorary Fellow, said that he would burn his cap and gown on the steps of JMU unless mine was taken away. His Twitter petition received 753 clicks. Not quite Rod Liddle's ten million threshold, and not necessarily all unique individuals, but who's counting?

Liverpool John Moores University, and the new Vice Chancellor, faced with such local pressure, had no choice, did they? Well, yes, they might have said that we should all await the outcome of the formal investigation about the serious allegations that I faced. Keep calm and carry on. They might even have asked for my response to the proposal to withdraw my honorary position and consider that response alongside what the *Echo* was reporting to be a 'guerrilla internet campaign'. They did neither. The Vice Chancellor's secretary sent me an unexpected email at 7.18 p.m. on 8 April 2013 to notify me that there would be a public announcement at noon the following day that my honour had been stripped.

That duly occurred. The announcement even included a placatory line, in case of any doubt, that the university supports the families' campaign for justice.

The University of Teesside were smarter, but no more courageous. On hearing of the JMU decision, they wrote to me to say that they had invoked a policy to regularly review their honorary connections and that, going forward and seeing as I was no longer a serving Chief, they would no longer need me as a Visiting Fellow on their Policing and Criminal Justice programme. As they had failed to use my services since granting me the honour, that was no loss for either of us.

The University of Huddersfield was more pragmatic. The avuncular and very successful Vice Chancellor Bob Cryan told me that there had been rumblings about my Honorary Doctorate, as a sizeable proportion of their student base hail from Merseyside. He had headed it off at the pass by a decision to invite me, for the time being, only to private events at the university.

The e-petition about my knighthood removal reached a sufficient threshold that the Forfeiture Committee at the Cabinet Office was obliged to convene to consider the question. They have strict criteria about these things since their earlier experience in the handling of the Fred Goodwin affair. They are, it seems to me, more mature in their dealings with e-petitions. Universities and other public institutions might take a leaf out of their book. Anyhow, the formal convention of the appropriate committee led to a decision that no action was required, at this time. The last three words are important, and also often absent in so many knee-jerk reactions to public outrage.

If the internet provides the technological platform for outraged individuals in the modern world, then the smartphone provides the technological means to populate it. I have been photographed in all manner of different situations and mentioned on Facebook and other social media, usually with a 'Disgraced Chief' tag or expletive-laden hashtag.

The most ridiculous brouhaha was created by a photograph of me attending a football match. I was a guest of the board of directors of a club unconnected with Merseyside or South Yorkshire.

I hadn't realised that my photograph had been taken whilst enjoying the game. The photographer later sent it to all manner of newspapers and media outlets highlighting my links to Hillsborough. A few carried it but most ignored it. What's the story? 'Man Goes to Football Match' – so what?

It was picked up by one provincial newspaper which used it to attack not me but the football club board, with whom the paper was at loggerheads. Their football correspondent expressed the rather haughty view that, whatever the bonds of friendship, 'someone like [me] should never be invited to a football match. It brings shame on the good name of the football club. It's like inviting Abu Hamza or Stuart Hall to corresponding events.' He didn't specify what kinds of exclusions might be relevant to those other two men, each convicted of serious criminal offences, but I presume his list might include church fêtes and children's parties.

I haven't accepted an invitation to be a guest at any football club since. Why share such a grotesque and hateful spotlight with friends?

———————

We fancy ourselves to be a modern, liberal and tolerant society. My experience of the last four years is that we are a long way from achieving that ambition.

We channel the Dark Ages in our visceral responses to untested allegations about people and events. The smartphone has simply replaced the pitchfork and the internet has replaced the gallows. The medieval clamour is alive and well, particularly online.

Yaël Farber, who directed Arthur Miller's play about the Salem witch trials, *The Crucible*, at The Old Vic in 2014, believes the play has an enduring relevance: 'We think we are above Miller's characters. We're not. We are them; they're just wearing different clothes and speaking with a different accent ... It's extraordinary what people can do to each other when they believe themselves to have righteousness on their side.'

CHAPTER 11

MIGHT THIS BE THE FINAL CHAPTER?

This is as far as my story goes, for the time being. It is only one story, one of thousands that could be told about the terrible day in 1989, about its aftermath, and of the aftershocks that still reverberate around the disaster. It is certainly not *the* story of Hillsborough. Others will claim the right to greater authority as objective historians. But I do know what should be included in any story about Hillsborough if it is to be authentic.

First of all, one should be wary of any account that seeks

to encapsulate the story of the tragedy and its aftermath in a few simple soundbites. The *Sun* newspaper failed, spectacularly, to summarise the event within ninety-six hours of the disaster unfolding. They focused, with obscene prejudice, on one constituent group that was present at the event. Based upon nothing more than third-hand gossip, they published an account to the world that has, ultimately, counted more against the reputation of tabloid journalism and its methods than the reputation of a city and its football supporters. *The Sun* was shamed by Lord Justice Taylor within sixteen weeks of the disaster and yet the bereaved families and other campaigners have had to strive, for twenty-seven years, to dispel the myth that was created.

The so-called Wain Report, an internal document to brief police lawyers, in which I played a part, was also a hopelessly incomplete account of the day. Unlike the *Sun* reports, it was based on first-hand testimony that was, if anything, toned down rather than sexed up. Unlike *The Sun*, it was never published, distributed nor asserted as being conclusive. Like *The Sun*, however, it was a partial account, some might say in both senses of the word, gathered within days of the disaster. It was an account that was shown to be insufficient in the light of the broader testimony given to the Taylor Inquiry.

To link or associate these two early summaries is to create an unsavoury whiff of establishment conspiracy.

The two institutions, of Fleet Street and Bow Street, were not seen, in the 1980s, as friends of the common man. Think miners dispute; think poll tax revolt. They were each, or jointly, determined, according to some conspiracy theorists, to pin the blame for the most dreadful tragedy on the poor unfortunates who found themselves on the terraces and in the cages beside the deceased. Throw in the protective cloak of Downing Street, and Margaret Thatcher's Tory government, and one could fashion a conspiracy theory fit for a place in folklore. Some have been keen, since 1998, to link me with the briefing of the Prime Minister when she visited Hillsborough stadium on the day after the disaster. It was an issue raised early in my very first interview with the IPCC. It would, if true, add more weight to the fable, created by Maria Eagle MP, of a black propaganda unit. Neither the specific insinuation nor the general accusation is true.

I am resolved to the fact that this conspiracy narrative will remain attractive to many. It will be presented in the future as emblematic of the 1980s. An era that is supposed to have witnessed a repressive political regime; a politicised and corrupt police force; and a compliant right-wing media. There is also an understandable reluctance, now, to challenge such a narrative in case one is misunderstood as being in denial of justice. '1980s establishment cover-up' is an easy label to apply and a difficult one to shift.

The word 'meme' has been employed, relatively recently, to describe the phenomenon, in the internet age, of the viral spread of an image or a story which appears within many blogs and persists over time. People in public life need to embrace a world in which they are at constant risk of becoming the symbol of a meme, and in which perceptions count for more than facts. Matthew Parris made the point in his column in *The Times* at the height of the controversy over David Cameron's offshore investments: 'It may be that the Prime Minister's financial conduct has been unimpeachable, but I'm afraid the story catches the wind. The meme this weekend, this year, perhaps this generation, is establishment hypocrisy. Allegations about Cameron's tax affairs play straight into that.'

So, if the enduring story of Hillsborough is likely to assert, or perhaps only imply, that there was a conspiracy within South Yorkshire Police and other institutions to cover up the true cause of the disaster for a generation, and if I have become associated with that charge, then what am I to do?

I marvel at the apparent nonchalance of the new generation, the millennials, who advocate ignoring the widespread and persistent defamations that are perpetrated through the World Wide Web. Perhaps they are merely commentators rather than casualties. 'Suck it up' is their contemporary motto as though any claim to accurate reporting is seen as somehow undemocratic or pedantic and quaint.

I have two granddaughters, aged seven and four. One
is currently reading Paddington Bear books, the second is
beginning to recognise the letters that make up her own
name. Nevertheless, they are both, even now, in thrall to
the internet. The iPad is the contemporary touchy blanket.
Each amuse, entertain, and occasionally educate themselves through YouTube and they are quietened on car
journeys through immersion in a personal, online world
far removed from the *I Spy* books and travel games that
I remember.

The internet will, in years to come, deliver to them,
whether they seek it or not, an encyclopaedia of knowledge
and also of half-truths. It may not always be clear to them
where one stops and the other begins. Although one hopes
that their generation might develop more mature means for
distinguishing the two. They may come to laugh at the fact
that we were once duped by phishers and exploited by vlog-
gers selling their wares. One hopes that they will have slain
trolls and be safe from online predators. That Wikipedia is
viewed by them as an adjunct to any research rather than
its conclusion. Such online sophistication, though, lies in
the future, for the frontiers of the new digital world are
still being settled and some of its territories remain uncon-
trolled and hostile.

There may come the day when one of the girls decides
to Google their grandpa, or whatever brand name then

provides a verb to describe the act of searching the internet. They will easily find the meme of 'establishment cover-ups' and, alongside it, the Hillsborough narrative. They will learn nothing about my forty-year career in policing. My web history will begin with Maria Eagle's denouncement of me on the floor of the House of Commons in 1998. That will be reinforced with the various accounts of my spectacular fall from grace in 2012 and a labyrinth of references, unsourced and unverified, that insinuate links to criminal conduct and shameful behaviour. They will find no formal record of exoneration and redemption. I have explained why that is a story that cannot easily be written by any third party in our current, victim-centred world.

I would not want either granddaughter to harbour a doubt that Grandpa was a criminal, or wrestle with the unanswered accusation that he acted dishonourably in the wake of a terrible human tragedy. I have therefore chosen an old-fashioned medium, increasingly unfamiliar to the millennial generation, to give each of the girls a point of reference to help them decide these matters for themselves. A printed book can be rejected, remaindered or criticised. It cannot, so easily as online content, be overwritten, deleted or lost.

This is not an account designed to bring down the meme. It will not dent the popular narrative. It is not intended to influence anyone who has already made up their mind that, after the Hillsborough disaster, there was an establishment conspiracy that persisted for twenty-seven years. It was not written for them. It was written for Olivia and Freya, and for future generations who may come to the story of the Hillsborough tragedy afresh.

The story of the disaster will echo through eternity and my own account and involvement may warrant no more than a footnote. There are other, much more important, elements to the story that need to be told.

Any story about the Hillsborough disaster should begin by telling of a time when the followers of Association Football were regarded and treated with contempt, not only by the game's authorities and the police, but also by journalists and politicians and through public stereotyping. It was this contempt that led to a common complacency about their welfare and safety and a widespread preparedness to believe that they may somehow be the ones to blame whenever a football tragedy occurred.

The story should also catalogue the missed opportunities that fell to many individuals, not all of them known by name, to make decisions and meet their professional responsibilities in a way that might have made the potential for disaster less likely. The football authorities; the engineers; those charged with public safety obligations; stadium owners and managers; the operational planners; event commanders and so on.

Every story of Hillsborough will undoubtedly focus on the actions of David Duckenfield, the police commander thrust late into the role of decision maker at the fateful and fatal moments on the day. No one will claim that he accepted the role nineteen days earlier, or came into work that day, with an intention to put anyone at risk of serious harm. The question that has never been conclusively addressed until the jury returned their verdict at the recent Coroner's Inquest is whether he was grossly negligent about those risks. It wasn't a question that was considered relevant by Lord Justice Taylor at his public inquiry; there was a different majority verdict at the original inquest in 1991; a hung jury determination in a subsequent criminal trial of Mr Duckenfield; and, because of the passage of time spent on those processes, there was a failure to impose any disciplinary sanction to at least acknowledge his professional failings.

Now, a Coroner's Inquest has decided, twenty-seven years after the disaster, that the ninety-six were unlawfully killed at Hillsborough and, whilst no Coroner's Court can find an individual guilty of a criminal offence, the Coroner has made clear that Mr Duckenfield's actions were not those of a careful and competent match commander. This particular, and central, aspect of the Hillsborough story may still have some way to go.

The story of Hillsborough that is to be retold in the

future will not end with the tragic deaths of the ninety-six and a Coroner's Inquest verdict. It is what happened after the deaths that gives the story its enduring human interest.

First of all, the story will recall the apparent slowness in the reaction of the emergency services to the unfolding tragedy and will acknowledge the heroic attempts of many members of the general public to bring help and succour to the injured, the dying and the dead. Early chaos, anticipated by professionals in the immediate aftermath of any major disaster, will be interpreted as indifference, or worse. It might mean, because of the generic criticism of the emergency services, that the occasional example of heroism and compassion amongst the uniformed personnel on duty at the stadium will pass without mention. That is a shame.

Any comprehensive account of the aftermath will highlight the bureaucratic treatment of the bereaved in the hours and days that followed the disaster. Viewed from any objective perspective, it will appear callous. The reporting and heartless identification procedures; the intrusive interviews by the investigating police force; the things that were done *to* the bereaved rather than *with* them. As a counterpoint, the story might record the way that the City of Liverpool and the region of Merseyside provided immediate and genuine comfort and support and acknowledge all the 'friends of the ninety-six' who have carried the burning torch of remembrance all these years.

Standing out amongst the raft of insensitive responses, and transcending the general charge of cold indifference, the Hillsborough story will recall the malicious misrepresentation of the facts surrounding the disaster, the *Sun* newspaper being a potent example. One might hope that the flagrant excesses of tabloid journalism, common in the last generation, also come to be seen as a historical footnote.

The story, if written thoughtfully, will acknowledge the judiciary as a keystone in the unwritten constitution of this country. The Hillsborough disaster has been examined, and poked at, and summarily disposed of, by many institutions over the last three decades. The issue has, in turn, been ignored or politicised and the facts and myths have been made to fit any number of pet theories, particularly about the actions of 'the fans' or of 'the police'. These one-dimensional accounts have been narrow and sterile. Standing out, like a beacon, in this superficial landscape are the various examinations and procedures employed by Her Majesty's judges.

Firstly, there was Lord Justice Taylor, who, in spite of the haste that was applied to his public inquiry, was able to give an account of the disaster and its causes that has stood as definitive for twenty-seven years. He needed only sixty pages to present his judgment and completed his task within sixteen weeks of the disaster occurring.

Later on, Lord Justice Stuart-Smith inquired into concerns that had arisen about the conduct of the original inquest. He criticised the approach taken by the Coroner and recommended that the Taylor Report should have served as the guide to how the ninety-six had died. Notwithstanding, it would be fifteen more years before the unsatisfactory inquest was overturned.

In 2000, Mr Justice Hooper decided, against fierce counter argument, that David Duckenfield and his number two, Bernard Murray, should face a jury trial in relation to their actions and omissions on the day of the disaster. He oversaw a thorough, and emotionally charged, trial, in which Mr Murray was found not guilty. He decided, in the light of the failure of the jury to reach an agreed verdict as to the culpability of Mr Duckenfield, that he should not have to face a future retrial. Each of Justice Hooper's judgments was bold.

In 2012, the Lord Chief Justice, Lord Judge, sitting with two other senior judges, laid down a carefully considered judgment that the original inquest should be set aside and that, regardless of the passage of time, there should be new inquests held. The recently retired Senior Presiding Judge for England and Wales, Lord Justice Goldring, was appointed Coroner in 2013 to conduct those proceedings. He has concluded, after the most comprehensive and detailed inquiry, that the ninety-six people who lost their lives at Hillsborough were unlawfully killed.

Each of these eminent judges have added clarity to the complex, and sometimes foggy, picture of the Hillsborough disaster. They have cut through controversy and swept away myth. I cannot think of any event or social issue that has enjoyed a greater amount of judicial scrutiny, and the balanced determinations of the courts should occupy a central place in any account of Hillsborough that is yet to be written.

Every story must also spend some time, as my own has done, recounting the long battle of those bereaved at Hillsborough. They were often met by heartlessness and apathy. They railed against false and malicious testimony wherever they found or perceived it. They overcame setbacks and disappointments in the formal and bureaucratic procedures that confronted them. When they seemed to be defeated they rallied, with an even greater resolve, in their campaign for a proper hearing. Finally, after battling for a quarter of a century, they achieved what was sought from the outset – a full and detailed examination of all the circumstances that surrounded the untimely deaths of their loved ones. The story of Hillsborough will conclude that this would never have happened without the families' struggle.

If my granddaughters ever get around to reading this book, or other authoritative accounts of the Hillsborough disaster and its aftermath, they will discover much more than Grandpa's story. They will learn how contempt for, or complacency about, others in society can lead to tragic consequences. They will be reminded of the strength of the judiciary in deciding the affairs of a just nation, particularly in a booming, buzzing world full of digital noise and chatter. They must also surely learn something about fortitude and the indomitability of the human spirit that can prevail over time and against all the odds. If they do, then they will have learned three important lessons for life. Ultimately, it may be these lessons for life that are the enduring legacy of the Hillsborough tragedy.

I hope that the bereaved families might soon find peace. They deserve it. It has been twenty-seven long years since their loss. I am always sorry for that loss and, today, pay tribute to their monumental struggle. The Family Support Group have announced that they wish the 2016 Memorial Service at Anfield to be the last of its kind. The large, public, set-piece event giving way, in future, to a myriad of personal and more private commemorations on each 15 April. They have said that there are to be no more fundraising campaigns, for no major battles are envisaged. The inquest, held over these last two years, may have delivered all that was ever fought for – a fair and comprehensive examination of all the circumstances surrounding the deaths of their loved ones in the spring sunshine at Hillsborough.